Thomas Morgan

Romano-British Mosaic Pavements

A History of Their Discovery, and a Record and Interpretation of tTheir Designs

Thomas Morgan

Romano-British Mosaic Pavements
A History of Their Discovery, and a Record and Interpretation of tTheir Designs

ISBN/EAN: 9783337020347

Printed in Europe, USA, Canada, Australia, Japan

Cover: Foto ©Andreas Hilbeck / pixelio.de

More available books at **www.hansebooks.com**

ROMANO-BRITISH

MOSAIC PAVEMENTS.

" Ex hac Britanniæ facultate victoriæ plurimos quibus illæ provinciæ redundabant accepit artifices."—EUMENES, *Panegyr. Constantii*, c. 21.

" Cum longi Libyam tandem post funera belli
Ante suas mœstam cogeret ire rotas ;
Advexit reduces secum Victoria Musas."

CLAUDIAN, *De II Cons. Fl. Stilichonis*, 17-19.

ROMANO-BRITISH

MOSAIC PAVEMENTS:

A

HISTORY OF THEIR DISCOVERY AND A RECORD AND INTERPRETATION OF THEIR DESIGNS.

WITH PLATES, PLAIN AND COLOURED, OF THE MOST IMPORTANT MOSAICS.

BY

THOMAS MORGAN, F.S.A.,

VICE-PRESIDENT AND HONORARY TREASURER OF THE BRITISH ARCHÆOLOGICAL ASSOCIATION,
MEMBER OF THE KENT, MIDDLESEX, AND SURREY ARCHÆOLOGICAL SOCIETIES,
AND OF THE ROYAL HISTORICAL SOCIETY.

LONDON:
WHITING & CO., SARDINIA STREET, W.C.
1886.

TO THE RIGHT HON.

THE EARL GRANVILLE, K.G., PRESIDENT,

LORD WARDEN OF THE CINQUE PORTS, ETC., ETC., ETC..

TO THE VICE-PRESIDENTS,

TO THE MEMBERS OF THE COUNCIL,

AND

TO THE HONORARY SECRETARIES,

WALTER DE GRAY BIRCH, ESQ., F.S.A.,   E. P. LOFTUS BROCK, ESQ., F.S.A.,

GEO. R. WRIGHT, ESQ., F.S.A.,

AND THE WHOLE BODY OF ASSOCIATES OF

THE BRITISH ARCHÆOLOGICAL ASSOCIATION,

THIS WORK IS, BY PERMISSION, RESPECTFULLY AND GRATEFULLY DEDICATED

BY

THE AUTHOR.

Hill-Side House,

Palace Road, Streatham Hill, S.W.

CONTENTS.

ILLUSTRATIONS.

INTRODUCTORY CHAPTER.

THE design of the present work is to bring together
descriptions of Romano-British tesselated pavements
which lie scattered through the writings of a great number of
separate authors; to add thereto what has come under my
own observation of the pavements themselves; and to
present authentic copies, in plain and coloured engravings,
of as many as may be found practicable or are within
reach. Some are of simple geometrical designs; others of
more elaborate composition, formed of lines, borders, and
floral decorations; but the most interesting, of course, are
those on which are depicted scenes of life or allegorical
figures, and allusions to the numerous *fabellæ* which made
up the atmosphere of the life and religion of the ancients,
and threw over them a charm in their every-day affairs,
whether at the dinner-table or in the bath, at the games
of the circus or in the hunting-field, and even amidst the
business and turmoil of the *forum* and the *comitia*.

If, in describing the pavements of England, county by

county, I am led sometimes, from the nature of the subject, into the depths of heathen mythology, let me neither elevate the gods and goddesses to the dignity of demons or sorcerers, nor yet treat them as the meaningless fabrications of the poet, the sculptor, or the painter. Chronologically, they have an interest as conveying to us the intellectual life of the time when they moved in the religious creed which gave a tone to the literature and intellect of the world; but I will limit my observations upon them to so much as is necessary for verifying my explanations of the mosaics and their pictured allegories.

By "nothing extenuating", yet "setting down nought in malice", if no other good is to be derived from such studies, at least they will inspire us with a feeling of thankfulness that we live in a more advanced age of the world than when these mosaics were laid down, and under a different dispensation of Divine Providence.

The aggregation of facts during the present century by the many antiquarian societies in this country and on the Continent has elevated archæology into a science, by multiplying in an extraordinary degree contemporary evidence of history, and hence a more critical system of studying it has been created. Our societies have done well in acting according to one of the laws adopted by the Institute of Archæological Correspondence, established in Rome in 1828—a society which laid down the rule that their work was to " define archæological facts, not to give academical treatises". Over fifty volumes of their *Annalli Monumenti*, filled with coloured engravings of sculptures and other antiquities, attest the assiduity of those who conduct the proceedings.

The Society of Antiquaries of London, the British Archæological Association, the Royal Archæological Institute, and the numerous county archæological societies,[1] have done much to extend the knowledge handed down by previous antiquaries of the progress of Roman civilisation in Britain from the date of the invasion of Claudius. This will be found to correspond very much with the first lines of occupation, which may be followed by mapping down the roads constructed by the Romans for military purposes, and specially particularised, with the mileage between each station, in the *Itinerary* of Antoninus—a roadster for the guidance of the military in the second century of our era.

Though the remains described in this work principally date from a period not earlier than the Gordians, it is proposed, nevertheless, to give, in an Appendix at the end of the volume, the text of the *Itinerary* of Antoninus, because this is an authentic document of the period when it was written, and is a good prelude to the advancing civilisation of the next and following centuries, about which this work will treat. The map which accompanies it is by no means intended to be a sure guide to the identification of every place, but rather to give a general view of the direction of the roads by which the scheme of the Roman engineer for connecting the main ports and fortresses together may be seen ; and for this purpose I have abstained from marking down any other roads, whether

---

[1] A general index of the writings and proceedings of the different antiquarian societies is much needed, for diffusing a wider acquaintance with their investigations than is now attainable, except with great loss of time in the search.

British or Roman, except those in the *Itinerary* of Antoninus.

Four sheets of autotype facsimiles, from coins in the British Museum, of some of the Roman Emperors most directly connected with British history, is also added. These present their portraits to the reader in a more accurate form than could be rendered by a mere outline; in fact, the view of the coins themselves will hardly teach more than can be learnt from the engraved facsimile produced by the new autotype process. The fifth chapter is dedicated to the subject of the perpetuation or imitation of forms and designs in art through Roman into Anglo-Saxon and mediæval times; and in the succeeding chapters the various mosaics of England are described county by county. The sixteenth and seventeeth chapters treat upon the native and foreign mosaics preserved in the British Museum; and the eighteenth sums up the whole subject-matter. The nineteenth is dedicated to an explanation of the coins before referred to; and the Appendix, besides giving a catalogue of the pavements, treats of the *Itinerary* of Antoninus, and furnishes the text of the document, as far as regards Britain, with a map. By following the lines on the map, not only will it be seen how in their vicinity some of the finest specimens of mosaics have been found, but it will also indicate in some degree where others might be sought which have not yet come to light.

The intermediate stations along the various roads have been amply discussed, and their correspondence with modern towns and localities not always agreed upon; but the main points and direction of the roads can hardly be controverted,[1] and the main *foci* of Roman occupation will

---

[1] With some few exceptions as to *Iter* x and the *Itinera* vii and xv.

be some guide to the villas of the rich and powerful of the time, and to the mosaics which adorned them. The counties of England south of the Thames were first formed into a province under the name of *Britannia Prima*, and this was entered from the Continent by roads leading from Richborough (*Rutupiæ*), Dover (*Dubris*), and Lymne (*Portus Lemanis*): three roads from which ports converged upon Canterbury (*Durovernum*), and from thence proceeded through Rochester (*Durobrivæ*) to London.

Here the river Thames intervened and bounded this province on the north. The next outposts on the west would be in Gloucestershire, the principal of these being the fortress and *Colonia* of Gloucester (*Glevum*). This was reached from London, perhaps by the Thames river as far as Silchester (*Calleva Segontiacûm*), and from thence by a direct road through Speen (*Spinæ*), near Newbury and Cirencester (*Corinium*). The next step was to subdue Wales; and a line of road was accordingly made by Ross (*Ariconium*), Kenchester (*Magna*), Wroxeter (*Uriconium*), and Mediolanum, a station on the Tanad, to Chester (*Deva*), the head-quarters of the 20th Legion, the "dutiful, faithful, and victorious". *Mediolanum*, a central town of Wales, as its name indicates, was conveniently situated in the midst of this country, now erected into the province of *Britannia Secunda*.

Wales being pacified, a pretty direct road was made to communicate from Silchester (*Calleva Segontiacum*), through Reading and Bath, with Caerleon (*Isca Silurum*) on the Usk, the head-quarters of the 2nd Legion, and the line was continued along the coast as far as Carmarthen (*Maridunum*). From Caerleon (*Isca Silurum*) a line was carried

c

northward to the great camp at Kenchester (*Magna*), near Hereford, and there was joined by the road from Ross (*Ariconium*) to Wroxeter (*Uriconium*), and on to Chester. The northern part of Wales was opened up by a line of road from Chester to Caer Seiont, near Carnarvon (*Segontium*).

The next progress of occupation was that of the large province called *Flavia Cæsariensis*, in honour of the Emperor Flavius Vespasianus, which included the whole country bounded by the Thames river on the south and the Humber on the north ; and to this was soon added the adjoining province northward from the Humber as far as the Wall of Hadrian, from sea to sea, under the name of *Maxima Cæsariensis*, and these provinces were then opened up by military roads, as well as that further north, the province of *Valentia*, between the two walls of Hadrian and Antoninus.

The original Dover and London road was continued, through Verulam and Dunstable (*Durocobrivæ*), to the river Trent, which was navigable to another *Mediolanum* in Staffordshire, the centre of the Flavian province, and thence it pursued its course in nearly a right line through Congleton (*Condate*), Manchester (*Mancunium*), through Wigan, Preston, and Lancaster, to Cockermouth, near Maryport, on the west coast of Cumberland. From London a road in a north-easterly direction embraced Chelmsford (*Cæsaromagus*), Colchester, the great camp of *Camulodunum*, to a port on the sea-coast of Suffolk, Dunwich (*Sitomagus*), with a line on to Norwich (*Venta Icenorum*). From the camp and colony of Colchester a thoroughly military way went round by Thetford to Cambridge

(*Camboricum*), Castor (*Durobrivæ*) to Lincoln (*Lindum Colonia*), thence through Doncaster (*Danum*) to York[1] (*Eboracum*), the head-quarters of the 9th Legion ("the Spanish"), proceeding thence northward to Hadrian's Wall, and through it as far as High Rochester (*Bremenium*).

This great road, which bisected the country in a course almost parallel with the line already described from Dover, London, Manchester, and Cockermouth, known in later times, through part of its course, as the Watling Street, communicated with it by two cross-ways, the one from High Cross (*Venonæ*) to Lincoln, and the other from Manchester to York, with a south-easterly line from York to Patrington (*Prætorium*) on the Humber, near its mouth ; and a branch must be mentioned which separated from the great military way (Colchester to York and Bremenium) at Catterick (*Cataracton*) in Yorkshire, and went off in a north-westerly course to Carlisle (*Luguvallum*).

At a later period the harbours of Portsmouth, South-ampton, Weymouth, and neighbouring inlets of the sea, seem to have been the most frequented ports of landing from the Continent; and the *Itinerary* points to a road from east to west, which ran along the south coast, connecting Worthing, Chichester, Portsmouth, Southampton, Winchester, Wareham, and Dorchester ; and from Havant two roads radiated, the one straight to London, in line with that from London to the Suffolk coast, and another due north to Silchester (*Calleva Segontiacum*), where the re-

---

[1] Though not in the *Itinerary* of Antoninus, there seems to have been a more direct road from Lincoln northward to York, by crossing the Humber at or near Winterton to Brough. (T. Wright, *Celt, Roman, and Saxon*, 1875, p. 153.)

mains of massive walls, forum, and buildings attest the importance of this central point of convergence.[1]

The cross-roads in the *Itinerary* to which I have not before referred are a line connecting *Etocetum*, near Lichfield, on the Watling Street, with Wroxeter, and one connecting Ross (*Ariconium*) with Abergavenny (*Gobannium*). It will be seen from this sketch of the roads where important positions as places of residence were situated in the vicinity of towns, such as Cirencester, Gloucester, and Bath.[2] The Isle of Wight, Southampton, Chichester, and neighbourhood, from their southerly position and easy access to the Continent, would be much frequented, as well as Kent, with its three ports before named, and Rochester (*Durobrivæ*), with the fertile country at the back of these places.[3] The neighbourhood of the garrisons of the northern legions, whose head-quarters were at York and Chester and along the stations of the Wall, were too much taken up with military works to afford the time and leisure required for the cultivation of the arts of peace, in the

[1] The most recent discoveries from excavations on this spot have been described by the Rev. James Gerald Joyce, F.S.A., in vol. xlvi, p. 344, of the *Archæologia of the Society of Antiquaries*, who had previously given an account of the investigations there in 1865 and 1867.

[2] The Rev. H. M. Scarth, M.A., the historian of Roman Bath (*Aquæ Solis*), has minutely illustrated this part of the country, and, indeed, many others, in a comprehensive manual of antiquities lately published, entitled *The History of Roman Britain*, to which I shall again have occasion to refer in the course of these pages.

[3] The latest guides to Kent in Roman times, since Hasted and the old county historians, are Mr. Charles Roach Smith, F.S.A., *Antiquities of Richborough, Reculver, and Lymne*, London, 1850; and the articles by Rev. Canon Scott-Robertson and Mr. George Dowker in the *Archæologia Cantiana; and Canterbury in the Olden Time*, by Mr. John Brent; and the various papers on the localities in the British Archæological Association and Royal Archæological Institute *Journals*.

laying out of spacious villas and mosaics, such as are seen
or might be found at Lincoln, Castor, Verulamium, Colchester, and Norwich. Wales, both north and south,
affords evidence of Roman peaceable occupation throughout the country, which was well guarded by the strong
garrisons at Caerleon on the Usk and Chester on the
Dee.

In the first chapters of this work are discussed the
two classes of subjects which in Romano-British mosaics
are generally combined, that is, the Orphic and Bacchic
myths, with astronomical references and symbolism; and by
comparing these with the writings of poets, contemporary,
or nearly so, with the mosaics, as well as with the prose
writers, we shall find them mutually to explain each other.
It would be long before the rich and luxurious Romans of
the higher orders would be induced to exchange their
Epicurean philosophy and habits for the principles and
practice of Christianity; and if they did, the banqueting-
hall would be the last place from which would be banished
the emblems and adornments of an ancient creed and
mythology. Epicurus considered the *summum bonum* to
consist in the attainment of happiness on earth by every
means which could procure peace of mind and tranquillity
through intellectual enjoyment and health of body—σαρκῶν
εὐσταθὲς κατάστημα. The tendency of such a system would
be to degenerate from the higher standard of its founder
into licentiousness and lust, which would entirely defeat
the end proposed by Epicurus. The Stoics and Cynics did
all they could to bring Epicurean doctrines into ridicule;
and one of the most moderate of these, the Cynic Hierocles,
may be named—who, nevertheless, was somewhat un-

measured in his satire, as appears by the testimony of Aulus Gellius (ix, 6-8).

The Romano-British tesselated pavements have been separately described, and most of those which are specially interesting on account of the subjects displayed in the pictures, have been figured in the works of S. Lysons, F.S.A., of which his *Reliquiæ Britannicæ Romanæ*, in three folio volumes, is a grand example of sumptuous illustration. Many are to be found in *Monumenta Vetusta* and the *Archæologia* of the Society of Antiquaries, and also scattered through the journals of the many archæological societies; in the *Corinium* of Messrs. Buckman and Newmarch; in the works of Sir Richard Colt-Hoare, Bart., and his *Pitney* (1831-4°); in the *Reliquiæ Isurianæ* of Mr. H. Ecroyd Smith, and in Mr. John Pointer's account of Stunsfield, Oxford (1713). The Rev. W. Hiley Bathurst published an *Account of Roman Antiquities in Lydney Park, Gloucestershire*, in 1879, with notes by C. W. King.

Mr. William Fowler, of Winterton, published twenty-six plates of Roman mosaics, 1796 to 1818,[1] and Mr. J. R.

---

[1] I am indebted to Mr. H. W. Ball of Barton-on-Humber, for the following testimonials to Mr. Wm. Fowler's skill and accuracy in publishing these drawings. The Rev. W. Gretton, D.D., Master of Magdalen College, Cambridge, writes, under date 20th March 1801:—"I recommend Mr. Wm. Fowler to the notice and regard of all who are admirers of the antiquities of this county, as a man of exquisite industry in his researches and of great ingenuity in the execution of the various species of tesselated pavements which he has drawn and engraved with the greatest fidelity and accuracy." Sir Joseph Banks, upon an occasion of addressing the Society of Antiquaries, said, in reference to the representations of mosaic pavements by Mr. Fowler :—"Others have shown us what they thought these remains ought to have been, but Fowler has shown us what they are; and this is what we want." Born in 1761, he died on 22nd September 1832, at Winterton, where he was born, and where he resided during

Smith, of Soho Square, another collection of plates of mosaics in 1850. Many accounts of them are given in the *Collectanea Antiqua*, seven vols., and *Roman Remains of Ancient London*, by Mr. C. Roach Smith, F.S.A.

Mr. J. E. Price, F.S.A., and Mr. F. G. Hilton Price, F.S.A., F.G.S., in describing the pavement found in Bucklersbury, have touched upon many other of the mosaics in Britain, and have given an account of the villa and pavements discovered in 1880 at Morton, near Brading, in the Isle of Wight, in a separate work. The Morton mosaics have also been described by Mr. Cornelius Nicholson, F.S.A., in the pages of the *Antiquary*, 1880. The county historians have but occasionally given accounts of the discovery of mosaics. Leland and Camden have described many, as well as Stukeley, Gale, Horsley, and others. In numerous instances the pavements have been destroyed or reburied, and, therefore, are only known by these descriptions in print; some also have been removed to public museums or private collections; and as I believe they have not hitherto been brought together for the purpose of comparison, a catalogue of them may be useful to future inquirers, and I have arranged more than a hundred and eighty examples, according to counties, without pretending that the list is complete, though embracing the principal figured pavements hitherto discovered, and it is a beginning for a work which others may continue and perfect hereafter.

One unintentional omission must be here mentioned, of a small portion of a pavement found at Bay's Meadow,

the whole of his long and active life.—Reprinted from the *North Lincolnshire Monthly Illustrated Journal* for April 1869.

xxiv INTRODUCTORY CHAPTER.

near Droitwich, on 3rd April 1847, particularly as no other mosaic has been reported in the county of Worcester. It is of geometrical pattern, of inch *tesseræ*, in about three colours; the lines form a diamond overlapping a square. In the centre is a guilloche knot in a circle. This pavement is now in the museum, Worcester.[1] A description is given of the principal examples, and references to the authors from whom my information is drawn, and I have added a notice of coins found in the vicinity, as some kind of clue to the chronology. My list will begin with Woodchester, once at the head of British pavements, but which now has even been excelled in interest by the late discovery in the Isle of Wight, with which I shall conclude. Coloured engravings, drawn expressly for this work, are also given of eight out of the seventy mosaics in the British Museum from Asia Minor and Northern Africa, with descriptions of each.

I shall not encumber my account with the origin and history of mosaics in general, and the date of their introduction into Italy, which has been often written upon; nor speculate as to how the floors of the Romans, at first stuccoed, came to be painted with representations of such objects as might have fallen from the table to the ground; nor how these first essays at art were succeeded by pictures in mosaics which acquired such repute, and came so much into use, that in the time of Seneca he was considered a poor man indeed who could not afford a tesselated floor[2] in his best rooms; nor need I repeat what is well known, that the far-seeing mind of the divine Julius, knowing

---

[1] *Journal Brit. Arch. Assoc.*, xxxvii, p. 432.
[2] *Lithostrotum.*

the effect of Roman civilisation upon the nations brought within its scope, did not fail to carry about with him *tesseræ* and *sectilia* for the decoration of the floor of his *prætorium*, wherever this might happen to be, so that the head-quarters of the general might always represent the style and dignity of Roman life.[1] Suetonius, in relating this (in *Vita C. J. Cæsaris*), little knew the puzzle it would be in after ages to discriminate accurately between the words *tesseræ* and *sectilia*. The probability is that the *tesseræ*, presenting four sides on the surface (from τέσσαρες, four), were originally the cubes of brick cast in a mould, and that when other substances, such as porphyry, glass, or marble, were cut into forms for the same purpose, these were called *sectilia*, as the word seems to be used in a wider sense than for the sections or slabs employed for decorating walls and ceilings, to which the word is sometimes restricted by modern interpreters. The *sectilia* were either square or shield-shaped, triangular or hexagonal (honeycomb form), and sometimes cut to special forms as required.

Britain was not behind the rest of the Roman empire in works of this nature, some of which were of great beauty and elegance. Foundations of Roman villas are spread through the length and breadth of the land, and accounts of them and their arrangements would bear greatly on the subject here treated of, but this present work must be restricted to the tesselated floors with which they were adorned. Grævius (*Antiq. Rom.*, viii) has the remark that

---

[1] Juvenal criticises such practices at a later period :

"Argillam atque rotam citius properate sed ex hoc
Tempore jam Cæsar figuli tua castra sequantur."— *Sat.*, iv, 133.

as the large number of slaves owned by the rich Roman
proprietors had each a separate *cella* allotted to him, it can
readily be seen how the villas came to be extended in width,
and, as Seneca observes (*Epist.*, 114), the private edifices
exceeded in extent even large towns. Olympiodorus (in
Bibliotheca Photii) informs us that each of the large villas
contained within itself whatever a moderate sized town
might require—that is, circus, exchange, temples, fountains,
and baths of all kinds; but it would be rather an exag-
geration to apply this description to those hitherto found
in England.

A large number of mosaics may yet see the light, for
in the country they lie only from one to two feet below
the surface, and the plough goes over without injuring or
exposing them to view, unless the finding a few Roman
remains happens to come to the ears of some neighbouring
antiquary. The south-western counties have furnished
the most numerous and some of the best examples; but
as instances are found in almost all the other counties
south of Yorkshire, it is probable that many more may
hereafter be exhumed. The pavements were formed of cubes
of various sizes, colours, and materials, and I may instance
as a good type the large pavement at Woodchester, in
Gloucestershire, described by Lysons, which consisted for
the most part of cubes of half an inch, and in which he
says that not less than a million and a half of them were
employed. The materials were mostly of the produce of
the country, except the white, which is of a very hard
calcareous stone, bearing a good polish, and resembling the
Palomino marble of Italy.

The Romans took much pains to keep out damp from

their floors and walls, and hence the mosaics have been so well preserved ; thus, the greater part were "suspended", that is, built on a platform of tiles which rested on pillars of brick-tile or stone, and into the hollow space below, or the hypocaust, was blown the heated air from a great furnace lighted outside the house, and the blast rushed into the hypocaust through one or two narrow channels. When the pavement had no hypocaust below it, then it was laid upon a thick bed of different materials, by which the same purpose of keeping out the damp was effected. Mr. Thomas Wright describes the foundations of one at Wroxeter as follows : " They consist of four distinct strata of materials, forming together a bed between two and three feet in thickness. On the native ground they first placed a layer of lumps of sandstone, rather irregularly disposed, and above eighteen inches thick, the uneven surface of which was made tolerably smooth by a bed of soft concrete or mortar, exactly like that now used in ordinary building. On this bed of mortar was placed the stratum on which the *tesseræ* were laid, about two inches and a half thick, exceedingly hard, and evidently composed of a mixture of rough pulverised burnt clay and lime, prepared with more care than the others, being of a very uniform thickness, and having its under and upper surfaces perfectly level. On this hard and even stratum the *tesseræ* were bedded in a layer of white and very hard cement, not more than half an inch thick." Mr. Lysons says of the pavement at Woodchester, that "the cement on which it was laid appeared to be about eight inches thick, and composed of fine gravel, pounded brick, and lime, forming a very hard substance, on which the *tesseræ* were laid in a fine cement consisting chiefly of lime. The next stratum was three feet thick, and appeared to be composed of coarser gravel, with which great quantities of *tesseræ* were mixed, and below this another of a reddish sand and clay, mixed with pieces of brick about a foot in depth, which lay on the natural soil." According to this, the foundations of the Woodchester pavement would be nearly five feet in thickness, though the previously named example at Wroxeter only measured between two and three feet. The thickness of these foundations was probably influenced by the nature of the soil,—a moist clay requiring a thicker foundation than a subsoil of gravel.

Seneca (*Nat. Quæst.*, vi, 31) instances a remarkable phenomenon in the case of an earthquake, when the entire nucleus of a pavement had been rent, and the water oozed up through the *tessellæ*. It will be seen that the English examples carry out very well the directions of Vitruvius: "*Super nucleum, ad regulam et libellam exacta pavimenta struantur, sive sectilibus sive tesseris.*" These mosaics were called *Opera segmentata, Opus musivum,* and *musaceum.* The workmen, in laying them down, kept the *tesseræ* of different colours in divisions, as does the printer his types.

The bed to receive them was of lime, sand, and ashes, and the cement used to set them in was composed of pounded slate, white of egg, and gum-dragon, which was to be moist when the *tessellæ* were laid on it, as it soon hardened, and these were then pressed down with a heavy roller, which fixed them in their places. The surface was then polished, or rather, such of the *tessellæ* as would take a polish; and this inequality of materials, some being polished and others retaining their natural dull surface, produced a very pleasing effect. The *Opus vermiculatum* seems to describe the sinuous lines of *tessellæ* when they were arranged in curves to follow the pattern, in opposition to those placed in straight lines. The *Opus Alexandrinum* was worked in two colours, black and white, on a red ground.

Eumenes, in his eulogium on the Emperor Constantius, who had restored Britain to Rome after the ten years' usurpation of Carausius and Allectus, invokes the Emperor's patronage in the restoration of his native town, *Augustodunum* (Autun), in Gaul, and cites the reconquest of Britain as the means by which the Emperor would be able to comply with his request, by sending artists from Britain, in whom that province abounded.[1]

For the purpose of reference, the value of a work such as the present is much enhanced by the excellence of engravings, that the pavements may be faithfully presented to the eye ; and I must acknowledge the obligation I am under to Messrs. Howe and Clark, of Messrs. Whiting and Co., the publishers, and the skilled artists under their direction, for the care bestowed on the coloured drawings from the mosaics at Morton, Bignor, London, and elsewhere, as well as those copied from the fine specimens in the British Museum.

Those discovered in far bygone times, which can only be represented by copies of engravings then made, may not so well represent the reality as the modern work referred to, but they are the best to be had. I have seen a

---

[1] Ex hac Britanniæ facultate victoriæ plurimos quibus illæ provinciæ redundabant accepit artifices (*Panegyric*, v, c. 21).

coloured drawing in the possession of Mr. Christopher
Bowly, of Cirencester, of a pavement described at its foot
as found " in Dier Street, A.D. 1820, in the house of Mr.
Jenkins, cheese-factor." It seemed not to be drawn with
that accuracy which would be required to substantiate a
discovery of which this drawing is the only record, still
the fact is worthy a place in the history of Romano-British
mosaics, and particularly as Mr. C. Bowly writes to me
that " it was very near to where the 1849 pavements were
found; but the house (No. 93, Dyer Street) is on the
opposite side of the street to the Mr. Smith's house
(No. 52, Dyer Street) in which the 1783 pavement was
discovered. The latter could not be the same as that discovered in 1849, though it may have been part of the same
dwelling. There are other pavements in Cirencester still
uncovered, and of which only the edge has been exposed,
and covered up as quickly as possible.

" There is an unopened villa on the estate of Lord Sherborne, at Bibury, about seven miles from here, where some
pavement was found, but has been covered up again in
order to preserve it ; the small piece that was exposed was
of a simple character." He further writes, in reply to
inquiries, that he regrets to say " the Barton pavement
has deteriorated, and is deteriorating, from the combined
effects of damp and frost. I am not aware that since its
discovery it has been injured by the roots of trees at any
rate : although it is quite possible, it is not very obvious
that such is the case. The pavement is under cover, but
rests immediately upon the soil, and is not flat, but undulating."

I have to express my obligation to Mr. Bowly for this

information, as well as to all those gentlemen whose printed works are referred to in this volume, and for the knowledge freely imparted to me by many of those who are still living, whenever required, as Mr. Joseph Clarke, F.S.A., of Saffron-Walden, Mr. Gordon Hills, Mr. Halliwell-Phillipps, LL.D., F.S.A., Mr. C. Roach Smith, F.S.A., Mr. Stephen Tucker (Somerset Herald), Mr. C. Warne, F.S.A., and others. I am also much indebted to Mr. Augustus W. Franks, F.S.A., Mr. Walter de Gray Birch, F.S.A., Mr. Charles T. Newton, C.B., F.S.A., Mr. A. S. Murray, and Mr. George Bullen, F.S.A., all of the British Museum, for facilitating the copying of the mosaics there and for information concerning them; and to the three first-named friends for looking through and correcting portions of my proof-sheets. To Mr. Walter de Gray Birch I owe the first idea of writing this work, by describing Romano-British mosaics, and throughout its performance he has assisted and encouraged me in the undertaking. I also gratefully acknowledge the many courteous acts of assistance in matters of archæology generally from his worthy father, Dr. Birch, F.S.A., Keeper of the Department of Egyptian and Oriental Antiquities in the Museum, as well as from Mr. E. Maunde Thompson, F.S.A., Keeper of the Manuscript Department.

To Mr. Herbert A. Grueber, of the Department of Coins and Medals in the British Museum, I am particularly indebted for the assistance he has afforded both to me and to Mr. Prætorius, the photographer, while engaged in reproducing the coins, and for his written descriptions of those coins and correction of the proof-sheets.

Mr. E. P. Loftus Brock, F.S.A., I have to thank very

much for the loan of many rare engravings of mosaics
from his rich collection, which has assisted me not a
little.

It is with great pleasure I acknowledge myself beholden
to Mr. Jno. G. Price, F.S.A., and to Mr. Fred. G. Hilton
Price, F.S.A., as well for their written descriptions of
Morton and other pavements, as for those given on the spot
vivâ voce, and for permitting the artist to make drawings
of the pavement at Morton.

I must not omit mention of the many friends who
have from time to time accompanied me to some of the
pavements; and I refer back with pleasure to the friendly
intercourse and free discussions kept up, during many
years, with Messrs. G. G. Adams, F.S.A., Geo. Ade,
Thomas Blashill, Cecil Brent, F.S.A., W. H. Cope, Arthur
Cope, C. H. Compton, H. Syer Cuming, F.S.A.Scot.,
Horman Fisher, F.S.A., J. W. Grover, F.S.A., George
Lambert, F.S.A., Douglas Lithgow, LL.D., F.S.A., Dr.
Phené, F.S.A., Rev. S. M. Mayhew, Walter Myers, F.S.A.,
Samuel B. Merriman, J. T. Mould, Geo. Patrick, W. H.
Rylands, F.S.A., Worthington G. Smith, and George R.
Wright, F.S.A., not forgetting Mr. Walter Mann of Bath,
all of whom have assisted me in these researches, the
latter having furnished me with drawings and plates of
the mosaics in Bath and neighbourhood.

Lastly, my acknowledgment is due to the learned ex-
Secretary of the Society of Antiquaries, Mr. C. Knight
Watson, F.S.A., and to Mr. G. C. Ireland, the Sub-Librarian,
for information they have at all times freely rendered as to
the books and records in the valuable collection under
their care.

Since this work has been written, notices have come to my knowledge of various other pavements lately found at Lancing, Yatton, near Weston-super-Mare, Leicester, and elsewhere; and the British Archæological Association paid a visit to the pavement at Bignor, Sussex, in August last, which was commented on by Mr. C. Roach Smith, F.S.A., who inclined to the belief that large villas such as this and the other recently found at Morton, Isle of Wight, were a kind of public building occupied by the *Procuratores*, or others who collected the revenues of the province; and for myself I have to remark that it seems to me probable that the head with a nimbus, attributed by Mr. Lysons to Venus, is rather that of Ariadne, the beloved of Bacchus. The pheasants seem emblematic of the country where she dwelt, and the *cantharus* of Bacchus also adorns the same compartment of the mosaic. She had the nimbus because exalted to the skies, where the crown of Ariadne among the northern constellations is still seen and acknowledged, though the fair lady has long ceased her lamentations here on earth. There are two letters, I R, on one of the mosaics at Bignor, which, transposed, may possibly be two letters of the name of Ariadne. This is purely conjecture, but I see no monogram or combination of letters here, but simply I R. This may be one of four divisions of the name; the remaining three may have occupied other three parts of the geometrical design, now destroyed. An article on the Bignor pavement, since the visit of the British Archæological Association thither, has been given in the *Builder*, vol. xlix, p. 487, for 10th October 1885, and the pavements there minutely described. The interest which all archæologists feel in this Bignor series of mosaics has been further stimulated by a paper read by Mr. W. de Gray Birch before the British Archæological Association on the 2nd December 1885, in which the Roman art was examined from new points of view; and the gradual decay of these and other Romano-British art-pictures in *tesseræ* deplored.

I will conclude these preliminary observations by pointing to an *erratum* on page 33, where Bignor is erroneously named as having on its mosaics a figure of Bacchus and panther; and also on page 36, Apollo and lyre is ascribed to Bignor pavement, which is equally a mistake, and the word Bignor should therefore be erased from those two paragraphs on pp. 33 and 36.

My many shortcomings and omissions are committed to the indulgence of my readers of this the first work specially dedicated to the description of Romano-British mosaic pavements.

ROMANO-BRITISH MOSAICS.

CHAPTER I.

AFTER the usurpation of Carausius and Allectus, the influence of the old gods of Rome, the *Dii majorum gentium*, appears to have slackened, both in Britain as well as elsewhere. The strongest argument which could be adduced in favour of their influence was the uninterrupted success of the Roman arms, under their supposed guidance, by which conquests had been made of new countries, and a vast empire consolidated. This was now appearing to wane ; and Greek modes of thought tended to carry back the Pagan world to earlier forms of nature-worship, such as were embodied in the Orphic hymns and the poetical rhapsodies of the Dionysiac epic. The follies and crimes of the gods of Olympus were successfully ridiculed by the voice of reason and philosophy, and such reasonings have been set forth in the elegant prose composition, *Octavius*, by Minucius Felix, an author well versed in the learning of the ancients, in whose work Christian principles and ethics are set forth in bright contrast to the licentiousness and degeneracy of the age. Lucian is more severe, though less serious.

The discoveries in astronomical science will be referred

B

to in another chapter, and the influence they had in
spiritualizing the anthropomorphic religion of the Greeks
and Romans. The beautiful order and regularity of the
heavenly bodies were an everlasting evidence of the unity
and immeasurable depth and greatness of a Divine mind, of
a great *effector rerum naturæ*, without which neither the
atomic theory of Anaxagoras, nor the forces of nature, the
vis consilii expers, could account for the presence of man
on earth, and the innumerable objects which are brought
together to administer to his mental and bodily enjoyments.
Much less could the marvels of the solar system, and of the
countless number of bodies in space beyond the orbits of
the planets, be explained as the work of chance, or be the
creations of such despicable divinities as Saturn and Jupiter.
Bœotian Thebes and Cadmus its founder, who introduced
into Europe the letters of the Ionian Greek alphabet, formed
a point of departure for the expansion of science among
mankind, and of the religious feelings which sprang from
increased knowledge. Hence we find that Cadmus married
Harmony, an embodiment of the "Music of the Spheres".

Euripides introduces her to the Athenians in those
beautiful lines of the *Medea*, which may be rendered into
English verse, however inadequately, as follows:—

> " Happy of old, ye sons of Erectheus,
> Children of good gods happy for ever,
> Nurtured on wisdom the most distinguished,
> In a land, sacred, untrodden by enemies;
> Leading refined lives in brightest of atmospheres,
> Where, as report says, the flaxen-haired *Harmony*
> Planted of old nine Pierian Muses,
> And where, as they say, the fair-flowing Cephisus
> Offered to Venus her pure stream to drink,
> As she breathed o'er the land odoriferous breezes,
> While braiding with chaplets of roses her hair,
> Sending her sweet loves attendant on wisdom,
> And help-mates in excellence, science, and taste."
>
> (EUR.. *Med.*, v. 820. *et seqq.*)

The antidote to this frame of mind was the later Epicurean system. Epicurean ideas had so strongly prevailed in the time of Juvenal in the Roman world, as to justify the satirist in saying that the hungry muse had migrated into the hall—

"Esuriens migraret in Atria Clio." (*Sat.* vii, 6—7.)

The Bacchic theogony, and the hours or seasons, took the place of the Muses, who, according to Cicero, were once only four in number, and whom he calls daughters of Memory (μνήμη).

The name *Mussivum* and *Musaceum*, applied to mosaic pavements, has been derived by some from the Muses, who at one time were often introduced into the designs of floors. Cean-Bermudez, in his summary of Roman antiquities in Spain, mentions two pavements at Ulia, near Montemayor, on one of which is a female head, with the letters EVTERPE, and on the other are female busts, which he supposes represent the Muses. The subject should be studied chronologically, as considerable changes were taking place in the social and religious ideas of the time, up to when our British mosaics were designed during the four or five centuries of Roman heathenism ; and we have, in fact, instances of floors upon three separate levels, and of different degrees of merit, representing the dwellings of successive generations; but as to the general tone of the pictured mosaics in Britain, it does not vary much.

The conservative ideas of the old Roman aristocracy, when heathenism was dying out, dictated the designs ; and at this time the eclecticism of the philosophers was striving to modify the mythology of the ancients, and to bring it more into harmony with the experiences of man and the lessons of nature. The spread of Christianity, too, had the effect of encouraging, on the part of its adversaries, the pictorial treatment of subjects which held up Epicureanism as the *summum bonum*. The old theogony of Homer and Hesiod, which formed the ground-work of the Roman system as well as the Greek, had been gradually giving place to the Orphic or Bacchic, which may be traced back to Onomacritus, who lived between 520-485 B.C. He seems to have collected the myths and traditions concerning Orpheus, reputed to be the pupil of Apollo, who taught him to play on the lyre, and with such wonderful effect, that not only wild beasts, but even trees and rocks, were moved by the power of his melody.

Dr. Smith, in his *Dictionary of Biography and Mythology*, has collected the opinions of the ancients upon Orpheus : Ibycus (*Frag. apud Priscian*, vol. i, p. 283, Krehl); Pindar (*Pyth.*,iv,315,s.176);Æschylus(*Agam.*,1612-13). Sophocles does not mention him, but Euripides repeatedly (*Med.*, 543 ; *Iph. in Aul.*, 1211 ; *Bacch.*, 561 ; *Rhes.*, 941-944 ; *Alcest.*, 357 ; *Hippol.*, 953), and this poet makes the first allusion to the connection of Orpheus with Dionysus, or the Theban Bacchus. The other Greek and Roman poets refer to him as the civilizer of mankind ; Aristophanes calling him the teacher of religious initiations, and of abstinence from murder (*Ranæ*, 1032). An inscription at Dium, near Pydna in Macedonia, says the Muses buried him there, Jupiter having slain him with a thunderbolt ; the more usual legend says he was buried by the Muses at the foot of Olympus (*Anthol. Græca*, No. 483 ; Pausanias, ix, 30 ; see Müller, *Hist. Lit. Grec.*, p. 231). The symbol of pure intellect and refinement melted away afterwards in the more sensual civilization of Bacchus or Dionysus; and hence, - in the myth of Bacchus we get two successive gods of this name who seem to represent the different stages of religious belief, the first of whom, under the name of Zagræus, is the oldest hero of the Orphic theology, and " his worshippers, instead of indulging in unrestrained pleasure and frantic enthusiasm, rather aimed at an ascetic purity of life and manners (Lobeck, *Aglaoph.*, p. 244). Their priests wore white linen garments, like Oriental and Egyptian priests, from whom, as Herodotus remarks, much may have been borrowed in the ritual of the Orphic worship (Dr. Smith, *in voce Orpheus*).

At about the same time that Onomacritus was establishing Orphic societies in Greece, Pythagoras was introducing his philosophy into Italy, and Meton had made that discovery in astronomical science, the cycle of nineteen years, when the sun and moon revert again to the same position relatively to the earth and to each other; a cycle still preserved and used in our golden number in the Calendar.

These three men mark an epoch in the world's history, and from them science and religion took a mould, which poets and artists rendered permanent, with progressive modifications, such as have been already referred to.

The Bacchic theology, under the auspices of the son of Semele, youngest daughter of Cadmus of Thebes, encouraged, and was acted upon by, the Epicurean ideas of the age, which were introduced not without a revolution, which spread from Thebes to the islands of the Ægean, to Argos, the stronghold of the stately and jealous Juno, where, though first opposed by Perseus, the system was also introduced, and finally into Athens. The history and ultimate stage of this mythology may best be studied in a long poem by Nonnus, a native of Panopolis, or the city of Pan, in Egypt, who wrote his *Dionysiaca* in forty-eight books, digested into Homeric hexameters. It has been translated into French, and the various texts collated by the Comte de Marcellus (Paris, 1856). This Nonnus was not only a contemporary of Claudian and Ausonius, but also of Cyros of Panopolis, and of Coluthus, Tryphliodorus, John of Gaza, Musæus, Comtos of Smyrna, and the poets of the *Anthologia*.

The coins found in and near the villas, to which reference is made in association with the description of each, will be some clue to the chronology of the mosaics, and from this it appears that, except in single instances, as in the coin of third brass of Hadrian, and one of Lucilla, found at Woodchester; the coin of third brass of Titus, found at Stanway, in Essex; one of Vespasian and of Faustina junior, at Gurnard's Bay, Isle of Wight; and one of Hadrian, in London, found near the Excise office in Broad Street, and perhaps a few more, the coins discovered on the site of the mosaics belong almost entirely to a date extending from the reign of Gordianus III, or say Alexander Severus, to that of Arcadius—a period of about 175 years. Cases of single coins found will, of course, not prove much in chronology. They were sometimes suspended round the neck as amulets or ornaments, as the holes bored through them testify, and therefore might have been in use long after they were first issued; but these would not greatly affect the question, the number of such coins being small.

Reference has been made to the progressive civilization of Britain along the Roman military roads; and the country abounds with remains of the early period of Roman dominion, both in coins, walls, architectural fragments, arms, and the various utensils of civil life; but it would appear from the coins found, either that the mode of decorating the floors with mosaics was not in use at the earlier period in Britain, or that at present such earlier floors have not yet been discovered; and it seems probable that the Gordians, father and son, who were elected emperors in Africa, to the joy of the Senate, may have been the means of introducing this fashion into Britain through their representatives.

Gordian III, who was grandson of the first Gordian, occupied a villa near Rome which was built on a scale of extraordinary magnificence. Gibbon says : " The family of the Gordians was one of the most illustrious of the Roman Senate. On the father's side he was descended from the Gracchi ; on the mother's, from the Emperor Trajan. A great estate enabled him to support the dignity of his birth, and in the enjoyment of it he displayed an elegant taste and beneficent disposition. The palace in Rome formerly inhabited by the Great Pompey had been during several generations in the possession of Gordian's family. It was distinguished by ancient trophies of naval victories, and decorated with the works of modern painting. His villa on the road to Præneste was celebrated for baths of singular beauty and extent, for three stately rooms of a hundred feet in length, and for a magnificent portico supported by 200 columns of the most curious and costly sorts of marble (*Decline and Fall*, vol. ii, p. 194).

If we consider the disturbed state of the empire ruled over by tyrants such as Maximin the Thracian, who was advancing with his legions upon Rome from the north, besieging on the way Aquileia, at the head of the Adriatic Sea, we should have supposed the provinces on the continent could seldom have enjoyed that repose which would be necessary for the cultivation of the arts of peace and the erection of sumptuous villas ; yet they seem to have been able to do so, and, moreover, to adorn them with metaphysical delineations and conceits. The state of affairs in the secluded island of Britain was scarcely less agitated by civil commotions than the continent, notwithstanding its insular position, yet its villas and mosaics show the same cultivated taste. The thirty years which followed the elevation of Gordian III, at the age of thirteen, could boast of little tranquillity, though the young man, under the guidance of

his father-in-law and prætorian prefect Misitheus, successfully defended the eastern frontier against the Persians.
He, however, finally lost his life in a renewed attempt
against the Persian kingdom, which had sprung up with
increased vitality under Artaxerxes and his successor
Sapor.

Philip the Arab, prætorian prefect in succession to
Misitheus, when raised to Imperial command, endeavoured
to amuse the people of Rome by celebrating the Secular
games, in commemoration of the thousandth year of the
foundation of the city.   His coin, bearing the effigy of
a hippopotamus, recalls the festivities of the circus.

The unfortunate reigns of the emperors Decius Gallus
and Æmilianus were succeeded by the disastrous events of
Valerian and his son Gallienus.   The former of these two,
whose attention was all fixed upon Persia and the East, and
who ended his career there by dying in captivity, could not
have exerted much influence over Britain and Western
Europe ; but not so Gallienus, his son, to whom was
entrusted the care of repelling the Germans and defending
the Gauls.   He had to encounter the opposition of the
thirty tyrants, the number of whom, however, has been
reduced by Gibbon to nineteen ; and as those in Gaul and
the western provinces more especially concern our present
subject, I will name only Posthumus, Lollianus, Victorinus
and his mother Victoria, Marius, and Tetricus.   Most of
their coins turn up occasionally in our archæological
researches, some often, particularly those of Tetricus, which
are very common.   He was governor of Aquitania, and
reigned four or five years.   The next period to be reviewed
in connection with our own history is that extending from
Claudius Gothicus to the reign of Diocletian.

Claudius, by his victories over the Goths, deservedly
earned his surname of Gothicus. If the origin of his ancestry

seems doubtful, his name is honoured in his posterity : his niece being the grandmother of Constantine the Great. A high character is given him by Trebellius Pollio, who lived under Constantius.

Aurelian, in his short reign of four years and nine months, put an end to the Gothic war, and recovered Gaul, Spain, and Britain out of the hands of Tetricus. After pacifying the Persians, he turned his arms against Zenobia, Queen of Palmyra, and defeated her two armies in the battles of Emesa and Palmyra. The pageant of his triumph at Rome was graced by the appearance of ten women of the Gothic nation, who had been made prisoners while fighting in the garb of men. Twenty elephants, bands of gladiators, and a variety of wild beasts swelled the triumphal procession, in which were seen captives of the nations of the Blemyes, Axomitæ, Arabes, Eudæmones, Indi, Bactriani, Hiberi, Saraceni, and Persæ, bearing gifts ; and of the Gothi, Alani, Roxolani, Sarmatæ, Franci, Suevi, Vandali, and Germani, with their hands tied ; and among these were some of the principal men of Palmyra, and Ægyptians on account of their rebellion.

We may hasten through the short reigns of Tacitus, Probus, Carus and his two sons, in which the ancient veneration for the Senate of Rome alternated with the turbulence of the Prætorian guards in the election of emperors. The reigns of Diocletian and Maximian, with the Cæsars Galerius and Constantius, appointed by them to assist in the government of the Empire, are illustrious in many ways. The august emperors who assumed the surnames of Jovius and Herculius ruled the East and the West from their two capitals of Nicomedia and Milan in their departments, and set the first example of abandoning Rome as the political centre of the Roman world. Maximian and Constantius exercised a particular influence over the province of Britain, but could not prevent the usurpation of Carausius and Allectus in the island, who for ten years succeeded in dismembering that province from the Empire, until Asclepiodotus, on the death and defeat of Allectus, restored Britain to the rule of Constantius and the harmony of the Roman system.

Eighteen years of discord and confusion followed, until Constantine the Great—from his palace in York, whither he had hastened to receive the last dying words of his father Constantius—by defeating his numerous opponents, restored order. We have coins of Magnentius, who took an important part in the civil war inherited by the numerous descendants of the family of Constantine, and among these a conspicuous part was played afterwards by his two nephews, Gallus and Julian ; the former from his capital, Antioch, ruling the East, and the latter, after a life of trouble, rising to the highest eminence in the West, and defeating the Germans at the battle of Strasburg. After saving Gaul, he delighted to make Paris his winter residence, and from thence was able to keep a vigilant eye on the province of Britain. He repaired the loss of food on the Continent, consequent upon the calamities of war, by importing large quantities of corn from Britain. Six hundred ships, built from the timber of the Ardennes, and making more than one voyage, were capable of transporting a very large quantity of corn. Such transactions argue strongly for the prosperous and fertile state of Britain at that time as regards agriculture, for the exportation thence seems to have been on a very large scale. We find memorials, in the shape of coins of the reigns of Valentinian and Valens, of Gratian, and as late as the reigns of Arcadius and Honorius, who divided the empire of the Great Theodosius between them.

Mr. C. Roach Smith, in describing a hoard of coins exhumed in 1883, in Cobham Park, Kent, makes this remark: " The finding of buried hoards of Roman coins from time immemorial is a well-known fact; but not generally considered in its historical signification as it deserves to be." In reference to this hoard, he goes on to say that, " with the exception of a single specimen of Constantine the Great, it is confined to coins of Constantius the Second, Constans, Gallus, Magnentius, and Decentius. As there is not one of Julianus, who was created Cæsar by Constantius in A.D. 355, when his coins were first struck, we may conclude that the hoard was deposited in A.D. 353, not long before the overthrow of Magnentius and Decentius by Constantius. This important event took place near Mursa, in Lower Pannonia. Magnentius, who in A.D. 350 had usurped the Imperial dignity, and reigned successfully over the Western provinces, had drawn together an immense army of legionaries and auxiliaries, and among the levies from Britain we may enrol the owner of the Cobham hoard now under our examination." The following will show the very limited range of the coins, as regards time :—

	No. of Specimens.	A.D.
Constantine the Great	1	306 to 337
Constantius II . .	148	337 to 361
Constans . . .	256	333 to 350
Constantius III, Gallus	1	351 to 354
Magnentius .	419	350 to 353
Decentius . .	11	350 to 353
Total	836	

From their good preservation, and the absence of attrition from circulation, these coins must have formed part of the vast stores sent by Magnentius from Gaul, and probably not long anterior to his overthrow.

Besides other towns in which the coins were minted, " we find on those of Magnentius and Decentius in the Cobham hoard, *Ambianum*, Amiens, AMB; and *Siscia* in

Pannonia, now Sissek, F.SIS., RSIS, etc., of the latter a few only."[1]

It has lately come to my knowledge that a Roman amphitheatre has been discovered in Paris, not far from the Thermæ of the Hôtel-Cluny, which are supposed to have been built by Constantius Chlorus, and improved and occupied by Julian. "The amphitheatre, which was not far distant from their palace, on the left bank of the Seine, under the hill on which the Pantheon and the church of St. Geneviève now stand, has not been forgotten in history, although buried by earth brought from the hill above since the beginning of the fifth century, when St. Marcel, relieving the people from the dragon of paganism, built the church of St. Etienne, and abolished the pagan amusements of the circus. Just south of the Jardin des Plantes, on the northern side of the Rue Monge, a large area of ground has lately been cleared of buildings which occupied the position of the amphitheatre in part.

"Under the direction of an influential committee, of which the late distinguished historian, Henri Martin, was president, a very considerable surface has been excavated, of twenty feet or more of earth, revealing the entrance to the arena, its outline, and still uninjured walls on the eastern side, a portion of a theatre connected with it, the approach to it gently sloping, the passages and recesses for the retreat of attendants, a very remarkable sewer or passage-way leading towards the river, and some of the seats for spectators. Enough has been opened to show that it was a very large and well-constructed building. It is of stone, like the Caen stone, in small, squared blocks, about twice the size of an English brick, and like those in the lower part of the Palais des Thermes."[2]

[1] *Archæologia Cantiana*, xv, p. 321, *et seqq.*

[2] From a letter to the author by J. Pierce, a member of the British Archæological Association.

It would be well if more attention were paid to the investigation of traces of amphitheatres in Britain. That in the neighbourhood of Dorchester was nearly being destroyed some years since, but for the efforts made to save it by Mr. C. Warne, F.S.A., the historian of Dorset, assisted by others. We have the authority of the Rev. Dr. Collingwood Bruce, the historian of the Wall, for the existence of other remains of the *Amphitheatrum Castrense* outside the walls of Corinium, Silchester, Caerleon, Richborough, and several other places ; and " in the north of England is one adjacent to the mural station of Borcovicus. It is, however, small in comparison with that at Cirencester, but large enough for the garrison, which consisted only of one cohort."

CHAPTER II.

Dionysiaca of Nonnus—Argument of the Poem—Europa carried off from Phœnicia—The Mimallones and *Thyrsus* of Bacchus—Cadmus and Harmony—Education and first Exploits of Bacchus—Re-establishment of the Spheres after the War with the Giants—The Progeny of Cadmus—Staphylus and Botrys; their Palace in Assyria—Prizes for Dancing — Lycurgus, Son of Mars; his Axe with double head—Deriades, the Indian King—Bassarides and Mænades—Morrheus and Chalcomedia—Bacchus defeats Lycurgus and Deriades—Agave and Pentheus—Athens at last converted.

A S reference has been made to the mythology which explains the subjects of the Anglo-British mosaics, this chapter will be devoted to a review of some parts of contemporary poems which appear to have exerted an influence upon the compositions. At the head of these is the *Dionysiaca* of Nonnus, before referred to.

He begins his work by the history of Europa, the Phœnician princess who was carried off from her father's grazing grounds by Jupiter in the form of a bull, who walked with her upon his broad back across the sea to Crete without wetting the feet of the princess.[1] She was met upon the sea-shore by Cadmus of Thebes, who plays a most important part in the poem. The author invokes the Muses to bring in the *narthex* (a bamboo-cane, the pith of which was used as tinder for striking fire), and to sound the cymbals, and to place in his hand the much celebrated *thyrsus* of Bacchus :—

[1] See the History of Europa in Moschus, *Idyl.* ii. Jupiter, he says, line 79—

" Κρύψε θεόν, καὶ τρέψε δέμας καὶ γίνετο ταῦρον."

" Ἄξατέ μοι νάρθηκα τινάξατε κύμβαλα, Μοῦσαι,
Καὶ παλάμῃ δότε θύρσον ἀειδομένου Διονύσου."

(Lib. i.)

Further on, he addresses the *Mimallones*, or bands of Bacchanalian women, who sang in divine raptures and delirium the praises of Bacchus. Their name, according to Strabo, was derived from Mount Mimas, in Asia Minor :—

"Ἄξατέ μοι νάρθηκα Μιμαλλόνες ὠμαδίην δὲ
Νεβρίδα ποικιλόνωτον ἐθήμονος ἀντὶ χιτῶνος."

They were to exchange the well-known tunic for the spotted fawn-back skin thrown over the shoulders. Nonnus then launches into the depths of the ancient cosmogony, and shows how the beneficent god brought all things out of chaos ; and how Typhæus led an army to fight against Jupiter, upsetting the constellations and the order of heaven ; and how Cadmus of Thebes, and Harmony his wife, re-established order, and imported into the heart of Greece the civilization and arts of Phœnicia and Egypt. After the first Dionysus, called Zagræus, had disappeared in the great war with the Titans and powers of darkness, appeared the second Dionysus, or Bacchus the Theban.

Born amidst the thunders of Jupiter, he had to flee from the vengeance of Juno and of Athamas, the husband of Ino, who had suckled the child, and brought him up. The young hero, after profiting by the education given him by Rhea or Cybele in Phrygia, the universal mother, proceeds to destroy the enemies of civilization, and to spread it over the earth. The arts of agriculture were promoted in every way, and particularly the cultivation of the vine. He taught the manufacture of wine from grapes all through India, following the line of march of Alexander the Great into that country at a later period. We find him at Tyre, the dwelling-place of his grandfather, Cadmus, and loading with his rich crops the valleys of Berytus and Libanus; and

passing through Cilicia and Lydia, he brings his influence
into Europe by way of Illyricum and Macedonia, towards
Thebes, where he was born. Athens is initiated into his
mysteries. At Naxos he dries the tears of the deserted
Ariadne, and marries her. Then comes his struggle with
Juno at Argos, and the episode of Perseus. He then con-
quers inhospitable Thrace, and makes rebellious Pallene
submit to be cultivated. After again repairing to Cybele
in Phrygia, the scene of his youth, where he had learnt to
drive great Rhea's chariot drawn by lions, and performing
many great and useful works in that country, he is admitted
to Olympus among the immortal gods. I will now refer a
little more in detail to the contents of those books of the
Dionysiaca which illustrate the designs of our mosaics.

In the first two books, Typhœus, after stealing the
thunderbolts of Jupiter, is described as upsetting the
beautiful order and harmony of the spheres, and causing
consternation among the gods and goddesses, so that

"Ἥβη λεῖπε κύπελλον, Ἄρης δ'ἀπεσείσατο λόγχην·
Ἑρμῆς ῥάβδον ἔθηκε, λύρην δ'ἔρριψεν Ἀπόλλων. κ. τ. λ."

But Cadmus helps to subdue Typhœus by the sound of his
flute, and Victory, under the form of Latona, addresses
Jupiter to urge him to use his power, and restore peace to
the distracted universe. He does, and the spheres assume
their accustomed order. The triumphant Hours or Seasons
stand at the gates of heaven to open them to Jupiter and
to Victory.

In the third Book appears the swallow, the plaintive
harbinger of spring ; and Cadmus of Thebes sails to Samos,
where, taking the hint given him by a raven, he marries
Harmony, the sister of the king of that island, and daughter
of Electra. The magnificent palace of Hemathion there
has some counterpart in the descriptions we have of the
gorgeous halls of Constantinople. Cadmus teaches the

islanders the ceremonies of Osiris, the Egyptian Bacchus, of whom he had been a pupil.

In the fifth book he dedicates the seven gates of his new city, the Bœotian Thebes, to Diana, Minerva, Mercury, Electra, Mars, Jupiter, and Saturn, but leaves it to Amphion to build up the towers, at a future time, by the sounds of his musical voice. The marriage of Cadmus and Harmony is celebrated with all honour, Apollo himself being present with his seven-stringed lyre, and the nine Muses also assisting. Polyhymnia directed the dance, and Venus brought presents for the daughters who were to be born, and who played important parts in the myth hereafter. The daughters' names were—

Antonoe, the eldest, who married Aristæus, and they had a son, the hunter Actæon.

Ino, who married Athamas.

Agave, who married Echion, and who had a son named Pentheus.

Semele, the youngest, who, though a mortal, had a son by Jupiter, called the Theban Bacchus. This child was born amidst the thunders of the gods, which burnt up the unfortunate mother.

The sixth book describes how the first Bacchus, Zagræus, was killed, and relates the story of the Deluge, and the dragons' teeth, and other marvels, which do not concern the mosaics.

The seventh book introduces σύντροφος Ἀιών, or Time and Eternity, and the wise and self-taught Cupid, or Ἔρως.

"Καὶ σοφὸς αὐτοδίδακτος Ἔρως αἰῶνα νομεύων
Πρωτογόνου Χάεος ζοφερὺς πυλεῶνας ἀνοίξας."

This clever boy produces twelve winged arrows to shoot at Jupiter, and the fifth brings down the god to the banks of the Asopus.

In the eighth book the jealousy of Juno is described.

D

but Jupiter contrives to assuage her wrath sufficiently to permit of Semele being placed among the constellations, one reason being that her mother belonged to the royal family of Olympus, being a daughter of Venus and Mars.

In the ninth book the palace of Ino is described. The seasons are crowning the infant Bacchus with ivy, Mercury having brought him in his arms to Ino; but her husband in the next book shows himself very jealous and furious.

The eleventh book is devoted to young Ampelos (the Vine), and the seasons Ωραι, particularly that one which is especially connected with Ampelos.

The thirteenth book gives the assemblage of a very mixed army of centaurs, satyrs, fauns, and others, too numerous to mention here, and among the first was Actæon the hunter; these were to accompany Bacchus on his Indian expedition, and a very curious series of campaigns are described.

In the fifteenth book Nicæa the huntress appears, and is courted by Bacchus. They had a child, who was called Teletes; and Bacchus, on his return from India, caused the city of Nicæa to be built in honour of the huntress.

In the seventeenth book he drives the car of Cybele, and pours wine into the Orontes, making his adversaries drunk.

The eighteenth book describes the splendid reception he met with at the Court of Assyria, in the palace of Staphylus and his son Botrys.

The nineteenth book introduces an interesting contest on the lyre, between the two great players, Œagrus, the father of Orpheus, and Erectheus, to compete for prizes. Erectheus sings first, and describes how, in divine Athens, Celeus, aided by his son Triptolemus and the ancient Metanira, had received the goddess Ceres as a guest; and how the latter had taught Triptolemus to plough and sow

corn, and how the latter had pursued a triumphant journey
in the chariot, drawn by serpents, spreading civilisation
and the arts of agriculture. Then Œagrus, the father of
Orpheus, varying his subject, sings of the immortality given
to Staphylus of Assyria for his hospitality to Bacchus, and
of the benefits he had derived from being made acquainted
with the juice of the grape. And when the contest is over,
the wreath of ivy is placed on the brow of Œagrus, who
receives the first prize of a young bull, whose neck has
never yet submitted to the yoke, while Erectheus of Athens
has to walk sulkily away with the long-bearded goat, which
was the second prize only.

The next prizes are for dancing : first, the wonderful
gold cup made by Vulcan, and presented by Venus to her
brother Bacchus ; the second prize for dancing is of silver,
adorned with festoons of ivy and enamelled with gold, and
Bacchus added a ton of new wine, to console those who gained
no other prize—" ὸυ νέμεσις γὰρ, ἀνέρα νικηθέντα πιεῖν ἀμέριμνον
ἐέρσην" ("No harm in the vanquished man to drink the dew
which drives care away").

The merits of a good dancer are wonderfully described,
the flexibility of the body, and movement in silence of the
hands and eyes, the silence which speaks—αὐδήεσσα σιωπή;
but after this poetical effusion the performers in the
dance are ludicrously chosen, being no less than old Mars
and Silenus ; the first obtains the gold cup, but the latter,
in dancing, is changed into a river, and his prize, the silver
cup, has to be thrown into the stream. The name of Silenus,
from ἴλλω or εἴλω, is expressive of his rolling motion.

The twentieth book introduces Lycurgus, son of Mars,
and king of Arabia, who is a great enemy to Bacchus, and
determines his destruction. Juno arms him with a double-
headed axe, with which he attempts to break the crown of
Bacchus ; the queen of heaven also sends Iris down to

Bacchus to threaten him with war. Iris puts on the *talaria* of Mercury, Lycurgus exclaims ἐγὼ βουπλῆγα τινάσσω (322), Bacchus has to throw himself into the sea to escape, and is well received by Thetis and old Nereus.

Homer describes the axe of Lycurgus, and calls it not πελακυς but βουπληξ, the axe of sacrifices.[1]

The punishment of Lycurgus is given in the twenty-first book, and the anger of Neptune described—

"Regna securigeri Bacchum Sensere Lycurgi."[2]

In the twenty-fourth the campaigns against Deriades, the Indian king, and his ally Hydaspes, are the occasion of many poetical adventures; and the following book shows how a war of seven years was not sufficient to bring to subjection the Oriental nations. The victories of Bacchus are contrasted with the feeble exploits of Perseus against a woman—

"᾿Αλλ᾿ οὐ τοῖος ἔην Βρομίου μόθος·"

The poet makes little of what Perseus accomplished by killing one woman—

"Οὐκ ἄγαμαι Περσῆα, μίαν κτείναντα γυναῖκα;"

and depreciates the fame of Andromeda and Celeus, who, though placed among the constellations, still, the former was perpetually being pursued by the Whale, and the latter was always unhappy at his daughter's distress. The shield is described after the manner of Homer, and Ganymede, the beautiful boy carried off by the messenger of Jove, is one of the subjects engraved upon it.

In the twenty-sixth and twenty-seventh books Argive Juno assists the Indian king Deriades and his allies, the Derbici, Ethiopians, Sacæ, Blemmyes, and different tribes of Bactrians; and Ceres also goes over to the enemy, out of envy of Bacchus and his invention of wine, which had effaced the glory of Zagræus, the ancient Bacchus.

[1] *Iliad*, vi, 135.   [2] Seneca, *Œdip.* Act II.

The Bassarides[1] and Mænades, on the side of Bacchus, take a prominent part in the fight.

" Βασσαρίδες καὶ δεῦρο χορεύσατε δυσμενέων δὲ
Κτείνατε βάρβαρα φῦλα καὶ ἔγχεσι μίξατε θύρσους."

In the twenty-eighth book the Cyclopes join in the mêlée.

In book twenty-nine, Hymenæus is wounded by Mars. War continues, and Morrheus slaughters the Bacchantes.

In books thirty and thirty-one golden-winged Iris appears, χρυσόπτερος Ἶρις, and there is trouble in the army of Bacchus.

In the next and following book is the episode of the Indian Morrheus and the Bassarid Chalcomedia. The former has left his black wife and made several Bassarides prisoners, tying their hands behind their backs and leaving them to his father-in-law Deriades. He sees the beautiful Chalcomedia wearing a transparent cloak and a brilliant tunic.

" φάρεα λεπτὰ φέρουσα καὶ ἀστράπτοντα χιτῶνα" (v. 266).

The image on his shield of his dark-coloured wife, Cheirobia, is effaced in the scuffle, and he pursues Chalcomedia, who flies before the winds, which expose her beautiful neck and shoulders, which rival the pallid moon.

" αὐχένα γυμνώσαντες ἐριδμαίνοντα Σελήνῃ".

She escapes, and hides herself among the troops of Bassarid women, who then disperse and fly towards Eurus, Notus, and Boreas. The Mænades exchange their *thyrsi* of Bacchus for the spindles of Minerva.

In the thirty-fifth book Deriades fights the women. An Indian woman attacks them to revenge the death of her husband, Orontes, and behaves like a new black Atalanta in courage. Morrheus again chases Chalcomedia, and is

[1] So called from the Bassaræ, or dresses of fox-skins, worn by the Thracian Bacchanals.

about to seize her, when a serpent, coiled about the nymph's waist, seizes the pursuer by the throat. He had been persuaded by the woman's stratagem to take off his breast-plate and to put down his arms, so that he was helpless against the attack of the angry reptile. Various events are recorded in the next three books. Bacchus takes divers forms, and Deriades meditates a naval attack upon him. Funeral rites to the dead are then performed, games are described, and Erectheus in these gains the first prize.

The hours bring in the seventh year of the war. The marriage of Clymene with the Sun is related, and the episode of Phaeton driving the horses till he upset the chariot and fell headlong. Lycurgus and Deriades then have a sea-fight with the merry god, and Bacchus gains the victory.

Book forty describes how, after the battle of the Caucasus on the banks of the river of the Amazons, Bacchus visits Arabia and goes to the land of the Tyrians, where he sees the wonderful colours and marvels of Assyrian art.[1]

The forty-first book is dedicated to love and Beroe, a scion of the Graces χαρέτων θάλος and Astræa.

The poem then goes on to describe the love of Bacchus for Beroe. Cupid goes to Tyre, and Bacchus spends the livelong day in creeping about in the forest.

" δείελος, εἰς μέσον ἦμαρ, ἐώιος, ἕσπερος ἕρπων."

Neptune falls in love with the same lady, and in the next book the rivals fight; but Jupiter parts the combatants, and gives her to Neptune. Cupid consoles Bacchus, and pro-mises him Ariadne.

---

[1] Claudian flatters Honorius by comparing him with Bacchus :
  " Hoc si Mæonias cinctu graderere per urbes,
    In te pampineos transferret Lydia Thyrsos,
    In te Nysa choros : dubitarent orgia Bacchi,
    Cui furerent : irent blandæ sub vincula tigres."
        De IV, Cons. Honorii. v. 602-605.

The forty-fourth book gives the tragedy of Agave much
as it is told by Euripides in the *Bacchæ*, and Pentheus is
killed by the hand of his mother, who mistook him for a
wild beast, indeed, his head is much like that of a lion.

In the forty-fifth, Agave holds up the bleeding head.
"Hang it up," she says, "under the portico of Cadmus, that
it may be seen how Jupiter has doomed the Cadmeian family
to destruction." Autonoe consoles her sister Agave, and
Bacchus consoles them both, and sends off Cadmus and
Harmony into Illyria, to wander there till they are petrified
into serpents; and two more books are filled with a variety
of incidents; among others, Bacchus falls in with a nymph
named Aura, whom he treats much as he did Nicæa before
referred to, and he has a young Bacchus by her, and closes
the drama with his Pans and Satyrs in immortal Athens,
the never-silent

$$\text{"} \dot{\alpha}\sigma\iota\gamma\dot{\eta}\tau\omicron\iota\sigma\iota\nu \text{ } '\mathrm{A}\theta\dot{\eta}\nu\alpha\iota\varsigma \text{,"}$$

where his divinity is at last acknowledged.

$$\text{"}\kappa\alpha\iota \text{ } \tau\epsilon\lambda\epsilon\tau\alpha\hat{\iota}\varsigma \text{ } \tau\rho\iota\sigma\sigma\hat{\eta}\sigma\iota\nu \text{ } \dot{\epsilon}\beta\alpha\gamma\chi\epsilon\dot{\upsilon}\theta\eta\sigma\alpha\nu \text{ } '\mathrm{A}\theta\hat{\eta}\nu\alpha\iota.$$
$$\kappa\alpha\dot{\iota} \text{ } \chi\omicron\rho\dot{\omicron}\nu \text{ } \dot{\omicron}\psi\iota\tau\dot{\epsilon}\lambda\epsilon\sigma\tau\omicron\nu \text{ } \dot{\alpha}\nu\epsilon\kappa\rho\omicron\dot{\upsilon}\sigma\alpha\nu\tau\omicron \text{ } \pi\omicron\lambda\hat{\iota}\tau\alpha\iota$$
$$\mathrm{Z}\alpha\gamma\rho\dot{\epsilon}\alpha \text{ } \kappa\upsilon\delta\alpha\dot{\iota}\nu\omicron\nu\tau\epsilon\varsigma \text{ } \ddot{\alpha}\mu\alpha \text{ } \mathrm{B}\rho\omicron\mu\dot{\iota}\omega \text{ } \kappa\alpha\dot{\iota} \text{ } '\mathrm{I}\dot{\alpha}\kappa\chi\omega.\text{"}$$

The Dionysian epic has been treated by no ancient author
so intelligibly and sympathetically as by Euripides in the
Bacchæ. Canon Brooke F. Westcott, in a late article in
the *Contemporary Review*, remarks that, "The significance
of Euripides as a religious teacher springs directly from his
position and his character. He looks from the midst of
Athenian society—a society brilliant, restless, sanguine,
superstitious—at the popular mythology, at life, at the future,
with the keenest insight into all that belongs to man, and
what he sees is a prospect on which we may well dwell.
He is, therefore, perfectly consistent when he affirms man's
dependence on the gods, while he denies the historic truth
of the ancient legends."

" From what has been already said, the profound significance of the Dionysian worship for Euripides will be at once clear. In that worship Nature found the fullest recognition as the revelation of the Divine. Man sought fellowship with God in the completeness of his being. The organ of knowledge was confessed to be, not the intellect, but life. Thus the *Bacchæ* is no Palinode, but a gathering up in rich maturity of the poet's earlier thoughts. Man cannot, he shows, with tragic earnestness, attain to communion with the divine by pure reason, a part only of his constitution. He must keep himself open to every influence, and so, by welcoming the new in time, prove his loyalty to the old. Seen in this light, the Dionysian worship is the witness to a real belief in the vitality of religion as answering to the completeness of man's nature. It does not aim at superseding that which went before, but at bringing it nearer to actual experience. Men must worship as men, feeling at once the richness and the limits of their endowments. The theology of Euripides takes its shape from his conviction that all Nature and all life is a manifestation of one Divine Power. All that is human claims his sympathy ; and it may be said, conversely, that all that claims his sympathy is seen in its connection with man. We can then study in Euripides a distinct stage in the preparation of the world for Christianity. He paints life as he found it when Greek art and Greek thought had put forth their full power. He scatters the dream, which some have indulged in, of the unclouded brightness of the Athenian prospect of life ; and his popularity shows that he represented truly the feelings of those with whom he lived, and of those who came after him."[1]

[1] Canon Brooke F. Westcott, " Euripides as a Religious Teacher", *Contemporary Review*, April 1884.

CHAPTER III.

THE poem referred to in the last chapter sufficiently
explains the myths as well as tone of thought pervading
the mosaics under review; and as the pavement at Morton,
near Brading, Isle of Wight, is about the fullest in subjects
of any, I will say a few words about its interpretation, and
there will then be little left to explain as to the pictures
displayed on the others. First, as to room numbered 3 on
Mr. Price's plan. This has a female head in the centre,
which I should be inclined to attribute to Harmonia; and
around it are three pictures which seem to represent the
three seasons of the day, that is, the early morn or cock-
crow, when the *lanistæ,* or keepers of the gladiators, were
in the habit of bringing out their men for practice, to fight
with wild beasts, as a training for the more serious contests
of the afternoon.

> " In matutinâ nuper spectatus arenâ."[1]

Horace relates such an early morning conversation :

> " Threx est Gallina Syro par ?[2]
> Matutina parum cautos jam frigora mordent."

> " Is the Thracian Gallina a match for the Syrian ?
> These morning frosts nip those who are not very careful."

---

[1] *Martial,* x, 25, and again xiii, 95.   [2] Hor., *Sat.,* ii, v. 44, 45.

Claudius, the emperor, was so fond of the sports of the amphitheatre, that he is said to have attended both the early performance at daybreak as well as that at midday.[1]

Seneca says, "Mane leonibus et ursis, homines meridie spectatoribus suis objiciebantur."[2]

The panthers on the mosaics have wings, which express the figurative ideal animal sacred to Bacchus.

The *lanista* is clothed in the woollen smock he is usually dressed in, as on the pavement at Bignor, and on the bas-reliefs from Cardinal Maximini's palace at Rome, figured in the *Vetusta Monumenta*, vol. i, plate 65. The man-cock is emblematical of the hour when the Romans began their day.

The next scene is midday, or when men fight with men, for the recreation of the Roman world.

The principal work of the day was then over; and, after a light meal and short repose, the Roman rose up refreshed for the afternoon amusements. Here we see the *secutor* with helmet and sword; the *retiarius* with net and trident. The latter endeavours to entangle his adversary in his net, and then attacks him with his trident, while the secutor has to avoid this, and follow up his antagonist sword in hand. The origin, perhaps, of this display of force is the personification of the land and sea combat.

In the third scene we probably behold the evening, or time of the principal meal of the Romans, the time being indicated by the fox stealing into the vineyard to eat the grapes at nightfall. The division of the Roman day was similar to that of the Greek; but Macrobius remarks how the space of a day was reckoned differently by different nations: the Athenians reckoned from sunset to sunset; the Babylonians from sunrise to sunrise; but the Roman day extended from midnight to midnight, and the first

---

[1] Suetonius *in vita Claudii*, xxxiv.   [2] *Epist.*, lib. 1, 7.

part was called *mediæ noctis inclinatio*; the next *gallici-nium*, or cock-crow; the third *conticuum*, or the silent, when not only cocks cease to crow, but men also take their rest; the last is the *diluculum*, when day begins to decline.[1]

In the centre of the long gallery at Morton is Orpheus, with Phrygian cap, *cothurni* on feet, the attributes of divinity, the lyre on left knee, and the flowing robe. This picture, both as to the principal figure as well as the animals, is small and inferior as compared with many other examples at Woodchester, Withington, and elsewhere.

The northern room, numbered 12 on the plan, extending 39 feet 6 inches from east to west, is a history in itself, and is divided into four principal compartments: a square towards the west; then an oblong panel; another square; and another oblong panel, eastward. The square towards the west is mutilated; the centre is gone, and we have no means of divining the subject. The corners represent the seasons of the year. The angry Juno seems to stand for the Spring, and Ceres for the Summer. Winter is placed to the north of the latter, and Autumn has been destroyed. The only one remaining of the four pictures which surrounded the centre in this western compartment is one which is attributed to Perseus and Andromeda, the former holding up the Medusa's head; but my interpretation would be more appropriate to the unity of the design, with reference to the poem, if we consider the two figures to be females, the one being Agave holding up the head of Pentheus, whose mangled remains appear at foot; and the other perhaps is Ino, or her other sister Autonoe. This is the catastrophe to the house and fortunes of Cadmus: here are his daughters, whose tragic end is well known; and the fourth, Semele, the mother of Bacchus, was burnt up by the lightning of Jupiter; represented, probably, by

[1] *Saturnalia*, lib. I, cap. iii.

the emblem of fire, which is clearly depicted on the western margin of the pavement, between the pictures and the western wall.   Autonoe, the eldest daughter, escaped the catastrophe, but it fell upon her eldest son, Actæon, whose fate has been referred to, and is depicted at Cirencester.

Then follows the oblong panel, with the astronomer seated; and who this may be it is difficult to conjecture. It might be one of the wise men of the age of Onomacritus, Pythagoras, or Meton; or, more probably, it is an abstract representation of an astronomer, without reference to any one individual.   It has been assigned to Hipparchus, of a much later age, who made a map of the fixed stars, and wrote a commentary on Aratus (cir. 146 B.C.).   The figure is seated by itself in a separate panel, and with the instruments around him which called forth the jealousy of the gods, according to Claudian.   The next square panel is a continuation of the story of the enemies of Bacchus, and I should be inclined to consider the central head as that of Pentheus, though usually ascribed to Medusa.[1]   The first picture in this square represents a man armed with the double-headed axe, who can be no other than Lycurgus.   The axe was given him by revengeful Juno, with which to crack the Osiris skull of Bacchus between the horns; but Bacchus was too much for him, as Ovid says, in addressing the god—

"Penthea, tu, venerande, bipenniferumque Lycurgum,
      Sacrilegos maetas."[2]

The myth of Ceres and Triptolemus shows how she

---

[1] The Bacchæ, or Bacchantes, were represented with snakes entwined in their hair.
      "Nodo coerces viperino
            Bistonidum sine fraude crines."—Hor., Carm., ii, 19.
      Met., iv, 22, 23.

rewarded those who had received her hospitably; and she taught the young farmer to sow corn and till the ground, as sung in the poem by Erectheus in honour of Athens; but she is represented as jealous of Bacchus for his gifts to men; and the other melody referred to in the poem was that sung by Œagrus, the father of Orpheus, about Staphylus, who was the son of Bacchus and Ariadne, and who received the first prize. This young man, from the island of Naxos, probably, is dressed in the costume of that island, and, with the Pandean pipe in hand, is educating a nymph for her part of a Bacchante. She plays the tambourine, and her attitude is not inelegant.

> "Motus doceri gaudet Ionicos
> Matura virgo," etc.,

was said by Horace of his young countrywomen, as it may be told of ours in this mosaic.[1]

This is the third picture of the eastern square; and the fourth has delineated upon it a nymph pursued, and with her drapery torn from her back. This seems to answer very well the description of the Bassarid Chalcomedia pursued by the Indian Morrheus. As a pair of thin legs is all that remains of the pursuer, these legs answer better to the Indian prince than they would to Apollo, on the supposition that the scene represented Apollo and Daphne. And here is another of the episodes in the expedition of Bacchus to India. On a portion of the stucco found in this villa, which once adorned the side of a room, is painted the head of a parrot, well designed, and perhaps emblematic of these Eastern campaigns —

> "Psittacus Eois, imitatrix ales ab Indis."[2]

The four female heads, having on them the wings of

---

[1] The Roman poet summarises the exploits of Bacchus in that beautiful ode addressed to the god, the nineteenth, in Book II.

[2] Ovid, *Amor.*, lib. II, Eleg. 6.

Mercury *(petasus)*, may represent Iris, sent down by Juno to proclaim war on Bacchus, which they do by the *tubæ*, or trumpets, they are blowing; but it is more likely they personify the Winds, with wings expressive of speed.

In the eastern panel the scene is changed to the realms of Neptune. Ino threw herself into the sea, and was well received by Thetis, and afterwards was changed into a rock, under the name of Leucothea, and her Sidonian women into birds. Bacchus, to avoid Lycurgus and the stroke of his axe, had also to leap into the sea, and was hospitably received by the queen of the deep, to whom he presented the golden vase which had been given him by Venus. The two figures with human bodies and the tails of fishes are probably intended for old Nereus and Neptune, each carrying his wife on his back; the former, Thetis, the latter, Amphitrite. If I have rightly interpreted the figures, the unity of the whole mosaic is thus established, and it is a beautiful illustration of the Dionysiac myth; the early Bacchus or Orpheus, Harmony and the seasons of the day and year, regulated and explained by the astronomer on his instruments; then the enemies of Bacchus, and his final triumph both by sea and land. The fearful catastrophe to the house and fortunes of Cadmus for opposing the worship of the god is here shown, while Staphylus (the vine) perpetuates the race of the Wine-god, and delights the agricultural population with the sounds of his Pandean pipes. It will be seen that this room (No. 12), in its entirety, is divided into parts corresponding with the four elements of nature: *fire*, in the semi-circular division at the west end; *earth*, on which are enacted the fables here pictured of the enemies of Bacchus and their fate; *air*, in the astronomical compartment; and *water*, at the eastern end.

If I have deviated a little from the interpretations of

some critics as to a few of the pictures at Morton, my reasons for so doing, and authorities, shall be given, that the reader may form his own judgment upon them.

The cock-man has been thought by some to be a caricature, having a religious, or quasi-religious character; and if the astronomer with his instruments is to be taken for Pythagoras, it might certainly remind us of the dialogue in Lucian between Mycullus, the shoemaker, and a philosophical cock who speaks with a human voice, and turns out to be a Pythagorean, and one who remembers the different changes his body had undergone since he was first a large white ant in India. From this he became a courtezan, changing afterwards into the form of a cynic philosopher; and even after this his metempsychosis did not bring him to his present form of a cock till after he had passed into the cold-blooded body of a frog. The shoemaker with difficulty restrained his anger, aroused by the cock crowing at midnight, instead of his proper time in the small hours of the morning ; and the more so, as this poor, half-starved cobbler had been awakened out of a delightful dream, in which wealth and plenty were at his command, and now the disenchanted cobbler awoke to his wretched hovel, his last, and his shoe-leather. However, whether the man-cock is to be interpreted as an impersonation of the before-named personage in Lucian, and a caricature of the Pythagoreans; or as a caricature of the Emperor Gallienus, from the similarity of name to *gallus*, a cock ; or as having some Gnostic signification, I think precedents are wanting to favour any of these interpretations, and a more simple one is that I have given, which harmonises also with the two other scenes in connection with it, which make up together the three parts of the Roman day, as given in the writers before referred to. A Gnostic signification has been given to a piece of sculpture found at Sea Mills, near

Bristol, in 1873, and figured in the Journal of the British Archæological Association, xxix, p. 372. It is a portion of a memorial stone, having a female head sculptured upon it. Above this is what seems to be a cross; on the right is a cock, and on the left a dog or a fox, in the same attitude as that on the Morton pavement. The lettering is SPES C SENTI, with a leaf stop on each side of the word "spes". The Rev. John McCaul, LL.D., President of University College, Toronto, after discussing the interpretation in various ways, says : " One other question remains for consideration: is it an ordinary Roman monument?" It appears to me to be so, and a dedication to the memory of a young daughter, the hope of Caius Sentius, who died early. The expression may not be in common use[1] on Roman monuments without the proper name, but the term agrees with the modern expression, "the hope of the family". She died in the midday of life, therefore lived only between the dawn, represented by cock-crow, and the evening, by the fox in the vineyards. This explanation may appear not altogether satisfactory; however, I offer the suggestion, and with due deference to the opinion of others who may differ from it.

If the interpretation is the correct one, it may some-

---

[1] Some analogy to it may be found in the epitaph in T. Reinesius, *Inscriptiones Antiquæ*, Classis xii, No. 30—

. . . . .

ORCVS . CVM . TE . VORAVIT

. . . .

BACVLVM . EXVCTIS . MEDVLLIS E
DENTVLÆ SENECTVTIS . SECVIT .
SPEM . NEPOTVM . ABSTRAXIT
SECVM . MAXIMAM .

. . . .

what corroborate two of the seasons of the day out of the three referred to on the Morton pavement. In confirmation of the popularity of the Bacchanalian myth, as represented in the large room at Morton, I may refer to the fact of its being quoted by Pomponius Lætus in his life of Julius Licinius Licinianus, when he deplores the wars and calamities of the empire. He says : " The Bassarid women, excited to madness at the name of Bacchus, did not murder each other. Agave—who did not kill another Bacchante, but an irreligious son—when she came to her senses, retreated into a cave and gave way to penitence. But we are never penitent for murder committed. In truth, we consider that we have gained an accession of praise and of glory the more men we have slain."

By taking a review of all the subjects delineated on the various mosaics which are classified at the end of the volume, it will be found that the subjects most frequently repeated are *Orpheus with his lyre*, taming the animals, as at Woodchester, Withington, Barton Farm, Winterton, Horkstow, Littlecote (Wilts), Chedworth, Cirencester, and Morton (Isle of Wight); *Bacchus and Panther*, as at Cirencester, Pitney, Thruxton, Stunsfield, Bignor, and London ; and without his panther at Frampton. His *Cantharus*, at Bignor, Cotterstock, Littlecote, Crondall (near Farnham), Lee (near Shrewsbury), Itchen-Abbas, Bramdean, Stunsfield, Carisbrook, Silchester, Morton (Isle of Wight). *Harmonia*, once at Morton. The *Seasons* of the year, at Littlecote, Thruxton, Morton; and at the latter place the seasons of the day also. The realms of Neptune, with his naiads, tritons, dolphins, and fishes, at Withington, Cirencester, Bramdean, Bignor, Frampton, Horkstow, Woodchester, and Littlecote. The enemies of Bacchus, as Lycurgus with his axe ; Pentheus, whose head is held up by Agave, his mother; and the head

F

itself, in the centre of another compartment at Morton.
The angry Juno is there represented, in her inter-
view with Lycurgus, armed with the axe; and she
appears also through her emblem, the *Peacock*, at Wellow,
London, and Morton, where also are depicted her winged
messengers, or *Iris*, sent to proclaim war against Bacchus:
unless these are meant for the Winds. Mercury is shown
five times at Frampton, and once at Bramdean; the episode
of the black king *Morrheus* and the nymph Chalcomedia,
one of the Bassarids, at Morton; another enemy of Bacchus
is disposed of in the death of the Indian king; while a
grandson of Cadmus, *Actæon*, son of his daughter *Autonoe*,
fills up the tragic catastrophe which overwhelmed the family
of Cadmus. The intrusion of the hunter Actæon upon
Diana and her attendants when bathing, was speedily
chastised by the goddess, who became purple with rage.
Ovid's simile from nature is admirable—

> " Qui color infestis adversi solis ab ictu
> Nubibus esse solet, aut purpureæ Auroræ;
> Is fuit in vultu visæ sine veste Dianæ."[1]

And she was not satisfied till, after changing him into a
stag, he had been torn to pieces by his own dogs—

> " Dilacerant falsi dominum sub imagine cervi
> Nec nisi finitâ per plurima vulnera vitâ
> Ira pharetratæ fertur satiata Dianæ."[2]

The goddess *Isis* is only once drawn, and that is at
Pitney, even if the figure should really be that divinity, who
holds what looks like a *sistrum*, the religious rattle of the
goddess, but may be something else. Sir R. C. Hoare, Bart.,
calls it a book, and thinks the personage may be the keeper
of accounts to a smelting establishment, to which he attributes the other figures scattering coin from a cylindrical
vessel, but which looks as much like seed or corn, and the

---

[1] Ovid, *Metamorph.*, III, v. 183.   [2] *Ibid.*, v. 250.

figures probably have to do with the various myths connected with Bacchus, as at Morton. Thus, we may conjecture
the horned figure No. 1 to be Neptune ; No. 2, Ceres; No. 3,
Triptolemus; No. 4, female figure, difficult to appropriate;
No. 5, Staphylus, with Phrygian cap; and No. 6, Nymph,
whom he is teaching to dance; No. 7, unknown figure;
No. 8, perhaps Isis, with *sistrum*. The animals at the
corners with cornucopiæ may perhaps represent the four
seasons.

Cupid,[1] addressed by name in an inscription at Frampton,[2] is represented at Leicester, and is seen riding on
the tail of a sea-horse at Horkstow.[3] Good-luck was
to be honoured—" Bonum Eventum *bene colite*"—as at
Woodchester ; and as this divinity was worshipped at
Rome, much more should it be in Britain, as to agricultural
results in our uncertain climate.[4] Reference is made to
agriculture in the young man fighting the Hydra, by which
was understood the swampy stream with many heads which
had to be drained. This is at Pitney; and at Woodchester
is seen foliage proceeding from the mask of Pan, a divinity
who seems to personify the woods, the country, and all
nature, and who was one of the most popular of the gods
of the ancients. A curious statue of him is figured in the
Monumenta Vetusta of the Society of Antiquaries.[5]

The occupations and amusements of men are shown in

---

[1] Chap. viii, No. 21.   [2] Chap. xiii, No. 11.   [3] Chap. ix, No. 2.

[4] Bonus Eventus was one of the twelve divinities who presided over
husbandry.—(Varro, *De re rustica*, lib. i.) " There was a temple to this
divinity in Rome, and Pliny mentions statues of this deity with *patera* in
right hand and an ear of corn and poppy in the left. He is represented in
the same shape on the reverse of a coin of Titus ; and the reverse of a coin
of Geta has a female figure holding a dish of fruits in her right hand, and
ears of corn in her left, with inscription, BONI EVENTVS."—(T. Wright,
Celt, Roman, and Saxon, 1875, pp. 233 and 327.)

[5] Vol. ii, Pl. 21 and 22.

the hunting scenes, as the "Tree and Animal," at Aldborough; "Three Dogs," at Cirencester; "Animals," at
Pitney; "Figure in a cloak standing by Stag," at Leicester; "An equestrian figure fighting a Lion," as at
Frampton and Withington. "Gladiatorial Combats" are
seen at Bignor and at Morton; "Chariot Races" at
Horkstow.

As the gladiators at Bignor are figures with wings as
well as the *lanistæ*, it is possible these may be the *umbræ*, or
ghosts, of an institution passed or passing away.

The old gods, *majorum gentium*, are represented in but
few cases, and these may be taken rather to designate the
days of the week over which the planets, under the names
of those gods, presided: as Jupiter and Mars at Frampton;
Mars, Venus, and Diana at Bramdean; Apollo and his lyre
at Littlecote and Bignor.

At Bignor, however, is Jupiter, by his messenger, an
eagle, carrying off Ganymede, the myth being referred to
in the poem of Nonnus,[1]—unless this should be taken for a
consecratio, that is, an eagle carrying up the deified man to
heaven.

At Bramdean is seen *Æsculapius* and *Hercules* and
Antæus. Hercules and Bacchus remained popular to the
last; the former specially encouraged colonisation, travel,
and hard work.

The *star* is introduced into many of the pavements:
astrology and astronomy being kindred sciences among the
ancients. Many of the personages referred to in this book
were transferred as stars to the skies; the Greeks called a
human being a light, and when it went out here it shone
forth in the sky above.

> "micat inter omnes
> Julium sidus, velut inter ignes
> Luna minores."

[1] See chapter ii.

The borders of the mosaics are not without their significance. The single, the braided, and double-plaited guilloches are beautiful designs, with their blended colours, which show off to advantage the pictures of which they form the frames.

The labyrinth, or fret border, is a combination of those emblems of fire which were used as such by the earliest nations, and are thought by some to be derived from two pieces of wood laid across each other on the ground, and into which, at the point of intersection, an upright stick is made to revolve rapidly, by means of a cord wound round it, till the friction causes the ignition of a certain dry kind of grass, still used in India for the purpose of obtaining fire; and the pith of the narthex seems to have served the same purpose, whence its sacred character. The narthex, a kind of cane or reed, was placed in the hands of divinities, as seen in nearly all these mosaics where gods or goddesses are depicted. Mr. C. Roach Smith, in alluding to the labyrinthine fret on a pavement at Wingham, seems to carry up the design to the celebrated labyrinth of Crete, of which he gives an example found at Saltzburg, which is an obvious reproduction "of the story of Theseus, Ariadne, and the Minotaur, in a series of pictorial scenes in rich colours and well designed."[1]

The element of water is represented by the spiral pattern, well known to students of Greek art, and of which an example is No. 27, chap. xii, found in London.

The axe of Lycurgus is often introduced as a border, as in that on No. 4, chap. vii; the earth is beautifully represented by lilies and foliage in flowing designs, and birds personify the air which they inhabit. The subjects treated of can be exemplified in scenes embossed upon the Samian

---

[1] *Archæologia Cantiana.* xv, p. 130.

ware which fills our museums; and I may refer especially
to a Bacchanalian cup, described by the Rev. S. Weston,
D.D., in the *Archæologia*, xvii.

The Emperor Septimius Severus was a devotee of
Bacchus, having been engaged in wars over the same
line of country as the conquering god. A coin of middle
brass, bearing the heads of Severus and Julia Domna face
to face, has on the reverse the figure of Bacchus in a *biga*
drawn by two leopards; he is hurling a spear in his right
hand against the enemy, carrying a leopard's skin over his
left arm, and with his left hand he holds a *cantharus*, towards
which one of the leopards turns round his head, as if to
drink. It is dedicated by the Seleucians on the river Caly-
cadnus, in Cilicia, and seems to refer to the defeat of Didius
Julianus, Pescennius Niger, and Albinus.[1]

[1] The coin is figured in Spon, *Miscellan. Erudit. Antiq.*, p. 26.

CHAPTER IV.

Emblems of the Elements—Anaxagoras and his Perception of the Neces-
sity for a Divine Ruler of the Universe—The Atomic Theory of the
Homœomeria—His Successors and Predecessors and their Theories—
Pythagoras and Meton—Astronomer figured on the Mosaics at Mor-
ton, Isle of Wight—Ptolemy—Claudian's Poem on the Loadstone—
Union of Astronomy and Philosophy—Astrology—Instruments, Con-
stellations, and Zodiacal Signs—Improved Observation of the Seasons
—Seasons of the Day, Week, Month, and Year depicted on Mosaics.

SOMETHING must now be said of Greek astronomical
science, to which honour is done in these mosaics.
We have seen the elements of air, earth, fire, and water
portrayed through their emblems, and made to adorn the
various scenes which have been referred to in the preceding
pages ; in the present chapter some remarks will be offered
upon the progress of the human intellect towards a recognition of one divine mind arranging and overruling the
wondrous cosmogony, which increased knowledge forced
upon the minds of men in a firm and serious conviction.
Perhaps it is due to Anaxagoras, among the Greeks, to have
first attributed to the Divine Mind the arrangement and
distribution out of chaos of atoms which made up the mass
of the globe and its contents. The *Homœomeria* of Democritus might account for the agglomeration together of atoms
of the same nature, which constitute the material world ;
but how could they be acted upon without a *summum
mobile*, a motive and active power, which must be nothing
less than eternal, omnipotent, omniscient ?

Cicero was aware of this when he briefly refers to the
tenets of the Greek philosophers, as of Thales, who supposed

all things to have been created out of the element of water;
and of Anaximander, who thought the gods were worlds
rising and setting at long intervals; and of Anaximenes,
who made a god out of the element of air, always in motion
and infinite; or of Strato, the physicist, who made Nature
his god; or of Zeno, who in like manner raised natural
law into divinity itself, the created into the creator; and,
when he interpreted the theogony of Hesiod, deprived it of
what inspired an intuitive perception of the existence of
the gods; but, continues Cicero (*De Nat. Deor.*, i), what
nation is there, or race of men, which has not, without
learning, a certain preconception of the gods which Epicurus
calls προλῆψις, that is, a kind of unformed idea of the thing
preconceived in the mind? Aristotle teaches that Orpheus
the poet never existed; and some Pythagoreans say the
Orphic poem was really written by one Cercops. Cicero
goes on to say that Democritus, who was certainly great
among the greatest, from whose rills Epicurus watered his
own gardens, yet seems to be asleep as to the nature of
the gods.

Anaxagoras, who resided thirty years at Athens, had
disciplined himself in the Ionian schools of Anaximenes
and Anaximander, who preceded him. He then went to
the fountain-head for attaining a knowledge of God, by
studying his works; pursuing especially the science of
astronomy with all the enthusiasm of his nature, and aided
by the use of the armillary sphere and the gnomon, instruments which Anaximander is said to have invented. If
Anaxagoras did not actually first discover the causes of
eclipses of the sun and moon, he yet did much to perfect
the discoveries of his predecessors; and our material age
will hardly give him credit for wisdom in abandoning his
sheep-walks and other property in Athens, to devote himself entirely to the contemplation of the heavens. He was

born about B.C. 500, and Pythagoras about seventy years before him. This great man, who introduced the wonderful discoveries of science from Chaldæa and Greece into Italy, has the credit of teaching there, if not of himself discovering, the obliquity of the ecliptic, the round figure of the earth and its rotation around the sun with the other planets, the reflected light of the moon, and the causes of eclipses. He considered the moon to be a world similar to our own, but inhabited by animals, the nature of which he could not determine.

Meton, B.C. 433, established the Metonic cycle on 16th July of that year; and such was the fame and the importance given to his discovery in Greece, that the order of the period of nineteen years was engraved in figures of gold upon plates of bronze. Hence the name of our golden number, still retained in the calendar.

Callipus, born at Nicæa in Bithynia, B.C. 338, corrected the Metonic cycle; and Hipparchus, born B.C. 160, rendered still more exact this periodical coincidence of the sun and moon. These ancient astronomers and philosophers have been referred to in order to show the connection between their observations of the great works of creation and their theological speculations, by which we can appreciate the juxtaposition of the various *fabellæ* on the mosaics at Morton, near Brading, and the figure of an old man, an astronomer, surrounded by his instruments, the armillary sphere, the gnomon and dial, and globe. The reader may appropriate to the figure any of the names of astronomers to which I have referred, but it is more probably an abstract impersonation of the science, rather than the portrait of any one philosopher in particular.

The age of Anaxàgoras and Pythagoras is separated by a pretty wide interval from the time when our mosaics were laid down. Epicurus was born in B.C. 341; he taught at

G

Athens thirty-six years, till his death at the age of seventy-
two (Clinton's *Fasti Hellen.*), and the four schools of philosophy about his time were represented by Arcesilaus,
Strato, Zeno, Epicurus, whose deaths occurred B.C. 267,
270, 263, 270.

Time ran on, and the Alexandrian school of astronomers
produced a Ptolemy, who had the advantage of the map of
the fixed stars, laid down by Hipparchus. His numerous
and valuable discoveries in astronomical science, such as the
inequality of the movements of the moon through evection,
or the attraction of the sun's mass, and his method of con-
centrating in writing the whole system of ancient astronomy
and geography, so blinded the world to his faults, that
nearly fourteen hundred years elapsed before mankind
were brought to see the fatal error he had fallen into, by
making the earth the centre of the system instead of the
sun, and thus undoing the discoveries of the early Greek
astronomers.

Having shown how increased knowledge of the heavenly
bodies, and of the laws which governed their movements,
produced in the minds of the Greeks the certainty of a
divine mover and ruler of this wonderful cosmogony, I will
now refer to a sense of something in and around us on this
earth—pure, ethereal, and pervading all created things—
which also served to draw the ancients to a sense of the
supernatural or divine. This was a certain electric or magnetic force, which, though not understood, was known to
exist; and that beautiful little poem by Claudian on the
magnet describes the feelings of the fourth century upon the
subject among the Romans. He seeks in this poem to find
out the causes of the sun's pale face and moon's disturbance
under eclipses; to account for the fiery tail of comets; the
movements in the bowels of the earth; the rents of the
clouds in a thunderstorm; the explosion of the thunder,

and the variegated light of the rainbow. He contemplates the loadstone, colourless, dingy, of little value. Where are its attractions ? It neither sparkles in the tiara of a monarch, nor adorns the white neck of a maiden, nor shines in the clasp of a belt; yet the miracles of this dusky stone attest its superiority over the brightest of ornaments, and the reddest of corals which an Indian may seek on his eastern coasts, for this stone gives life to iron and feeds upon it. It knows the sweet food, and from it extracts its native strength. The hard aliment is infused through its whole frame ; without it the stone perishes, its dying limbs grow stiff from gnawing hunger, and thirst consumes its dried-up veins.

The simile is then given of Mars, the smiter of cities at the point of the sword, and Venus, who relaxes human cares during a period of ease, and they occupy one common fane inside a golden temple. Their figures are very dissimilar, but the iron form of Mars and the magnetic stone as Venus, unite in wedlock at the altar. She entwines her arms around his helmet ; he is drawn by secret cords to his stony wife, and they are united by unseen attractions. What congenial heat has welded the two metals together ? What attraction has drawn two hard heads into one, and made the steel alive to the charms of love ?

So Venus has power to compel a savage king, drawn sword in hand, to relax his features when boiling over with bloodthirsty rage, just as she does in the case of the lower animals. " What power, too, is not given to you cruel boy," says the poet, addressing Cupid; "you are greater even than the Thunderer, and bring him down from heaven to roar as a bull in the middle of the waves.¹ You wound a cold stone, and, struck by your weapons, the rock begins

¹ An inscription of a modern wit (Voltaire ?), below a figure of Cupid, runs as follows :—" Qui que tu sois voilà ton maitre."

to burn ; the iron is held by enchantments, and flames
pervade the rigid marble."

This power, then, is held by the ancients as one beyond
our mortal ken.   Cupid pervades the mosaics ; he rides on
the dolphins, is present at the sports, and subdues the
hydras in the field.   Lucretius gives his mother the first
place in the government of the world, and she can hardly
be said to have quitted her pedestal ever since.

The union of philosophy with astronomy resulted in
many a mythological tale and many a religious dogma.
Goddesses, as Venus Urania, descended from heaven ;
mortals were taken up to shine in the sky, like the crown
of Ariadne, Orion the Hunter, Perseus and Andromeda,
and many others.

Astrology sprang from a knowledge of astronomy. Some
of the instruments of the period have come down to us, as
the two armillary spheres, said to be of the fourth century,
preserved in the Archæological Museum of Madrid.   The
view of three instruments depicted on the mosaic at
Morton, Isle of Wight, is a contemporary record of high
interest.   The progress of astronomy in after ages, which
was remarkable in Spain during the Moorish occupation of
that country, may have been due in part to its cultivation
in North Africa, under Mussulman rule ; succeeding, as
did the Arabs, the famous schools of Alexandria and the
many learned astronomers, philosophers, and writers who
flourished in the Roman provinces of North Africa.   The
reformation of the calendar by Julius Cæsar was the result
of increased knowledge derived from the schools of Egypt.
The practical application of this knowledge gave a great
impulse to agricultural pursuits, and caused a more accurate
observation of the seasons ; hence the mosaics in this
country take the seasons for their theme oftener than any
other. We find the seasons of the day at Morton, the days

of the week at Bramdean, and the seasons of the year repeatedly. The months are not separately emblematised in England, as far as we know at present, but they are on that pavement in the British Museum brought from Africa, which will be treated of in a separate chapter at the end of the work.

The Romans, in naming the days of the week after the sun and moon and five planets, generally began the enumeration with Saturday, or Saturn's day, then following with Sun-day, Moon-day, Mercury, Jupiter, and Venus days, as on the bronze forceps found in the bed of the Thames at the close of the autumn of 1840, by Charles Roach Smith, and described by him in *Archæologia*, xxx, p. 548, where, beginning at the bottom of one of the handles, the heads of the gods representing the days appear in the above order, four appearing on one handle and four on the other ; an eighth head being added to complete the uniformity, which may be that of Ceres. Professor Migliorini, of Florence, compares the heads with those on a calendar discovered in the baths of Titus, in Rome, in 1819 (see C. R. Smith's *Collectanea*, vol. ii). On the Bramdean pavement, Saturn's head has been destroyed, as well as the eighth head, inserted to complete the even number, as was the practice. The other heads remain. The order of the days of the week is made to begin with Sunday by Ausonius, as is seen in the well-known lines—

> " Primum supremumque diem radiatus habet Sol ;
> Proxima fraternæ succedit Luna coronæ ;
> Tertius assequitur Titania lumina Mavors ;
> Mercurius quarti sibi vindicat astra dici ;
> Inlustrant quintam Jovis aurea sidera zonam,
> Sexta salutigerum sequitur Venus alma parentem,
> Cuncta supergradiens Saturni septima lux est ;
> Octavum instaurat revolubilis orbita Solem."

Before leaving astronomers and the stars, it would not

be right to omit mention of three very celebrated MSS. of Cicero's metrical translation of Aratus, one of which is considered by Mr. W. Young Ottley (*Archæologia*, xxvi) to have been written as early as the second or third century, while the other two are not earlier than the end of the tenth century. The difference in characteristics and costume is very marked. The first MS. (*Harleian*, No. 647) is accompanied by drawings of the constellations, with a preliminary dissertation in proof of the use of minuscule writing by the ancient Romans, and it is a corrected edition of the poem itself, including nine lines not heretofore known.[1]

The figures of the constellations are in colours; they are of somewhat large size, and within the outlines of the figures, the prose accounts of these constellations, as given by Hyginus, are written in small capitals, like the small poems of Simmias Rhodius, which are often inscribed within the shape of an egg, a pair of wings, a battle-axe, an altar, etc., as in the *Poetæ Minores Græci*.

The scheme gives—

Aries.	Deltolon.	Pisces.
	Δ	
Perseus (18 stars).	Pleiades (7 stars).	(Lyre).
Cygnus.	Aquarius, Capricornus.	Sagittarius (16 stars).
Sagitta.	Aquilla.	Delphinus (9 stars).
Orion (18 stars).	Syrius (20 stars).	Lupus (7 stars).
Argo (26 stars).	Cœtus, the sea-monster, coming to destroy Andromeda (13 stars).	Eridanus, the Po (13 stars).
Piscis (12 stars).	Ara (4 stars).	Centaurus (24 stars).
Hydra.	Anticanis.	Five heads (the planets Jupiter, Saturn, Mars, Mercury, and Venus).

[1] In a tabular arrangement of typical Latin MSS. and handwritings, to the tenth century, given in the *History of the Utrecht Psalter*, p. 43, by Walter de Gray Birch, F.S.A., so great an antiquity is not given to this MS., which is described as of the ninth century—rustic and minuscule duplicate text.

The Sun is represented in a chariot drawn by four horses, ascending. The Moon is represented in a chariot drawn by two oxen, descending.

The early MS. above referred to is 12⅞ in. in height and 11⅛ in. in width. There are upon it extracts from Pliny, Macrobius, and Martianus Capella, by another hand, and a planisphere by one Geruvigus, a monk. Under this is written : " Ego indignus monachus nomine Geruvigus repperi ac scripsi, pax legentibus." Among the writings in this hand are treatises *De Concordia Solari et Lunari, Item de eadem Ratione, De Concordia Maris et Lunæ.*

The following are the nine lines, the existence of which, says Mr. W. Young Ottley, are not even hinted at in any printed edition, and he concludes thence that, except in the ancient MS. referred to, and the two Saxon copies from it, they are nowhere to be found.

> " Sed cum se medium cœli in regione locavit
> Magnus Aquarius, et vestivit lumine terras,
> Tum pedibus simul et supera cervice jubata
> Cedit equus fugiens ; at contra signipotens nox
> Cauda Centaurum retinens ad se rapit ipsa ;
> Nec potis est caput atque humeros obducere latos ;
> At vero Serpentis hydræ caligine cæca
> Cervicem atque occulorum ardentia lumina vestit ;
> Hanc autem totam properant depellere pisces."

The poem of Aratus was put into Latin verse by Cicero, when quite a young man, as Q. Lucilius Balbus informs us, who was so pleased with this Latin version that he was in the habit of reciting passages of it by heart.

We may now descend from "the clouds", and conclude this rapid sketch of the scientific investigations of the ancients by referring to a conversation or disputation in matter-of-fact Rome, or at the Tusculan villa of Cicero, held on the occasion of the *Feriæ Latinæ*, the great national holiday.

The greatness of Rome, her glorious history, and the

general belief in the overruling providence which had been
instrumental in building it up, was present to the minds of
those here assembled, who were C. Cotta, the intimate
friend of Cicero, and a *pontifex*; Velleius, a senator and an
Epicurean; and Q. Lucilius Balbus, a Stoic, dignified in
Cicero's description of him as *Græcis par*. This latter
weaves an intricate web of history, showing the direct
action of the gods in bringing about prosperous events,
and their anger as the cause of misfortunes; instancing the
latter in the first Punic war, when P. Claudius insulted the
gods by making a joke at the chickens of the State, who,
when brought out of their coops, refused to eat. " Let them
drink, then," he said, and ordered them to be drowned. The
Sybilline oracles, the great authority of the Augurs, and
the numerous other religious institutions of ancient Rome,
are adduced in support of his cause; and he is careful to
distinguish between what he calls religious and superstitious beliefs.

We should have a difficulty in perceiving the definitions
of the boundaries of each, but he points them out to his
own satisfaction, and dwells particularly on the dignity of
man's nature; he alone, of all created things, having a
knowledge of the risings, settings, and courses of the
heavenly bodies, by which he defines days, months, and
years; he knowing also the eclipses of the sun and moon,
and when and where they will occur. This study leads his
mind to the knowledge of the gods, from which springs
piety, the handmaid of justice and of the other virtues.

Cotta, the *Pontifex*, anxiously endeavouring to draw
out the philosopher's reasons by a closer line of argument
than he seemed able to give, took care at the same time to
maintain his own official dignity by saying that he always
believed and defended the religious opinions, and the
sacred acts and ceremonies connected with the worship of

the gods, which had been handed down by those who went before; that he always would defend them, and would place more faith in the teaching of the High Pontiffs, and in C. Lælius the Augur than in all the speeches of Stoic philosophers; but, he goes on to say, I am bound to expect reasoning about religion from you, a philosopher, as I am bound to believe, without any reasoning, what our ancestors have handed down.

He then begins to take exception to some of the marvels recorded, as the foot-print of Castor's horse's hoofs on the stone at Lake Regillus, and of the supposed appearance of gods on horse-back who have formerly lived on earth. Balbus rejoins, " What! do not you believe in the temple dedicated to Castor and Pollux in the forum by A. Postumius?" etc. "I believe in the gods", said the pontifex, " but not in your reasons for proving their existence." He then goes on to object to the numerous natural objects being made into gods, as well as abstract qualities, such as Harmony, Faith, Prudence, Honour, Hope, etc.; and those who have been made gods by the vulgar and ignorant, as a Fish by the Syrians, and every kind of animal by the Egyptians. He objects to Greece making gods of mortals who have once lived on earth, as Leucothea, who had been Ino, and her son Palæmon; and Italy, who had enrolled Romulus, and many others, among the new citizens of Heaven. But you philosophers are no better, for you number each of the stars as a separate god, giving them the names of beasts or objects of still-life.

If, then, such are accepted as gods, why do we not as well include among them Serapis and Isis, and all the beasts and birds and reptiles of the barbarous nations? He names a number of foreign divinities, such as Circe. Medea, etc., and if they are not admitted, what shall I say then of Ino, called by the Greeks Leucothea, and by us

II

Matuta, she having been a daughter of Cadmus ? He then objects to the old gods being multiplied by having a different parentage and origin given them. He winds up a long speech, by saying to Balbus, " I see I must go elsewhere to find the proofs of the existence of the gods and of their nature, rather than take them as you make them out to be."

The result of the discussion was that the whole subject was declared to be very obscure. Velleius, the Senator, thought that dreams, said by the Stoics to be sent down to us from Jupiter, were as shadowy as their own exposition of the nature of the gods; it seemed to him that the arguments of the pontifex Cotta were the truest, but that those of Balbus were nearer the semblance of truth.[1] I have inserted this episode to mark a stage in the progress of polytheism in Italy and the signs of its decay. Socrates had died for teaching what was not considered the orthodox view of religion, four hundred years before Cicero lived ; and four hundred years afterwards, the legend of Cadmus, Ino and Bacchus still survived to be represented on the floors of dining-halls by the men of Rome in distant countries. In the intermediate time, Lucian perhaps represented the opinions of his day, when he said the number of new gods introduced into Olympus was so great, and of so many nations and languages, some being really quite unpresentable in such high society, that the ambrosia and nectar were beginning to run short there, and were selling as high as a *mina* for a *sextarius*, or eighty shillings a pint. He further makes Jupiter notify the fact by proclamation,[2] and declare that every god should mind his own business, and not be jack-of-all-trades like Apollo, who was patron of the four arts of music, archery, medicine, and divination.

---

[1] Cic., *De Natura Deorum*, lib. II and III, *passim*.
[2] Θεῶν ἐκκλησία, 14 and 16.

51

CHAPTER V.

Transitional Times—Policy of Theodosius—Absorption of the Gothic Nations—Destruction of Roman Villas—Continuation of Roman Arts and their Mosaic Patterns by Sculptors and Scribes—Wall Painting and Sectilia for Walls—Floral Decorations and their Influence on early Church Architecture and Glass Windows.

IT will be my endeavour in this chapter to penetrate, if possible, the darkness of the transitional times which led to the universal adoption of Christianity in this country; or at least to trace the permanence or revival of many arts and appliances of civilisation for which we are indebted to the Romans. We must be satisfied to grope through a misty atmosphere with little light from contemporary evidence in writing. The end of the mosaics and the villas which they adorned can only be conjectured from their present appearance; such portions only of the buildings as have from time to time been disinterred remain to tell their imperfect tale; but a fair idea of their ground-plans may yet be pretty accurately ascertained.

The Dacian conquests of Trajan have been perpetuated on the column of marble which still stands in the forum, bearing his name, at Rome; and the 2,500 human figures of the triumphal procession which surround it may be studied in London on the full-sized cast of the column in the South Kensington Museum; but the unification of the various tribes of northern and eastern Europe under the name of Goths, by the civilisation and language of Greece, and the written gospels of Bishop Ulphilas in the Mœso-Gothic tongue, combined to form a monument more durable than the marble of Trajan, and more efficacious in the re-constitution of nations than the exploits of his sword.

The archæologist may obtain some insight into what was going on from the very many relics of those times disinterred of late years and subjected to the scrutiny of attentive criticism. It has been said, in reference to the introduction of Christianity in Ireland, by one who has an accurate knowledge of such relics, that "the facile conversion, or rather passive reception of the gospel by the natives, forms a feature in Irish history almost unparalleled in the history of any other country. The favour shown to the new faith and its disciples prompted many a neophyte to seek that peace and safety in Erin which was denied in other lands, and the welcome and hospitality exhibited to distressed and persecuted strangers, were the means of turning to its shores men of learning, genius, and piety from distant regions. Through the agency of these foreign refugees a tinge of Byzantine taste was infused into the decorative arts of Ireland, and the bold, simple, and severe style which characterises the productions of the Bronze period, was soon lost in the elaborate ornamentation which followed in the wake of the Christian missionary. Three varieties of bronze are found in Ireland : one the ordinary bronze, another of a dark-red colour, and the third, of a yellow colour, much like brass."[1]

It may be here remarked that besides the vast collections of objects which illustrate this transitional period, and which fill our national and provincial museums, much benefit has accrued to archæological science by the constant handling and exhibition of such relics before our antiquarian and archæological societies ; for this the private collections of individual members have proved very useful, and I may particularly name, from my own experience, the

[1] H. Syer-Cuming, F.S.A.Scot., in *Brit. Arch. Assoc. Journal*, x, p. 172.

collections of Mr. Bailey; of the three brothers Brent, of
Canterbury, Bromley, and Plymouth; of Mr. E. P. Loftus-
Brock, of Mr. H. Syer-Cuming, of the Rev. Sam. M. Mayhew,
of Mr. Stephen Tucker, *Somerset Herald;* of Mr. C. Warne,
and Mr. E. Way, with many others, members of the British
Archæological Association.

We are indebted to Dr. Birch for an exhaustive account
of Roman tiles and pottery, both as to their manufacture
and uses. He informs us that stamps on tiles give the
names of proprietors of the estates, or *prædia,* where they
were made. This has enabled him to draw an ingenious
deduction therefrom, which shall be given in his own words:
"The most remarkable fact connected with the history of
the proprietors is the prevalence of female names, and the
quantity of tiles which came from their estates was enor-
mous. The occasional renunciation by the Emperors of
their private fortunes in favour of their female relatives;
the extensive proscription by which, owing to a defect of
male heirs, estates devolved upon females, as well as the
gradual extinction of great families consequent on the
corruption of public morals, may be traced on a tile as
readily as on the pages of a historian."[1] Future excavators
may bear this in mind, and endeavour to trace out some of
the names in this country in case any should appear on
tiles or mosaics of villas.

The alteration of Roman names into the language of the
country is another subject which needs investigation. It has
been said that no Roman proper names have survived; but
this is not altogether correct, and some have, no doubt,
through syllabic alterations, become difficult of recognition
unless a special search were made with good philological
experience.

[1] *History of Ancient Pottery,* by Samuel Birch, LL.D., F.S.A. London,
1873, p. 483.

The legislation of the emperor Theodosius did as much
to destroy artistic remains, as well as the memory of the
ancient civilisation, when this ran counter to the new order
of things, as did the arms of the barbarians or the raids of the
sea kings; yet most interesting records of his time have re-
appeared, and none more important can be mentioned than
the disc of silver, twenty-nine inches in diameter, being the
largest of this kind of memorial dishes extant, which was
found in 1847 at Almandralejo (province of Badajoz), not
far from Merida, and now in the Museum of the Royal
Academy of History, Madrid. The subject, in relief, is
altogether historical. The Emperor Theodosius is accompanied by the two princes, Valentinian II and Arcadius,
who were associated with him in the empire, and surrounded
by his guards; he is handing a scroll to a consular personage. The legend around reads :

" D.N. THEODOSIVS PERPET AVG OB DIEM
    FELICISSIMVM   X

which fixes the date to 19 Jan. 389, being the tenth anni-
versary of the accession of Theodosius to the throne[1], unless,
as is probable, it was a presentation dish on the 1st January
of that year. The latest of these dishes known was one of
nineteen inches diameter, with the legend :

" GEILAMAR REX VANDALORVM ET ALANORVM",

showing it to belong to the first half of the sixth century
(530-534). It was found on 20th Jan. 1875.[2]

The prestige, however, of Rome remained, and the skill
of her lawyers and ecclesiastics was strong enough to rule
Britain and absorb any number of the northern Gothic

---

[1] See Anto. Delgado, *Mem. Historico-Critico Sobre el Gran Disco de
Theodosio*, Madrid, 1849, 4to.; and an essay upon it by Merimée in *Revue
Archéologique* for July 1849, p. 263.
[2] *Journal des Savants*, année 1877.

confederacies. It is probable that the large towns would remain constant in orthodoxy and in their allegiance to Roman ideas of government, and true to the memory of the great soldier Theodosius, as well as to his son the emperor ; but, as in the olden time, the populations of the villages and country hamlets were probably left much to themselves, and if slow to be converted to Christianity, the force of example and the zeal of the missionary would, in the end, weld them together in a compact nationality.

The skilful policy of Theodosius, the emperor, retrieved the fortunes of Rome, which had suffered so severely at the fatal battle of Hadrianople (A.D. 378), in which Valeus had lost his life. The Eastern Goths, under Odothæus, were routed on the Danube in the reign of his son Honorius, when each of the five mouths of that river was tinged with the blood of the slain, to use the language of a contemporary historian, and the fish fled in trepidation ; but a writer of more recent date thinks that a large pike in the Danube would have caused more consternation among the fishes.

The Western Goths were absorbed and amalgamated under Roman institutions. The poet Claudian could boast, when addressing Honorius in his fourth consulate,—

> " Tua Sarmata discors
> Sacramenta petit, projectâ pelle Gelonus
> Militat : in Latios ritus transistis Alani."

In Britain, the partizanship of Greek or Roman ideas was often the primary cause of those conflicts between Saxons, Britons, and Welsh, which are irreconcilable upon any other hypothesis ; and as there is not reason for supposing that the permanent government of Britain suffered collapse, such quarrels would only partially affect our villas and mosaics.

The plan of warming the house by hot air conveyed through tiled passages inside the walls from the hypocaust beneath the flooring, furnishes a good proof of the skill of the Romans in the conveniencies of social life. The system was intricate, from the difficulty of admitting heated air without smoke; vapour or steam, as well as cold air, were judiciously sent into the rooms at different levels, producing a circulation and uniform temperature above and below.[1] The subject is one of considerable interest, which it is not my purpose to enter upon here; but the heating flues may have been the cause of many of the conflagrations which appear to have been frequent; and these have been attributed, perhaps in many cases without reason, by historians, to the effect of civil strife or incendiarism.

Our island has twice been invaded by Greeks and twice by Romans, paradoxical as this may at first sight appear. The visits of Greek navigators to our shores before the time of Julius Cæsar are certainly recorded by several trustworthy authors of antiquity; but it is doubtful whether any remains of such visits can be traced, or any other evidence than that of the few authors referred to, unless it is the gold coinage of the ancient Britons, which has been investigated with success by the Rev. Beale Poste in the early volumes of the British Archæological Association, and by Mr. J. Evans, F.R.S., in his work *The Coins of the Ancient Britons.* The second invasion, though of a peaceful and more permanent character, was gradually brought about through the extension of the dominion of Rome over Greece and her dependencies, and may date, probably in England, from the immediate successors of the emperor Septimius Severus, if not from his reign; and Greek influence was greatly stimulated by the removal of the seat of civil government to Byzantium by Constantine the Great. If, however, Greek was the language of the court, it is not probable that it would supersede the tongue of the natives

[1] Seneca, *Epistle* xc.

in these islands, any more than would the Latin. These two languages of the educated classes had been formed by some of the finest intellects which the world has ever produced ; and doubtless were as different, even in Greece and Italy, from those in use among the lower orders of men as is the provincial country English of Yorkshire or Dorset from that spoken in our large towns. The history we have of the inhabitants of the different countries of Europe shows that they consisted of a great number of separate tribes, and the march of civilisation among them would cause those individuals who might be gifted either by nature or education to rise to positions of command.

We are, by a wide conventionality, in the habit of calling all the old inhabitants of north-western Europe under the general name of Celts and Teutons, and of tracing their earliest origin and migrations: a system leading to no result. The Greeks were more rational than ourselves in this respect, who, in writing of the antiquities of their country, found that, as they could neither tell who the native inhabitants may originally have been, or whence they had come, gave them the name of *Autochthones*, or born of the soil. The movements of nations may be compared to the old and new theories of light. The expounders of the former describe a ray as proceeding from the sun and travelling at so many miles in a second. The advocates of the new theory show that a ray is the oscillation of the waves of light set in motion, and thus reaching us by a very different process. So, we find nations set in motion on the page of history by new combinations, and wave appearing to succeed wave ; yet the masses of the people, like the ocean or the atmosphere illumined by the light, remain unmoved, and the surface only or the crests of the waves are presented to our observation. What England owes to that regeneration out of which Christian feelings and ideas have sprung, with

J

their civilising influence upon social life, let our own history
tell. The spirit of God has moved upon the face of the
waters, ruffled though they have been. We might almost
as well search for the fountains or sources of the Atlantic
and Pacific Oceans, or attempt to analyse the waters of each
for the purpose of separating the infinite number of rills
and rivers which have flowed into them from time immemorial, as seek to trace out the primeval origin of nations,
and analyse the combinations of which they are composed.

To return from this digression, let me call attention to
its application, by first claiming the necessity of studying
the chronology of history in disquisitions concerning the
origin of nations. This is too often disregarded and de-
spised, though really the only test of the soundness of any
system. My object has been to show the infiltration of the
Greek element into Roman civilisation, which is manifest
in these mosaics, by the not infrequent use of Greek words
or letters in the few inscriptions which remain. The
quartering of cohorts of the Roman army raised in Asia
Minor, Syria, Thrace, Illyricum, and elsewhere in Greece,
throughout our island, and particularly in the northern
parts of it near the Wall, accounts for Greek inscriptions
which have often been found and continue to come to
light.

Now, as to the two Roman invasions before referred to,
the first was by Claudius, when a permanent occupation was
effected; for the invasions of Julius Cæsar were only in the
form of reconnaissances in force, unless there should be any
truth in the supposed intercourse between Rome and Britain
under the Emperors Augustus and Caius, which some think
is implied by the words of Xiphilinus in his abstract of
Dion Cassius, and put by him into the mouth of the British
queen, Boadicea. Cæsar's narrative of his two invasions
shows that in his time, and somewhat before, Roman influ-

ence in Britain was considerable in promoting the disunion of the tribes, and in the gradual formation of a Roman party. It is hardly likely that this influence would have been allowed to drop, and it probably was the principal cause that the permanent annexation was made under Claudius with so little bloodshed.

The second invasion may be called that of New Rome, by Augustine, at the end of the sixth century. The impossibility of effecting a reconciliation with the Greek Church in the matter of religion, rendered it the interest of Rome, and her safety, to retain the old lines of the Roman or Latin dominion with her language, and to do away with the memory even of everything Greek in Western Europe. This seems to have been in a great measure accomplished ; and even if the civil arm may have been inclined to Greek institutions and ideas, through Constantinople and the later emperors, it was gradually, in the seventh and eighth centuries, subdued to the ecclesiastical. This phase in the history of England is interesting, and may be further elucidated.

Mr. C. R. Smith, in describing a so-called Anglo-Saxon urn from North Elmham, in the museum of Joseph Mayer, Esq., remarks that "these urns are of ruder fabric than the Roman, and less elegant in shape, but the Roman influence is more or less apparent in them all, as it is in the Frankish pottery found in France and Germany. The urn in Mr. Mayer's museum must be regarded as influencing to a certain extent our opinions on the so-called Saxon mortuary urns, and if not to modify, at least to reconsider them. The inscription is in every respect a Roman one, written in a well-known and very common funereal formula. The inference that may be drawn from these facts is antagonistic to the popular idea that the advent of the Saxons into Britain was attended universally with hostility, and with the carnage and extermination of the population of Britain."[1]

Old Roman civilisation has never ceased to prevail; and though the difference of religion would prevent this being fully acknowledged in the writings of the cloister, yet it is very manifest as to the arts, which are brought to light by the excavations made of late years.

Mr. E. P. Loftus Brock, F.S.A., one of the honorary secretaries of the British Archæological Association, in an article in vol. xv of the *Archæologia Cantiana*, pp. 38-55, has collected the earliest evidences of Christianity in Britain in Roman times. As to mosaics, he refers to the ☧ found on the pavement at Frampton, Dorset.

Let us now refer to those artistic evidences which have not been buried, and they are the stone memorial crosses, called Anglo-Saxon and Celtic, which show how the interlaced patterns upon them have been the outcome of patterns on the Roman mosaics. It will be enough to refer to the Copplestone Cross in Devonshire, of which a drawing by Sir Henry Dryden, Bart., has been figured in the *Journal of the British Archæological Association*, vol. xxxiv, p. 242, and to those interlaced crosses at Penally Church, Pembroke-shire, and one at St. David's Cathedral, which have been drawn by Mr. J. Romilly Allen, and figured in the same *Journal*, vol. xxxiv, p. 354; and also to a cross at Winwick, Lancashire, and figured in vol. xxxvii, p. 92, of the same *Journal*; all which plates have been kindly lent by the Association for reproduction in this work. It is not necessary to multiply examples, which are very numerous throughout the country.

The next evidence in support of this position is that derived from interments, wherein buckles, or *fibulæ*, are found with the same interlaced pattern, and the jewellery,

---

[1] C. Roach Smith, *Collect. Antiq.*, vol. v, p. 115.

3, 4. FRAGMENT OF SHAFT OF CROSS FOUND IN PENALLY CHURCH, PEMBROKESHIRE
5, 6. HEAD OF CROSS, FROM ST. DAVID'S CATHEDRAL, PEMBROKESHIRE.

To face p. 60

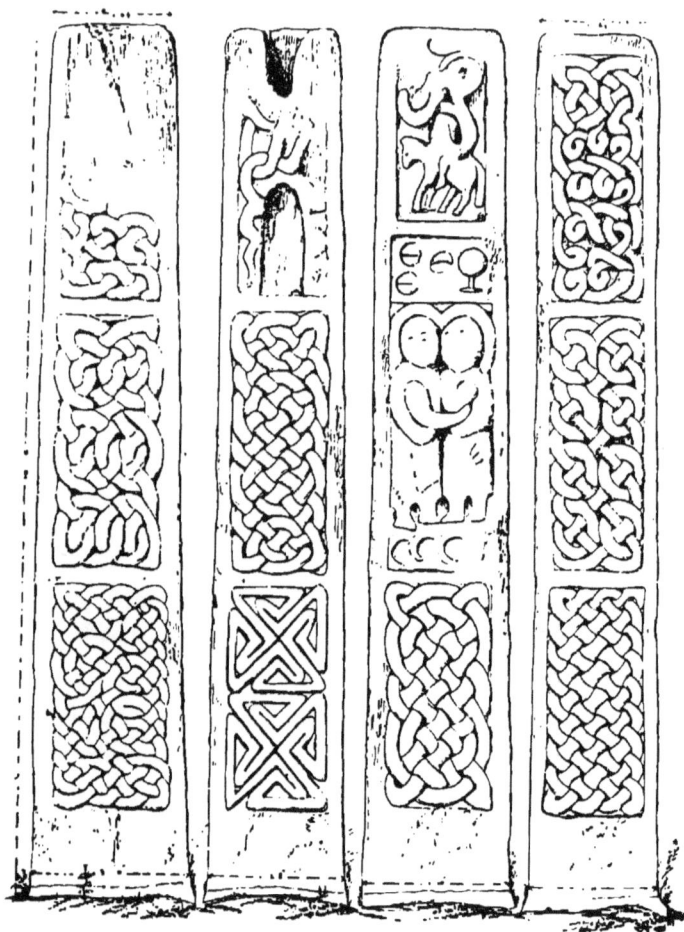

generally of a Roman style, as well as the arms and implements. The excavation of a tumulus recently made at Taplow, near Maidenhead, caused a grave to be reached below the level of the natural soil, which proved to be that of a king or chieftain, to judge by the pattern of his arms and accoutrements. The buckles to fasten the belt at the waist have the interlaced Roman pattern very marked; and the gold thread of the border of his vestments indicates Byzantine influence. The bronze vessel found there, also, is quite Roman in make and taste. These remains are to be seen in the British Museum, where also is a fine collection of objects of the same period found in the various Anglo-Saxon cemeteries of Kent, in one of which, at Sarre, near Canterbury, were four gold coins of Emperors of the East.[1]

Mr. C. Roach Smith, in speaking of mosaic floors, has remarked that " the mode of constructing them was preserved by the ecclesiastics to a very late period, as continental examples testify. At St. Omer is preserved a fine specimen worked in the twelfth century, which is a close copy of the Roman in every respect except that the subjects are scriptural, surrounded by the signs of the zodiac."[2]

In our own country may be named the mosaic in the Prior's Chapel at Ely, figured in *Archæologia*, xiv, Plate 28 ; and the series of encaustic tiles in Derbyshire and elsewhere, described and illustrated by Mr. Llewellyn Jewett in the *Journal of the Brit. Arch. Assoc.*, vol. ii, p. 261; iv, p. 216 ; and vii, p. 384, particularly in the Plates xli and xlii of the last-named volume.

The farther we recede from Roman times the more the patterns diverge from the original model, but still the ornaments retain the unmistakable characteristics of their origin.

[1] C. Roach Smith, *Collect. Antiq.*, vol. i, pp. 63 and 177 ; and Jno. Brent, *Canterbury in the Olden Time*, p. 29.

[2] *Journal of the Brit. Arch. Assoc.*, vol. v, p. 402.

As to Anglo-Saxon charters, it is curious to find the Greek name of Albion used instead of Britannia for this island ; and I will refer to one of Edgar, A.D. 966, for the foundation of Newminster Abbey, in which he is styled *Totius Albionis Basileus;* but this is only one out of many others which could be cited.

To trace further the continuity of Roman ideas, we may notice the construction of the early religious houses, which conform very much in their cloistered arrangements to the peristyle form of Roman villas. The Roman pavements had, of course, to be done away with on account of the allusions on their face to the old mythological worship; but it is probable that if we were to dig beneath the old tithe-barns of the monasteries, which are often extensive and well-preserved, we should find they were not unfrequently built over mosaic pavements of old Roman times, for this reason, that the hypocaust below them, and their solid construction, rendered them impervious to damp, and therefore well-adapted for granaries; and they seem to have been used as such in the middle ages, from the frequent remains of wheat found upon the surface of mosaics.

The monks, in cultivating the language of Rome, seem to have been well acquainted with the best ancient authors, and used them freely as far as they served their purpose. Precedents for government were at times taken from Roman examples, and these in some cases had better have been forgotten. Mischief is often produced in after times by immoral political examples, as Horace well knew when he quoted one from Roman history.[1]

---

[1] " Hoc caverat mens provida Reguli.
    Dissentientis conditionibus
        Fœdis, et exemplo trahenti
        Perniciem veniens in ævum,
    Si non periret immiserabilis
    Captiva pubes."
                    Hor., *Od.* III, 5-13.

The assemblies of the tribes of this country, in their open-air meetings at such places as Abury, Arbor-Lowe, Pennenden Heath, and elsewhere, speak of the state of the country when these meetings prevailed, and it can be traced how the isolated Moots came to be gradually drawn into one central government as civilisation progressed among them. Mr. G. Laurence Gomme[1] has investigated this subject, and more yet remains to be told.

In the meantime this is enough to show how the transition took place from heathen Roman to Christian Roman ideas, and without that violence having been resorted to which is generally asserted or implied by the historians of a later epoch. It is hard to think that the men who could produce in the seventh and following century the beautiful MSS., each one being almost the work of a life, could have been working in times of bloodshed and slaughter. The writing has all the signs of a civilisation uninterrupted, continuous, and peaceful. Whether we take the Gospels of St. Chad, c. A.D. 700, from Lichfield, or the *Book of Kells* of the seventh century, from Ireland, or the Lindisfarne Gospels from Scotland, the interlaced work in the ornamentation of the three is strongly suggestive of an old Roman origin.[2]

To continue the successive stages of the decorative art, we may pass from the illuminated MSS. to the system of wall-painting by means of sectilia or thin slabs cut into shapes to form pictures, which were used by the Romans, and gave, perhaps, the idea of painting the walls of churches. One of the earliest examples of the latter in England is on the small church of Kempley, in

---

[1] *Primitive Folk-Moots.* London, 1880.

[2] See *Facsimiles of MSS. and Ornamentation*, with letterpress, of the Palæographical Society, Parts I-VIII, Nos. 21, 35, and 58, 89, and Nos. 4, 5, 6, 22.

Gloucestershire, near Ross, visited by the British Archæological Association at their Congress at Great Malvern, in
1881. Of wall decorations of Roman times in this country
by means of these mosaic pictures, however, I am unable
to name an example, because the walls no longer exist,—.
unless we except a very small portion of the lower part of
the wall at Wingham so ornamented,—but must refer to
the account of three fine specimens of such decoration
described by Mr. Alex. Nesbitt, F.S.A., in vol. xlv, p. 267,
of the *Archæologia*. He describes them as at the church
of Saint Barbara, originally perhaps the great hall or
basilica of the Bassi in Rome on the Esquiline Hill. The
three subjects are Hylas and the Nymphs, a consular
procession, and a tiger seizing an ox. Mr. Nesbitt says the
ground of both the large pictures was originally green
porphyry (or as it is commonly called at Rome, " serpen-
tino"), and still remains so in that representing the rape of
Hylas ; but in that of the consular procession a great part
of the ground is now of the soft stone known as " verde di
prato", so much used in buildings in Tuscany, this having
no doubt been used to replace pieces of green porphyry
which have dropped out. The rocks, in the rape of Hylas,
are of " alabastro fiorito", variegated alabaster ; the figures
of Hylas and the nymphs, of the marble known as " gialo,
antico"; the hair, I believe, of some variety of alabaster ;
the præfericulum held by Hylas, and the armlets and
bracelets of two of the nymphs, of mother-o'-pearl. The
water, the blue portions of the garments of the nymphs,
and the cloak of Hylas, are of glass ; the drapery flying
out from the nymph on the right of Hylas is of marble, the
paler portion of that known as " palombino". The band,
representing embroidery, below the figures of Hylas and the
nymphs, is wholly of glass, with the possible exception of
the green ground on which the small figures are placed.

The other large picture represents a consul (or other official), clad in the *toga*, or *lœna picta*, or *triumphalis*, of purple and gold, proceeding in his chariot to preside at the games. The white horses are of "palombino", the chestnut of "gialo antico"; the stockings worn by the men on horseback of "palombino"; the garments, as well as those of the consul, of glass ; as also are the trappings of the horses, with the exception of the discs in the breasts and head-bands of the horses attached to the *biga*, which are of mother-o'-pearl. These two mosaics are preserved in the palace of the Prince del Drago, at the Quatro Fontane in Rome. Of the palace of the Bassi, Mr. Nesbitt considers the founder to have been the Bassus who was Consul in A.D. 367. This art of joining together sections of polished stones, marble, or glass, to form a picture or a pattern, was carried to great perfection throughout the Gothic period in Europe. An instance is given in *Archæologia*, xlvi, p. 237, of two gold ornaments of the time of Theodoric, preserved in the Museo Classense at Ravenna ; they are supposed to have been "fastened on the fore part of a cuirass or of some leather garment or *lorica*". The author of the article referred to—Count Ferdinand de Lesteyrie—describes them as the most perfect specimen of workmanship of the kind he had ever seen, and goes on to say : "They are not flat, but consist of a central raised band with a border on each side. The pattern throughout is the same, composed of nine fillets of various designs running symmetrically, so as to make the transverse section of any part of the bands the same. Nothing can give an adequate idea of the regularity and delicacy of the work, in which thousands of minute pieces of oriental garnets are inlaid, and separated from each other by thin gold partitions. It has been remarked that the exterior border of the band on both sides presents to the eye the same pattern as the cornice of the well-

K

known mausoleum of Theodoric, which the Italians call
the Rotonda."

The buckles lately discovered in the grave at Taplow,
before referred to, show a similar skill in the execution of
this kind of work. If the evidences of its continuance in
England fall away in the lapse of ages, a revival of mosaic
work is manifest in the thirteenth century, when the
European influence of the Anjevin kings caused it to be
introduced largely for the decoration of churches and
tombs. An instance ready at hand is the work in Westminster Abbey, of the pavement before the high altar, and
in the chapel of Edward the Confessor. The floral decorations of the old Roman mosaics, in which they abound, are
again manifest in the varied floral ornaments of the capitals
of the Early English architecture, and the flowing decorations of the coloured glass windows then introduced, of
which specimens are given in an article on stained glass
by Mr. W. H. Cope, in *Journal of the Brit. Arch. Assoc.*,
vol. xxxviii, p. 249, and *Salisbury Volume, R. A. I.*, p. 158.
Roman tesselated pavements for flooring in small cubes do
not seem to have continued in England, but the idea was
accepted of producing a somewhat similar effect by encaustic tiles, which could be produced with much less
labour and expense.

CHAPTER VI.

GLOUCESTERSHIRE Mosaics — Situation of the Villas — Woodchester and Cirencester described in Lyson's great Work—Catalogue and Description of these and other Mosaics—The Localities where found— Coins —Authorities.—HEREFORDSHIRE: Mosaics at and near Kenchester referred to by our early Writers on Antiquities.

I WILL now, county by county, refer to the principal mosaics, with a description of each, and especially of those which have pictured scenes of life upon them, authorities being also quoted, and will begin with GLOUCESTERSHIRE, where attention seems first to have been directed to Roman pavements in England by Camden's translator (1695), and then by Lysons, in his great work on the pavements, in 1797. The situation of each pavement will at the same time be given, and a note of the Roman coins which may have been found in the locality, as some clue to the chronology, though some of these are mentioned in too vague a manner.

In Gibson's *Camden* (1695), it is said that "south of the river Stroud, and not far from Minchin Hampton (a pretty market town once belonging to the nuns of Sion), is Woodchester, famous for its tesseraick work of painted beasts and flowers, which appears in the churchyard, two or three feet deep, in making the graves." No further discoveries are reported, and damage must have accrued to the pavements, which, though covered up, were constantly interfered with in the churchyard by coffins being placed upon them, and sometimes they were even cut through if a grave of extra depth were required. The pavements were again uncovered in 1880, for inspection by the Bristol and Gloucestershire

Archæological Society. Mr. William George, in an account of this inspection, in *The Bristol Times and Mirror* for August 9, 1880, especially refers to the interest taken in this relic of antiquity by the rector of Woodchester, the Rev. F. Smith, and to the precautions taken for its preservation from further injury. Woodchester is described by the late Thomas Wright, Esq.,[1] as " situated in a beautiful valley in the high grounds bordering on the bank of a stream, which runs down thence into the plain to join the Severn, and at about four miles from the Roman road from (*Corinium*) Cirencester, to the (*Trajectus Augusti*) Aust Passage across the Channel. It was about twelve miles from the town just mentioned, and the same distance from (*Glevum*) Gloucester. If we left Corinium by the ancient road just mentioned, we should first have seen on a hill to the right, between this road and the road to Glevum, a villa of some extent, the remains of which have been discovered at Daglingworth, about three miles to the northwest of Cirencester. Close to the road on the left, under a hill about five miles from Corinium, was a Roman station, or building, at a place now called Trewsbury. About two miles further, on the right-hand side of the road, stood another handsome villa, which has been excavated to some extent, at Hocbury, in the parish of Rodmarton. Two miles more brought us to a villa on the opposite side of the road, and like the last, close to it, which has been discovered in the parish of Cherington. About six miles further, on the same side of the road, extensive buildings have been found at a place called Kingscot, which belonged either to a villa or a station. About half-way between the last two places, a by-way probably led to the villa at Woodchester, among the hills to the right. Eight or nine miles from Kingscot, at a place called Croom Hall, remains

[1] *Celt, Roman, and Saxon.* London, 1875.

of another villa or mansion have been found close to the left-hand side of the road, where it passes over an eminence. A few miles carried the traveller hence to the shores of the Bristol Channel. If we had taken the road from Corinium to Glevum we should first have seen the villa at Dagling-worth, on the hill to the left ; and then on the right hand, and near the road, about seven miles from Corinium, we should have seen a finé villa which has been discovered at Combe-end. On the other side of the road, in a fine valley among the hills, about half-way between the road and Woodchester,was another rich villa, the remains of which have been discovered at a place called Brown's Hill. In the vale of Gloucester, at the foot of the hills, about four miles to the west of Woodchester, stood another handsome villa, or perhaps a small town, at Frocester. All these places are within a very small circuit, and have been discovered accidentally, so that there may be others within the same compass."

The Roman villa at Chedworth was situated in an equally picturesque and commodious situation as that at Wood-chester. It has been graphically described by Mr. J. W. Grover, F.S.A. (in *Journal of the Brit. Arch. Assoc.*, vol. xxv, p. 129-35), as situated at the bottom of a steep Cots-wold valley, two miles to the west of the Fosse Bridge Inn, which stands at the seventh mile from Cirencester. "The villa occupies the extremity of a ravine, which opens into the vale, and looks upon the river Coln, the parent stem of the Thames, which at this point is about six or seven miles from Thames Head, near Cheltenham.

"The buildings of this villa, or rather the foundations which remain, are placed at the base of the natural slopes surrounding them closely on three sides and covered with a thick growth of wood. The spot is one of remarkable beauty and seclusion, eminently calculated for the site of an elegant

retired sylvan residence, where its lord might enjoy at
leisure the beauties of undisturbed nature, and in the
neighbouring woods find good sport to enliven his more
active moments. Although the aspect of the villa is north-
east, yet so closely do the hills surround it that few winds
can disturb its precincts, whilst the dense foliage is sufficient
to protect it from the heats of the summer sun.

" On entering the nearest building of the extremity to
the left, the antiquary finds himself in a large room paved
with a very bright and beautiful mosaic in singularly good
preservation. The centre compartment is divided into
various divisions, some of which are destroyed by rabbit-
burrows. They contain dancing figures in various attitudes. At the four corners, in triangular spaces, are the
four seasons, wrought out with singular art. That of Winter
is very interesting, exhibiting the dress, probably, of the
Roman sportsman in primæval Britain. His head is enveloped in a capote or hood, similar to that worn by the
head of Winter in the great Bignor pavement. Round the
waist goes a belt, and below this there is a lappeted kilt.
The wind appears to be blowing a loose cloak from his
shoulders ; in his left hand he holds a bare branch, and in
his right a rabbit—indeed, rabbiting must have formed a
leading amusement amongst the proprietors of this villa, for
in another room there is a sculpture of a man holding a
rabbit with a dog at his feet. The figure of Spring is very
vigorous and artistic. It represents a divinity girt with a
sash, and holding in the left arm a basket, whilst with the
right she is apparently scattering seed. Upon her hand
stands a bird.

" This pavement is surrounded with an ingenious, entwined band, beyond which comes a broad and graceful
Greek device. It has also some very pleasing patterns in
scroll work, and is generally of a very elaborate and tasty
character."

The Rev. Preb. H. M. Scarth furnishes some further particulars (in vol. xxv of same *Journal of the Brit. Arch. Assoc.*, pp. 215-227), with a plan of the villa. He refers particularly to the tesselated floor at the south end, "on account of its elegant pattern and execution." He says: "It seems to contain the figures of a dance, eight in number, in which the couples gradually approach or move round each other, till in the last figure the gentleman places a chaplet on the head of the lady. This may be seen in his hand in the first figure. Unhappily, several of the compartments have been broken up by the burrowing of rabbits."

My principal authority for the following descriptions is the large work of Saml. Lysons, *An Account of the Roman Antiquities discovered at Woodchester*, imp. folio, 1797, and the larger work of the same author in three volumes, folio, *Reliquiæ Britannicæ Romanæ*.

This author describes the villa at Combe-end in *Archæologia*, x, p. 319, as follows : "In 1779, some labourers digging for stone in a field called Stockwoods, at Combe-end, farm, belonging to Saml. Bowyer, Esq., in the parish of Colesburn, in Gloucestershire, discovered the remains of a very considerable building, at a small depth below the surface of the earth ; which, on further investigation, appeared clearly, from the remains of tesselated pavements which were found in several places, to have been a Roman house. The floor of one room was preserved quite entire, the walls remaining in many places near three feet in height. Its dimensions were 56 feet in length and 14 feet in breadth. The entrance to it was by a stone step on the south side. Immediately above this pavement were found many of the slates with which the roof had been covered ; they were of a rhomboidal form, and several of them had the nails with which they had been fastened remaining in them. This

room, in its size and situation, bears a near resemblance to
the *cryptoporticus*, described by Major Rooke in his account
of the Roman villa at Mansfield-Woodhouse, Nottinghamshire, and was in all probability designed for the same purpose. The above-mentioned building was pleasantly situated on the side of a hill, facing the south, at the distance
of about a mile from the great Roman road leading from
Cirencester to Gloucester, seven miles from the former, and
about eleven from the latter, and must undoubtedly have
been the villa of some Roman of considerable eminence.
About two feet above the level of the cryptoporticus, before
mentioned, appeared the remains of another tesselated
pavement, of a red and white chequered figure, in a very
indifferent state of preservation."

The beautiful pavement found at Cirencester, and now
one of the two preserved in the Museum there, has upon it
three heads, described as Flora, Ceres, and Pomona, which,
following the precedents of other pavements, I take to be
the seasons of Spring, Summer, and Autumn, as they are
usually depicted.

A small fragment of a corner of a pavement was seen
by Mr. Inskip in August 1843, at Oxbody Lane, now Mitre
Street, Gloucester, figured in *Brit. Arch. Assoc.*, Gloucester
volume, p. 316.

We have no special descriptions of pavements in Herefordshire, only observations upon them of a general
character, thus reported in Gough's *Camden*, vol. ii, p. 449 :
" Kenchester standeth a three mile or more above Hereford upward, on the same side of the river as Hereford dock,
yet it is almost a mile from the rise of the Wye. This
towne is far more auncient than Hereford, and was celebrated
in the Romans time, as apperith by many thinges, and
especially by antique money of the Cæsars, very often
found within the town, and on ploughing about, the which

the people there call Dwarfes money . . . . Of late, one Mr.
Brainton, building a place at Stretton, about a mile from
Kenchester, did find much tayled (hewn) stone there
towards his buildings. There hath been found *nostra
memoria lateres Britannici et ex eisdem Canales, aquæ ductus,
tessellata pavimenta, fragmentum catenulæ aureæ, calcar ex
argento,* byside other strawnge things."[1] " At Kenchester
was a palays of Offa, as sum say. The ruines yet remain,
and vaults also. Here hath been and is found a *fossoribus
et aratoribus,* Romayne money, *tessellata pavimenta,*[2] etc."

Ariconium stands on a little brook called the Ine, which
thence, encompassing the walls of Hereford, falls into the
Wye. The form of the station is an irregular hexagon. Mr.
Gale says the site is oval, of 50 or 60 acres, with four gates or
openings, two on the west, two on the north side.[3] In 1669
was found here a great vault with a tesselated pavement and
a stone floor. About fifty years ago a very fine mosaic floor
was found entire, but was soon torn to pieces by the ignorant
vulgar. Dr. Stukeley took up some remaining stones of
different colours and several bits of fine red pottery. Mr.
Aubrey, in his MS. note, says, " In 1670 old Roman buildings
of brick were discovered underground, on which oaks grew.
At the same time was found here by Sir John Hoskyns an
hypocaust about 7 feet square, the leaden pipes intire,
those of brick a foot long, 3 in. square, let artificially into
one another. Over these probably was a pavement. In
another place is a hollow where burnt wheat has been taken
up. Col. Dantsey sent some to the Society of Antiquaries.
Numbers of Roman coins, bricks, leaden pipes, urns, and
large bones, have been formerly dug up here."

This large camp and station at Kenchester is now generally considered to be the Magna of the *Itinerary,* that is,

---

[1] *Leland,* v, 66.   [2] *Ibid.,* vii, 152.
[3] *Reliquiæ Galeanæ,* pp. 120, 122.

L

the Magna Castra, or Great Camp, and not Ariconium, as
was supposed by Camden, this latter place being now appropriated to Ross. On the 10th June 1830, Thomas Bird,
Esq., F.S.A., communicated the following account of the
discovery of a Roman pavement at Bishopstone, in Herefordshire : " The Rev. Adam Jno. Walker, rector of the
parish, has answered my inquiries in the following form.
The distance from the station of Kenchester is nearly a mile
and a half. This is directly east of the site at Bishopstone,
which was probably the commanding situation of the Prætorium for the general at Kenchester; Credenhill and
Dinevor being perfectly under his eye from this spot."[1]

GLOUCESTERSHIRE.

WOODCHESTER, *twelve miles from Cirencester ; same from*
Gloucester.[2]

1. The large pavement, 48 feet 10 inches square, was
discovered in 1797. A circular area of 25 feet diameter is
enclosed within a square frame consisting of twenty-four
compartments, enriched with a great variety of guilloches,
scrolls, frets, and other architectural ornaments, edged on
the inside by a braided guilloche and on the outside by a
labyrinth fret, between a single fret and a braided guilloche.

The large circular compartment in the centre is surrounded by a border consisting of a Vitruvian scroll, edged
on each side by a guilloche and enriched with foliage proceeding from a mask of Pan, having a beard of leaves.
Immediately within this border are representations of

---

[1] *Archæologia*, xxiii, p. 417.
[2] S. Lysons, 1797 ; and *Rel. Brit. Rom.*, by same author, 3 vols., fol.
Gibson's additions to Camden's *Brit.*, 1695. *Mon. Vetusta S.A.*, vol. ii, for
pl. xliv, Brown's drawing. *Brit. Arch. Assoc.*, Gloucester vol., p. 327.

various beasts, originally twelve in number, on a white ground, with trees and flowers between them. The figures of a gryphon, a bear, a leopard, a stag, a tigress, a lion, and a lioness are now remaining. Those of a boar and a dog, which are to be seen in Mr. Brown's drawing, together with that of an elephant, have since been destroyed, and no part now remains of the two others necessary to fill up the whole space. Most of these figures are about four feet in length. Within the circle occupied by the animals is a smaller circle, separated from the larger by a guilloche and a border of acorns, in which various birds are represented on a white ground. In this circle is also the figure of a fox. Within the circle of birds is an octagonal department formed by a twisted guilloche, in the south side of which, and also of the border of acorns above mentioned, are openings to admit the principal figure of the design, now much mutilated. When Mr. Brown's drawing was made the head only was wanting. The figure is that of Orpheus playing on the lyre, which he rests on his left knee.

No part of the pavement within the central octagon exists at present, but it appears from the memorandum on the margin of one of Bradley's drawings that it contained figures of fish, and that about the centre there was a star-like figure.

In the four angular spaces between the great border of the pavement and the great circular compartment are the remains of female figures, two of which appear to have been in each of these spaces. The figures in the north-east angle, which are more perfect than any of the others, were Naiads. One of them is represented in a recumbent posture, with her right hand over her head, and in her left holding what was intended for an urn, though very rudely expressed ; the other, supporting her head with her left hand, extends her right over an urn placed under her left arm.

The *tesserœ*, for the most part, are cubes of half-inch; those of the outer border are larger, and those near the centre much smaller. Many are triangular and of various other shapes. The whole, when entire, could not therefore have contained less than a million and a half of them. Most of the materials are the produce of this country, except the white, which is of a very hard calcareous stone, bearing a good polish, and nearly resembling the *palombino* marble of Italy. The dark bluish grey are of a hard argillaceous stone found in many parts of the vale of Gloucester, and called blue-lias. The ash-colour are of similar kind of stone, frequently found in same masses with the former. The dark brown are of a gritty stone found near Bristol and in the Forest of Dean. The lightest brown nearly resemble a hard calcareous stone found about two miles from Woodchester. The red are of a fine sort of brick.

The cement on which the pavement was laid appeared to be about eight inches thick, and composed of fine gravel, pounded brick, and lime, forming a very hard substance, on which the *tesserœ* were laid in a fine cement consisting chiefly of lime. The next stratum was three feet thick, and appeared to be composed of coarser gravel, with which great quantities of the *tesserœ* were mixed; and below this another of a reddish sand and clay, mixed with pieces of brick, about a foot in depth, which lay on the natural soil.[1]

2. At the east end of the above-named pavement another was laid over it, a foot above its level, of much coarser materials and very ill-executed; the design being nothing more than stripes of white, blue, and red, very irregularly put together.

3. Another pavement is shown on Lysons' Pl. xiii.

---

[1] See *Vitruvius*, vii, c. 1. Plin., *Nat. Hist.*, xxxvi, c. 25. Pavement of a passage is shown on Lysons' Plate xii. Cubes of one inch.

The design is simple and elegant, consisting of a mat of three colours, dark grey, red, and white, surrounded by a double red border. The mosaic is of same degree of coarseness as the preceding.

4. There is another in a gallery running on south side of the great mosaic. The labyrinth pattern at the east end has been very coarsely patched with rude stripes of blue, red, and white. Other plates, xix and xx, show four fragments found 25 feet from the churchyard wall.

5. Three feet below the surface was a floor of very hard cement, and six inches below this were found the fragments referred to. Five octagonal compartments are seen, with figures on a white ground, surrounded by a double labyrinth fret, immediately within which, on the north side, is a scroll of flowers having a vase in the centre. In the remains of the compartments at the north-west and south-east corners, are fragments of Bacchanalian figures. The octagonal compartment at the south-west corner is entire, and contains figures of two boys holding up a basket of fruit and leaves, with the words BONVM EVENTVM inscribed under them. The compartment at the north-east corner had nothing remaining within the octagonal border except the letters B H N H C, being part of the remainder of the foregoing inscription ; the last word has probably been COLITE, which would exactly fill the space which is effaced. The inscription would then be *Bonum eventum bene colite.* The room in which this was found seems to have been 22 feet 10 inches square. The walls remained to the height of about three feet on every side, and several fragments of stucco-painted in fresco were found among the rubbish and adhering to the walls.

6. Another pavement, shown on Lysons' Pl. xv and xvi, was in a room 20 feet by 12 feet 8 inches.

7. The pavement of a passage is shown on Pl. xii, fol. 2.

8. Another, south of this passage, in room 19 feet 3 inches by 13 feet 8 inches, simple and elegant in design. The *tesseræ* were of the coarser kind, none being smaller than a cubic inch in size. The coins found within the walls of the room numbered 25 on the ground plan were two large brass of Hadrian and Lucilla, and here and in other parts of the building were found a considerable number of small brass of the Lower Empire, chiefly of Tetricus junior, Victorinus, Probus, Constantinus, Constantius, Constantius junior, Crispus, Magnentius, Valentinianus, and Valens ; none of them were remarkable either for their preservation or for the peculiarity of the "reverses".

WITHINGTON-UPON-WALL-WELL, *nine miles from Cirencester; fourteen from Gloucester*.[1]

In eight rooms were pavements of coarse *tesseræ*, cubes of one inch ; not inelegant ; very ruinous. One very good pavement in five compartments ; two nearly entire, the others almost destroyed ; in cubes of half-inch.

9. In compartment at east end, Orpheus surrounded by various animals, eight in all,—leopard, boar, wolf, entire ; bull and stag, nearly so ; horse and lion much mutilated, as was also the figure of Orpheus.

10. On each side of the circle was a narrow compartment, that on the south being ornamented with a peacock and goblet, much mutilated.

In oblong compartment, north of circle, were figures of pheasants and other birds. This division was much better than that which joined it, which was probably the work of

---

[1] *Brit. Arch. Assoc.*, i, p. 44.   *Arch. Journal*, ii, p. 42.

a much later age. The second compartment, which was an oblong, the sides of which were not parallel, contained figures of dolphins and sea-monsters, and a large head of Neptune, represented with horns, apparently formed of crabs' or lobsters' claws, and two dolphins proceeding from his mouth. The other three compartments were much mutilated, yet could be seen a figure on horseback in the act of hunting some wild beast, apparently a lion ; another contained figures of fish, etc.; and the third con-sisted only of ornaments. The pavements were on different levels. That marked A in the plan was 4½ inches higher than D, and 9½ inches higher than E. The pavement B was 4½ inches above C, and D was the same height above E. (See *Archæologia*, xviii, p. 118.)

1223 coins were found near, of third brass, from Valerian to Diocletian, including Carausius and Allectus.

Four pieces of this pavement are now in the British Museum.

———

CHURCH PIECE, *near Lilly Horn and Bisley*.[1]

11. *Tessellæ* of different sizes and colours by thousands.

———

COMB-END FARM, *seven miles from Cirencester, parish of Colesbourn.*

12. Pavements in two rooms. No. 1, coarse *tesseræ*.

13. No. 2, circles and double-fret border. Passage chequered blue and white bordered, with several stripes of brown. Twelve feet remain. No. 3, no pavement, but stucco painted on walls *in situ*.

Coins of Valentinian, Valens, and Gratian.

[1] *Brit. Arch. Assoc. Journal*, ii, p. 326 ; plan of villa, p. 325.
[2] *Archæologia*, xviii, p. 112 ; by Sam. Lysons.

HOCKBURY FIELD, *a quarter-mile N.E. of Church, Parish of Rodmerton.*

14. Pavement with stripes of blue, red, and white. 200 coins (copper) were found here, in perfect preservation, from Constantine to Gratian.[1]

CHEDWORTH, *seven miles from Cirencester.*

15. A large room, 28 feet 9 inches by 18 feet 6 inches, paved with bright and beautiful mosaics. In centre compartment are dancing figures; and in the four corners, in triangular spaces, are the Seasons, surrounded by an ingenious entwined band, beyond which is a broad and graceful Greek device. It is much mutilated; three of the corners only remain. Winter is represented by a man warmly clothed, and holding a hare or rabbit in his hand. Discovered about 1864. Moulding and columns of best period of Roman art, and pavements in smaller rooms.[2]

CIRENCESTER, *in Dyer Street.*

16. Discovered in 1783. The space within borders filled with marine subjects—Cupid on a dolphin; Nereid on dolphin. In field are marine dragons—the sea-leopard, sea-horse, and fishes, among which the conger-eel is conspicuous. There are also lobster, crab, star-fish, spiral shells, bivalve shells, etc. This seems to be the same as that discovered in 1849.[3]

QUEEN'S LANE.

17. Another discovered in 1837. Geometrical patterns, and a flower in the centre.

---

[1] *Archæologia*, xviii ; by Sam. Lysons.

[2] *Brit. Arch. Assoc. Journal*, xxiv, p. 130 ; xxv, 219.

[3] Buckman and Newmarch, *Corinium*, p. 29.   Lysons' *Reliq. Rom.*, ii, p. 7.

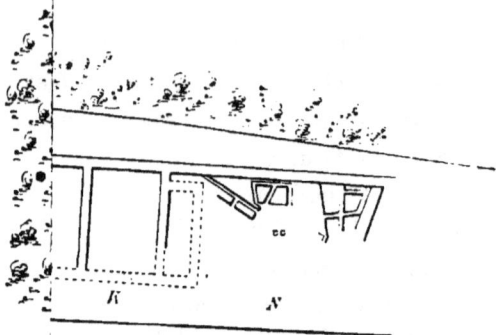

K N

Garden of the Villa, with *Cryptæ* or Ambulatories

trance to Ambulatory. (*d*) Steps.
ypta or Ambulatory in front.

nk,—perhaps for fish. In this room the small Altar

gings for Attendants.

rs for sundry purposes.
bath.

end of the *Villa Rustica*.

ulatory.
RTICI, or Ambulatories, used also for storing grain
ildings (Vitruvius vi, 5, 2; Varro, R. R , i, 57)
oms.
n.
ins.
ff water from the bath.

feet to an Inch .

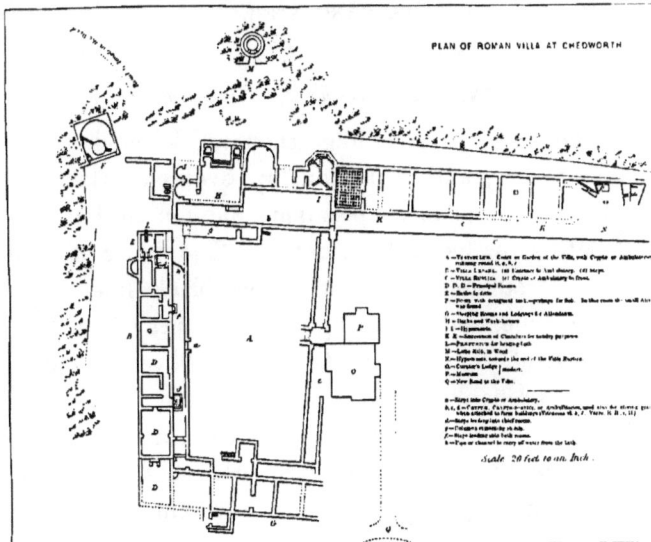

PLAN OF ROMAN VILLA AT CHEDWORTH

Scale 20 feet to an Inch.

To face p. 9.

BARTON FARM, *in Earl Bathurst's Park, near Cirencester.*

18. Orpheus,[1] resembling that at Woodchester, but *tesserae* smaller, and workmanship even superior. It is imperfect to the extent of about one-fourth, but enough remains to show most of the details. The figure of Orpheus in centre is surrounded by a simple black line. Outside this black line, and encircling it, is a series of birds of rich plumage strutting from right to left. Seven remain, and there are probably more. Outside these is a concentric border filled in with a wreath of laurel leaves. The space between them is occupied by figures of beasts. The whole circle had six originally, but four only remain, more or less imperfect—a lion, a tiger, a leopard, and another animal of the panther tribe.

Orpheus,[2] as described above, in Phrygian cap, occupies the centre of a room 21 feet square. He rests his lyre on his left knee ; a dog dances on his hind legs. Around the circle walk with rapid strides a duck, goose, hen, peacock, the common and the silver pheasant. In another circle animals are running in a contrary direction to the birds—that is, a lion, panther, leopard, and tiger occupy half this circle ; the remainder is destroyed. Guilloche border surrounds the circle, which is in a square, and the spandrils are filled up with a floral pattern. This pavement may still be seen *in situ* at Oakley Park, by application, and within reasonable hours. It was discovered in the year 1826 ; a walnut tree was then growing near the middle of it.

19. Pavement of a room, 15 feet square, discovered in Dyer Street, Cirencester, in 1849. There is a central circle, and four semicircles placed at right angles form the sides of

[1] *Brit. Arch. Assoc.*, ii, p. 381 ; xxv, p. 103.
[2] Buchman and Newmarch, *Corinium*, p. 32.

M

the figure, whilst the corners are filled with quadrants. These forms are brought out by the twisted guilloche, and greater relief given to the design by various dark-coloured frets. In centre are three dogs : a large one, around whose neck is a collar, and two smaller in full chase ; but the opposite side of the design is worn away. Of the semicircles only three remain, in which are a winged sea-dragon in pursuit of fish ; a sea leopard with legs, also in pursuit of fish ; sprig of a plant with leaves. In the quadrants, three only remaining entire, are petals of flowers and a Medusa's head. In one of the lozenges is a head of Neptune, with tangled sea-weeds and lobster's claws entwined in the coronet which crowns the head, as also in the side hair and flowing beard ; there is also a flower with four heart-shaped petals and an endless knot. This appears to be the same pavement discovered in 1783. (See No. 16.)

20. The last discovered in the town is on the floor of a room 25 feet square. There were nine medallions when perfect, each nearly five feet in diameter, and each included in an octagonal frame of twisted guilloche, in which bright red and yellow *tessellæ* prevailed. Within the octagons are the circular medallions, surrounded by twisted guilloche borders, but in *tessellæ* of a subdued colour, in which olive-green and white prevail. The central medallion is distinguished from the rest by a double twisted guilloche circle, in which are the colours black, green, ruby-red, yellow, and white. This is a good study for the chromatic effects displayed. The groups were originally five, one in the middle and one on each side. The central is much injured, but is supposed to represent a Centaur.

The two last-named pavements, discovered in a Roman villa in Dyer Street in the year 1849 during drainage operations, were removed in blocks, together with the concrete on which they were laid, and were transferred to their present position in the museum at Cirencester. The larger pavement is thus described by the learned curator, Mr. Arthur H. Church, who says it is of "singular merit and design, and excellent in execution. In its perfect state it originally consisted of nine medallions, each nearly five feet in diameter, and included in octagonal frames, formed of a twisted guilloche, in which bright red and yellow *tessellæ* prevailed. Within all the octagons, with the exception of the central one, are circular medallions, surrounded also by the twisted guilloche, but with *tessellæ* of a subdued colour, in which olive-green and white prevail, this arrangement giving greater effect to the pictorial subjects within each circle, an effect which is heightened by inner circles of black frets, of various patterns, in the different medallions. The central figure, which is supposed to have been a Centaur, together with some other parts of the pavement, was unfortunately injured by the pressure of the foundation wall of a dwelling house.

"The first figure on the south side is the goddess Flora. The head has a chaplet of ruby-coloured and white flowers, intermixed with leaves ; the ruby *tessellæ* here are of glass ; they are now covered with a green crust. A bird, probably a swallow, is perched upon the left shoulder ; against the right rests a flowering branch.

"The next figure is Silenus. He is sitting backward on an ass, and has a cup and bridle in his right hand, while the left is extended.

"Next appears the goddess Ceres. She is crowned with a chaplet of leaves, intermixed with ripe and partially ripened corn ; against the left shoulder rests a reaping-hook.

"The next figure represents Actæon the hunter at the moment when he is being changed into a stag, and is on the point of being devoured by his own dogs.

"The goddess Pomona is next. She has a coronet of

fruits, interwoven with autumnal leaves. Against her
right shoulder is seen an edged instrument, which may be
a knife for gathering grapes.

" The materials used in the manufacture of the *tessellæ*
appear to have been carefully selected, and many of them
obtained from a considerable distance. The white *tessellæ*
are from a singularly hard and pure limestone of the neighbourhood, the uppermost bed of the great oolite; the
cream-colour, from the great oolite; the grey, the same
stone altered by burning; the light yellow, from the oolite;
the chocolate, from the old red sandstone; the slate, or
dark colour, from the limestone of the lower lias; the
brown are of Purbeck marble; while the light and dark
red, the yellow, and the black, are of burnt clay; and the
ruby-red, glass. The last-mentioned colour is used for the
flowers which adorn the head of the goddess Flora, and
for the blood dropping from Actæon's wounds. The glass
is coloured red by sub-oxide of copper, but by lapse of
time it has acquired a green crust of carbonate."[1]

The following are further descriptions by other authors
of the same beautiful pavement:—No. 1. Actæon; young
stags' horns surmount his forehead, and a couple of dogs
are attacking him. The figure is beautifully drawn. No. 2.
Silenus, sitting backwards on an ass, holding the bridle
and a cup in right hand, and extending his left. Trousers
and shoes are of Eastern fashion. No. 3. Bacchus; the
head and Thyrsus remain, much injured. Three out of
the four heads are distinguishable—(A) Head of Flora, with
chaplet of ruby-coloured and white flowers, intermixed
with leaves; a bird is on the left shoulder, against the
right is a flowering branch. (B) Ceres, crowned with

---

[1] *Guide to Corinium Museum.* By Arthur H. Church, M.A.Oxon.,
Professor of Chemistry in the Agricultural College, Cirencester; Local
Secretary to the Society of Antiquaries of London, etc.

chaplet of leaves, intermixed with corn; against the right shoulder rests a reaping-hook, and against the left some ears of corn. (c) Pomona; head with coronet of fruits; against the right shoulder is an instrument which may either be a pruning-hook or a knife for gathering grapes.[1] There are squares and triangles: in one a dancing figure, scattering flowers, and in another, a Medusa's head.

There is a similarity of design and ornaments to those at the grand Imperial villa at Woodchester. The ornaments are those prevailing at the time of Hadrian; and the floors in the Vatican, rescued from Hadrian's villa, may be compared with these.[2] Colours of the *tesseræ* are white chalk; cream-coloured, of hard, fine-grained freestone, from the great oolite; grey, the same, altered by heat; yellow, oolite, oolitic and Wilts pebbles; chocolate, old red sandstone; slate-coloured or black, limestone bands of the lower lias. Artificial are the light red; dark red and black are of terra-cotta; the transparent ruby-coloured are of glass. The foundations consist of the regular *Nucleus*, *Rudus*, and *Statumen*, making up the *Ruderatio*. Coins of the Emperors in great quantities, from Augustus to Arcadius. The reparation of the pavements when injured by time was in many instances done by inserting simple stripes, as shown in the mosaic at Woodchester, of blue, red, and white colours.

The same coloured stripes are observed at Hockbury Field, Rodmerton, and it occurs to me as possible that these stripes may have had some party significance, as being of the colours originating in the circus at Constantinople, which, as badges of party, caused dissensions throughout the empire. Gibbon (*Decline and Fall*, chap. xl, 2) says, "The race, in its first institution,

---

[1] Lysons' *Reliq. Rom. Brit.*, iii, Plates 15, 22.
[2] *Arch. Journal*, vi, C. Tucker's "Observations".

was a simple contest of two chariots, whose drivers were distinguished by *white* and *red* liveries; two additional colours, a *light green* and a *cærulean blue*, were afterwards introduced. The four factions soon acquired a legal establishment and a mysterious origin, and their fanciful colours were derived from the various appearances of nature in the four seasons of the year—the red dog-star of summer, the snows of winter, the deep shades of autumn, and the cheerful verdure of spring. The four colours, *albati, russati, prasini, veneti,* represent the four seasons, according to Cassiodorus (*Var.* iii, 51), who lavishes much wit and eloquence on this theatrical mystery. Of these colours, the first three may be fairly translated *white, red,* and *green. Venetus* is explained by *cæruleus,* a word various and vague: it is, properly, the sky reflected in the sea; but custom and convenience may allow *blue* as an equivalent. Baronius (A.D. 501, Nos. 4, 5, and 6) is satisfied that the blues were orthodox. The partiality of Justinian for the blues is attested by Evagrius (*Hist. Eccles.,* lib. iv, c. 32). At the accession of the younger Justin, the proclamation of equal and rigorous justice indirectly condemned the partiality of the former reign. 'Ye *blues,* Justinian is no more! Ye *greens,* he is still alive!' He goes on to say that party spirit caused such a sedition and tumult in the Hippodrome at Constantinople, that 'thirty thousand persons were slain in the merciless and promiscuous carnage of the day'."

An inscribed slab, now to be seen in the grounds of Lord Stanhope, at Chevening, bears the name of one Fuscus, a charioteer, who belonged to the "blue" faction. My attention was called to it by the Rev. Canon Scott-Robertson, on the visit to Chevening of the Kent Archæological Society, and I at once recognised the stone as one I had seen described by Ambrosio de

Morales (in his *Antiquities of Spain*, Alcala, 1578) as then lying in a garden at Tarragona. It appears that this, among other stones, was brought from thence by the first Earl Stanhope, they having been presented to him by the municipality of that town as an acknowledgment of his military services to Spain during the war of the succession. The inscription, as illustrative of the period which followed that under review, shall be given in full.

```
FACTIONIS VENETAE FVSCO SACRAVIMVS ARAM
DE NOSTRO CERTI, STVDIOSI ET BENE AMANTES
VT SCIRENT CVNCTI MONIMENTVM ET PIGNVS AMORIS.
INTEGRA FAMA TIBI LAVDEM CVRSVS MERVISTI
CERTASTI MVLTIS NVLLVM PAVPER TIMVISTI
INVIDIAM PASSVS, SEMPER FORTIS TACVISTI.
PVLCHRE VIXISTI, FATO MORTALIS ORISTI
QVISQVIS HOMO ES QVAERENS TALEM . SVBSISTE VIATOR
PERLEGE SI IMMEMOR ES SI NOSTI . QVIS FVERIT VIR
FORTVNAM METVANT OMNES, DISCES TAMEN VNVM
FVSCVS HABET TITVLOS, MORTIS HABET TVMVLVM
CONDITVS HOC LAPIDE, BENE HABET FORTVNA VALEBIS
FVNDIMVS INSONTI LACHRYMAS, NVNC VINA PRECAMVR
VT IACEAS PLACIDE, NEMO TVI SIMILIS.
```

TOYC COYC AΓΩNAC
ALΩN . . . AΛΛACCE.

"Thy contests for a prize
Eternity doth change."

CHAPTER VII.

Mosaics in SOMERSETSHIRE, MONMOUTHSHIRE, WILTSHIRE, and SHROPSHIRE
—Situations of the Villas and Remains described by various Authors
—Particular Descriptions of the Mosaics with the Coins found near
them, and the Authorities quoted.

LET us follow Mr. Thomas Wright's introduction into
SOMERSETSHIRE. He says, "Taking as a centre the
ancient town of Somerton, situated on a Roman road
leading from Ilchester in the direction of Glastonbury.
If we follow this road towards Ilchester, two miles from
Somerton, two extensive Roman villas have been traced in
the parish of Kingsdon; one near the Roman road, and
the other a little to the east, on the bank of a small
stream, called the Cary. Further east, on the other side
of the stream, a third villa has been found at Lyte's-Cary.
These three villas are included in a distance of about a
mile. In the parish of Hurcot, joining Somerton to the
east, two villas have also been found ; one near Somerton,
the other about three-quarters of a mile to the north-east.
Barely half-a-mile to the south-east of the latter is another
extensive Roman villa at Charlton-Mackrel ; and, in the
opposite direction, somewhat more than half-a-mile from
the Hurcot villa, is another at Copley. To the east of this,
in the parish of Littleton, close to the Roman road just
mentioned, a group of several Roman villas has been
found. Proceeding along the road northwardly, at about
four miles from Somerton, we arrive at Butleigh Bottom,
where a Roman villa of considerable extent has been
traced. Villas are found in equal abundance within two

or three miles to the west of Somerton, among which the most extensive is that at PITNEY, covering an acre and a half of ground, and containing a very remarkable pavement. It may be noted that the walls of the villas in this district abound in herring-bone work."

A pavement at EAST COKER, near Yeovil, in this county, has been commented on by Mr. C. Roach Smith, who compares the account of one given by Collinson with the discovery of a villa, presumably the same, by Mr. Moore, who says: "About forty years ago, I was riding from Yeovil to East Coker; a mile and a quarter south-west of Yeovil, in a field called Chessles, I saw a crowd of people inspecting the pavement in question. It formed part of a pavement which had been laid down in a concrete of lime, sand, and pounded brick, about eight inches thick, and beneath this was some masonry of herring-bone work, containing flues. I found it was intended to remove the fragment by sawing it off about an inch below its surface. Of course it fell to pieces. It was tolerably put together again, but is now gone to decay. It was, therefore, fortunate that I made the drawing before it was removed. There were other fragments of pavements close by, but shattered to pieces, and one quite entire, but that was composed of large *tesserae* of blue lias, of no interesting pattern. The room in which the hunters' scene pavement was found had been painted; the pieces of plaster which remained were coloured in white, blue, and red stripes. I saw coins picked up on the pavements; they were of Faustina (much worn), Constantine, Crispus, Constantius, Julian, and Valens."

Collinson makes mention of a Roman villa and pavements at East Coker, discovered in 1753; one of several rooms discovered was floored with a most beautiful tesselated pavement, representing, in strong

N

colours, a variety of figures, among which was a female
lying on a couch, in full proportion, with an hour-glass
under her pillow, and a cornucopiæ in her hand; over her
head a hare flying from a greyhound in the act of catching
her in his mouth; and at her feet a bloodhound in pursuit
of a doe, just before him.   Another female appeared,
dressed in her Roman stola, with the purple laticlave; and
a third, much damaged, helping to affix a robe round a
naked person on a couch.   Under this pavement was a
hypocaust.   Not a piece of this pavement is now left, the
whole of the field wherein it was found having been
ploughed up, and the antique fragments dispersed among
curious visitors." [1]

Mr. Smith remarks upon this, that "the fragment
of Mr. Moore's, of which he gives a coloured representation, is probably one of those referred to in the
above account, which had escaped destruction, and would
complete the picture of the hunting scene—the dog
chasing the doe."   Mr. Smith says the group is altogether
well-designed, and, allowing for some defects of drawing,
spirited and characteristic.   From the costume of the
hunters, its execution may be ascribed to a period as late
as the fourth century.   Hunting subjects are of unusual
occurrence in tesselated pavements found in this country,
unless we except that of Actæon and his dogs.   Almost
the only one that occurs to me is that of the Frampton
pavement, in which a man with a spear is pursuing a stag
and some other animal." [2]

A pavement at WELLOW, near Bath, was discovered in
1737, and described in the *Archæologia*, with plates.   It
was opened out in 1807.   Five plates of the mosaics, and

---

[1] Collinson, *Hist. and Antiq. of the County of Somerset*.   Bath, 4to.,
1791, vol. ii, p. 340.

[2] C. R. Smith, F.S.A., *Collect. Antiq.*, ii, pp. 51, 54.

plan of the villa, were made by Rev. J. Skinner, F.S.A., and engraved by H. and E. Waddell, Walworth, Surrey, on a scale of an inch to a foot. The ground plan shows three sides of a quadrangle ; the portion on the eastern side is formed of chequers of different sizes in white lias and pennant stone, measuring ten feet in width ; and, parallel to this, beyond the suite of apartments, is another passage of 12 feet wide. " Plates I, II, III, and IV give excellent coloured views of the designs. The principal of these, Plate IV, measures 34 feet by 26 feet, and appears to correspond with No. 3, Plate LI, of my previous description, occupying the central apartment at the head of the quadrangle; on each side of this is a passage-room, that on the left measuring 26 feet by 6 feet, and the one on the right of similar dimensions. In the corner, at the back of these grand apartments, is a room 20 feet by 15 feet, which has been much injured since the year 1807, when it was last opened. This appears to be the room No. IV in my first description."

In BATH, a pavement has been found on the premises of the *Bluecoat School*, and two others within the precincts of the *General Hospital;* and some rich mosaic work was found in November 1837, in a villa at NEWTON-ST.-LOE, Twerton, near Bath, on the line of the Great Western Railway.

In MONMOUTHSHIRE, the mosaics discovered at Caerwent, more than a hundred years ago, have not left very perfect records of their forms and features. When Giraldus Cambrensis, in the twelfth century, referred to the mosaic pavements, hypocausts, and Roman buildings of Caerwent, they were probably then in a fair state of preservation. Since then, the first mention of pavements there was by Dr. Gibson, in his *Addition to Camden's Britannia*, who says that in the year 1689 there were three chequered

pavements discovered in the garden of one Francis Ridley,
which being in frosty weather exposed to the open air, upon
the thaw the cement was dissolved, and this valuable piece
of antiquity utterly defaced, so that at present there
remains nothing for the entertainment of the curious but
the cubical stones whereof it was composed, which are of
different sizes and colours, and may be found confusedly
scattered in the earth at the depth of half a yard.
Another chequered pavement, the same learned author tells
us, was discovered in the year 1692, in the grounds of the
learned Henry Tomkins, of Caerleon, Esq., in the same
county.   It lay no deeper than the ploughshare, and that
at Caerwent not much lower.   See the figure of it in
Gibson's *Camden*, p. 697.   The diameter is 14 feet.   All
the arches, and that part of the border they touch, were
composed of white, red and blue stones, varied alternately.
The bills, eyes, and feet of the birds were red, and they
had also a red ring about the neck ; and in their wings
one or two of the longest feathers were red, and another
blue.   The inside of the cups was also red ; and, elsewhere,
whatever we have not excepted of this whole area is variegated of umber or dark-coloured stones and white.   Mr.
Tomkins took care to preserve what he could of this valuable piece of antiquity, by removing a considerable part of
the floor, in the same order as it was found, into his garden.

    In Monmouthshire, two other remarkable pavements
have been described ; the one at Caerwent by Henry
Penruddock Wyndham, Esq., in the Appendix to *Archæologia*, vii, p. 410, which was discovered by Mr. Lewis of
Chepstow, in 1777.   It measured 21 feet 6 in. by 18 feet
4 in.   " The pieces of which it was composed are nearly
square, of about the size of a common die.   These are of
various colours—blue, white, yellow, and red ; the first and
second are of stone, and the yellow and red of terra-cotta.

By a judicious mixture of these colours, the whole pattern is as strongly described as it would have been in oil colours. The original level is perfectly preserved, and the whole composition is so elegant and well executed, that I think it has not been surpassed by any mosaic pavement that has been discovered on this, or even on the other, side of the Alps. In my opinion it is equal to those beautiful pavements which are preserved at the palace of the King of Naples, at Portici. Several pieces of tesselated work have been frequently ploughed up at Caerwent, but none have been preserved. Mr. Lewis informed me that within these few years several have been discovered in small parts, but that their continuation was never pursued." The other, a pavement at Caerleon, has been referred to by Mr. C. Roach Smith,[1] and it was discovered in the churchyard. He says : " It presents a novel design so far as regards works of this kind found in England. Though not in the best state of preservation, enough remains for us to understand the pattern. It represents a labyrinth, which is precisely of the same kind as one depicted in a pavement of great beauty discovered at Saltzburg, which was published in colours by the late Professor Joseph Arneth, in his valuable *Archæologische Analecten*, taf. v. The plan of the labyrinth is the same in both ; but while that of Caerleon is merely surrounded by scrolls proceeding from two vases, the Saltzburg example is of elaborate and elegant designs and pictures—the adventures of Theseus to destroy the Minotaur. In the centre, Theseus is about to give the fatal blow to the monster, who has fallen upon his knee. On one of the sides the hero and Ariadne join hands over the altar ; and in the fourth Ariadne sits alone and disconsolate. In the Caerleon pavement, the centre, which must have been small, is wanting, and in other parts

---

[1] *Collectanea Antiqua*, vol. vi, p. 258.

it is also mutilated ; but the Monmouthshire and Caerleon
Antiquarian Association have done all they could to save
what remains of it, and it is deposited in the museum of
local antiquities."

The list of coins found near the pavements at Caerwent
is interesting as showing the occupation of *Venta Silurum*,
at a late period of the Roman dominion.

Proceeding into WILTSHIRE, which can boast of several
interesting mosaics, I will refer to one, not much known,
which was discovered as far back as 1741, and may be
called the wandering mosaic.   It was brought to the
notice of the British Archæological Association, at their
congress at Winchester, in 1845, by Mr. Wm. Webster, of
Great Russell Street, London ; Mr. Charles Beauchamp,
Captain Smith, R.N., and Mr. Hatcher, of Salisbury.   Sir
Richard Colt Hoare, in his *Modern Wiltshire*, part the last,
p. 30-31, has the following account of it.

"In a carpenter's shop in the village of West Dean are
the remains of a Roman mosaic pavement, which was
discovered here in the year 1741, and of which the
following notices occur in the minute-book of the Society
of Antiquaries of London: ' 1741-2, February 18.—The
Secretary read part of a letter from the Rev. W. Rowlston,
intimating that a tesselated pavement was lately found at
West Dean, about seven miles from Salisbury, which was
sent to Mr. Ward, who promised a further account when it
came to hand.   April 1.—The Secretary presented the
Society with a drawing of the tesselated pavement lately
found at West Dean. October 14.—One Mr. Daniel Reeves
of West Dean, attended with the entire centre of the pavement lately found there, about four feet square superficies.'
This is what Mr. Ward had given some notice of by letter
February 18th, and March 11th, 1741.   This travelled
piece of pavement was subsequently made a public exhibi-

tion at the sign of the 'Golden Cross', Charing Cross, and
its authenticity vouched for by William Sterne, Rector of
West Dean; Richard Stern, Gent., and John Coster,
churchwardens; Philip Emmot Hand and John Thistle-
thwayte, overseers. The number of 'cheques' as named in
the advertisement is 12,000."

Besides the square pavement referred to, was found
another (from which the centre had been previously taken),
composed of coarse red and white *tesseræ*, in stripes; both
of these are figured in the Winchester volume *Brit. Arch.
Assoc.;* and another, described by Mr. Hatcher, 1846, as a
highly finished tesselated pavement, of which only a few
fragments remained, though, when entire, the pattern must
have been perfectly beautiful. The *tesseræ* are scarcely
half-an-inch square, and laid with peculiar care and
regularity. Mr. Hatcher sent a sketch to the meeting,
which is also figured in the Winchester volume before
referred to, on page 244. He considered the building, or
rather this portion of a larger building, to be 62 feet by 55.
He believed the ornamented pavement was destroyed by
the breaking down of the flue, as fragments of it were
found deep in the ground. On the outside of the foundations was a mass of chalk, two feet wide, probably to keep
the floors dry. His remarks on the neighbourhood I will
give *in extenso*, as illustrative of the widespread influence
of Roman civilisation : " The discovery of these remains
confirms me in the opinion I have long entertained, that
the forest of Clarendon was much anterior to the Conquest,
and that it probably contributed to the pleasures of the
officers commanding the neighbouring garrison of Old
Sarum. I suspect, indeed, that if the foundations of the
old palace were thoroughly explored, traces of Roman
occupation would be found there also. In a field below
the ruins, many small Roman coins have been discovered

after the plough.   West Dean is about midway between
the palace of Clarendon and the royal park of Melchet." [1]

Another pavement in this county is recorded in
Archæologia, viii, p. 97, found in *Littlecote Park*, the seat
of the Pophams; it has been engraved by Vertue from a
drawing made by Mr. George, steward to Mr. Popham : in
the margin is a verbal description of it, drawn up by the
late Dr. Ward, of Gresham College.   This curious piece of
antiquity has since been destroyed, but Mr. George made
an exact drawing of it on several sheets of paper, in which
all the parts and figures were expressed in their proper
colours.   From this drawing his widow afterwards made a
beautiful carpet in needlework, reduced to the size of
about one inch to a foot of the original.

In SHROPSHIRE, reference is only made to a mosaic at
Wroxeter (*Uriconium*), where important excavations were
made, and described by Mr. Thomas Wright, who calls it
"one of the largest Roman cities in Britain.   It was surrounded by a wall and fosse, the remains of which may be
traced all round, and are upwards of three miles in extent,
and enclose a space of about double that of Roman London.
The town occupied a picturesque and strong position at the
foot of the celebrated Shropshire hill of the Wrekin, which
perhaps gave its name to the place, and on the bank of the
river Severn, just where it is joined by the Tamer.   It was
evidently of considerable importance, and well inhabited; it
had a forum of great extent, and it possessed a theatre of
considerable size in the heart of the town, as well as an
amphitheatre outside."   (See *Uriconium*, by Thomas
Wright, M.A., F.S.A., 8vo., London, 1872.)

Seeing the importance of the place, it might be
expected that more ornate examples of mosaics might
have occurred than have been found here; but the very

[1] *Journal Brit. Arch. Assoc.*, i, p. 62.

fact of its importance may probably account for the dis-
appearance of its figured mosaics. Mr. George Maw, of
Benthall Hall, near Broseley, has minutely described them
in *Journal of the Brit. Arch. Assoc.*, vol. xvii, p. 100. He
has given a plan of the building in which they were found,
and a drawing of one in a long corridor, consisting of
oblong panels of simple patterns of dark grey and cream-
coloured *tesseræ*, and, as in most Roman pavements,
surrounded next the wall with a broad field of uniform
colour, in this instance of a greenish grey tint. Narrow
bands, about five inches wide, branching from this, divided
the pattern into panels of about 8 feet by 11 feet. In
point of design, as far as fine detail is concerned, the pavements were decidedly inferior to many that have been
found in this country. Those at Cirencester and Woodchester, for example, are not only finer in mechanical execution, but are admirable as works of high and refined art.
In the pavements of *Uriconium* the designer appears to
have been satisfied with producing a bold arrangement of
simple geometrical forms. Considerable variety has, however, been obtained, no two of the panels being exactly
similar ; and doubtless these two long pavements, although
wanting in high artistic excellence, must have had a very
noble appearance in their original entirety.

I would here notice the close similarity that exists
between several of the patterns forming the filling in of the
compartments, and those that occur in the pavements of
some of our early mediæval buildings. The subjoined cut
represents part of a mediæval pavement from Beaulieu
Abbey, Hampshire. A close similarity will be found with
the pattern forming the panel enlarged on p. 102 in vol.
xvii of the *Journal of the Brit. Arch. Association*.

SOMERSETSHIRE.

Pitney, a village west of Somerton [1]

1. Mosaic discovered by S. Hasell of Littleton, in A.D. 1827. The ruins of the buildings cover an acre and a half of ground, on the north side of a steep hill bordering on Sedgmoor. Eight rooms had tesselated pavements, but three afford the richest specimens, in rooms connected with each other. The largest is the central, of a square form, with an octagon within it, divided into eight compartments, and one in the centre of an octagon shape. In this centre is a figure seated, holding in left hand a slender rod with small cross at the top of it. In his right hand is a cup. In the compartments around are—No. 1, a man walking hastily, having on his head a pair of horns, and mantle on his back ; in his left hand is one of the rods before mentioned, which has a cross at the bottom and three prongs at the top. No. 2, a female figure, seated, scattering something from a canister which she holds in her right hand. No. 3, a young man naked, and running ; he holds a cloak on his right arm, and in his hand holds an instrument bent at the top, and in his left some drapery and a canister similar to that held by the female in No. 2. No. 4, a female figure, enveloped in a large cloak, and holding in right hand one of those rods described, having a cross at top and bottom of it. No. 5, a man dressed in what looks like armour, with Phrygian bonnet. His chin reposes on left hand, and he holds in right one of the crooked rods as in No. 3. No. 6, female figure, much mutilated, bearing in each hand a musical instrument. No. 7, a male figure in the act of running, with a cloak at his back. His right

<hr/>

[1] Sir R. Colt Hoare, Bart., *Pitney Pavement; Gentleman's Magazine* for 1827.

hand presses his breast, and in his left one of the rods before described. No. 8, a female figure, seated, having left hand raised to her chin, and an open book (or the sistrum of Isis) lying on the ground by her side. In the angles of this pavement are four beasts, three of which have *cornucopiæ* on their shoulders.

The other rooms are divided into square compartments, four of which are decorated with figures, the others with arabesque patterns. Three of the former are nearly perfect, and represent winged boys. No. 1 holds in his right hand a pair of pincers and a rake. No. 2 has a bird perched on right hand, and in left holds one of the crooked rods, on which a canister is suspended. No. 3, the figure also holds in right hand the crooked rod, on which are suspended some quatrefoil flowers, of which others are scattered around. Each of the boys has a piece of drapery round his waist.

2. In another room is the figure of a young man within a circle, striking at the hydra, or serpent, which is darting furiously at him. He holds a bent stick in his right hand, and in his left the canister as before, with the coin or the corn running out of it. Excepting as to the right leg, the figure is perfect. Another small room has a mosaic bust with ornamental head-dress. Coins mostly of the Lower Empire.

The villa is surrounded on all sides by relics of antiquity.

———

HURCOT, *near Somerton.*

This site was examined in 1827 by Mr. Hasell. It is situated at the foot of a hill facing the south and commanding a fine view of the neighbouring country; it covers about half an acre of ground, and a clear spring of water

rises at a short distance from the ruins. Traces of hypocausts, baths, and mosaic pavements were discovered.

Another site, also at Hurcot, but nearer to Somerton, has
been dug into, and Roman pottery, tiles, flues, and coins of
Constantine, Antoninus, Victorinus, Porthumus, etc., with
foundations of tesselated floors, have been found.[1]

EAST COKER, *one mile and a quarter south-west of Yeovil.*

3. Two hunters hold each a spear in right hand, and
with left support a pole, on which is suspended between
them a doe, having her legs tied together and head hanging
down. On the ground beneath the animal is a dog
seated.[2]

WELLOW, *near Bath.*

4. Oblong, chiefly of geometrical pattern, found in
1737; elegant borders; one of the labyrinth pattern. In
centre is a bird, either a peacock or a pheasant, and the
hinder part of an animal in one of the corners of the central
oblong. The size, 32 ft. by 22 ft.[3]

5. Another found in same place. Geometrical oblong
figure in centre, and at top and bottom a floral pattern
with two animals in each, in outline, badly executed. 20
ft. by 15 ft.[4]

Of the large mosaic, No. 3 in this enumeration, only the
upper part now remains, presenting borders so beautiful as
to cause regret for the loss of the remainder. One particularly deserves notice, formed of a double row of axe-heads
placed horizontally and perpendicularly to form the pattern.

---

[1] *Pitney Pavement.* By Sir R. C. Hoare, Bart., 4to., 1831.
[2] C. R. Smith, *Collect. Antiq.*, ii, p. 51; Collinson's *Somersetshire*, vol.
ii, p. 340.   [3] *Vet. Mon.*, Pl. L. vol. i.   [4] *Ibid.*, Pl. LI.

PAVEMENT DISCOVERED AT WELLOW IN 1737

Each axe-head is in two colours, black and red, divided down the middle, and the background is white. The other mosaic referred to as No. 4, consists of an outer border of lines, black, white, red, and blue, then a Greek fret, more lines of the colours as before, and the interior is made up of a square and two oblong panels, one on each side. The centre is an elaborate pattern of guilloches, ingeniously combined. The oblong panels contain each two animals like dogs, amidst plants with heart-shaped leaves. The two passage-rooms on each side of the large mosaic No. 3 are particularly remarkable for the geometrical designs, which are uncommon, particularly that formed of right-angled triangles.[1]

BATH BLUE-COAT SCHOOL.

6. Portion of pavement removed here, measuring 6 feet by 5. Three animals of good design. Horse with hindquarters of a fish. Panther or leopard, terminating in the same way, and a dolphin. A portion of the tail remains of a fourth animal. The *tessellæ* are of white lias and pennant slate of several shades, giving the picture an artistic appearance.

BATH GENERAL HOSPITAL.

7. A large square pavement of geometrical design, found on the premises and preserved in one of the galleries of the hospital, where it is well cared for and protected.

8. At one of the outlying parts of the premises where building is going on, a small portion of a pavement of good design has been uncovered (1884), but the remainder runs under the modern houses, and this small fragment will soon be again covered up.[2]

[1] Skinner and Waddell, plates.
[2] Shown to the editor by Mr. Richard Mann, Contractor to the Corporation of Bath.

NEWTON ST. LOE, TWERTON, *near Bath.*

9. A long corridor, running north and south, is paved with chequers and subdivided by panels of geometrical design. At the southern end of the corridor three principal apartments with pavements are shown upon the plan.[1]

10. The mosaic in the central and largest chamber, marked No. 3, consists of a square surrounding a circle in the centre, wherein is the figure of Orpheus, with lyre, and an animal, apparently a dog or fox, standing on his hind legs. Around this circle are seven animals, lion, stag, leopard, panther, bull, perhaps wolf, and hind. The spandrils between circle and square are fitted with triangular figures; a guilloche border surrounds the whole, and outside is a bold frame of various geometrical figures composed of Greek fret, guilloche knot, etc.

11. Nos. 2 and 3 on each side of this large apartment have good mosaics, though the latter much destroyed. To the north of the above-named large apartment is another, with pavement of good design, with a border of chequers, and in the centre a square containing a guilloche knot.

12. Eastward of this room is an oblong chamber to complete the space to the wall which bounds the large apartment No. 3. The mosaic here consists of circular figures of considerable variety of design.

13. Northward of room No. 4. is a small fragment of mosaic which covered room No. 5, but the remainder has been destroyed.

At the north end of these buildings which have been uncovered is a hypocaust, with adjoining rooms, connected, probably, with a bath. The Bath and Bristol highroad running east and west here cuts off any remaining portion of this fine villa, the portion uncovered measuring 125 feet

[1] Plates by W. B. Cook (Bath) and T. Hearne (London), 1839.

by 55 feet. The pavements were 5 feet below the surface of the ground, and composed of half-inch *tessellæ*. The remaining walls of the building were from 1½ to 3 feet in height.

MONMOUTHSHIRE.

CAERWENT.

14. Mosaic discovered in 1763 in an orchard adjoining the street. "The colours are lively enough, but the figure of a dog or other animal under a tree very ill-expressed."[1]

15. In 1775, John Strange, F.S.A., communicated a long paper, accompanied by an engraving, in which he describes a pavement, on which was still preserved part of a vase and a bird, and on which there had been figures of a lion, a tiger, and a stag.[2]

16. In 1778, a beautiful pavement discovered in previous year, of which, fortunately, an accurate drawing has been preserved. Figured in *Archæologia*, vol. xxxvi, p. 428, Plate 34. Many geometrical figures and floral designs. Mr. O. Morgan refers to the above in describing the excavations in Caerwent, in summer of 1855, when a villa was discovered.

17. In the room No. 6 were traces of a ruined tesselated pavement. Coins of Magnentius and Valentinianus. A well-preserved silver coin of Julian, A.D. 360. In another room were coins of 3rd brass of Gallienus, Tetricus, Constantine, Constans, Caráusius, and Arcadius.

18. In room No. 7 is a fine tesselated pavement, covered to a considerable depth with stucco and plaster, as if of the walls or ceilings. It is divided into four compartments, each four feet square. The baths, paved with coarse *tesseræ* of dark reddish sandstone, about 1¼ inch square.

[1] *Archæologia*, ii, and xxxvi, by Octavius Morgan, M.P., F.S.A.
[2] *Ibid.*, v, p. 58.

19. Square of 14 feet discovered in 1692. *Tesseræ*, white, red, and blue, birds, and a geometrical pattern.[1]

20. "Octavius Morgan, Esq., F.R.S., F.S.A., exhibited a fragment of a Roman pavement which had been recently accidentally discovered in a cottage in the walls of Caerwent, about 10 inches below the surface cell ; the rest of the pavement would appear to have been destroyed many years ago by building a wall and constructing a path. Enough, however, was left to give a clue to the pattern of the whole pavement, showing that there had been four spandrils with a fish in each (a salmon), and eight hexagons, each containing two fish ; one of the hexagons had a trout with an eel coiled up by the side of it."[2]

WILTS.

LITTLECOTE PARK, *Parish of Ramsbury.*[3]

21. Discovered in 1730. A square floor with semi-circular apses or recesses on three sides ; is wholly covered with mosaic work, and on the fourth side is an oblong panel of mosaic leading to another room of larger dimensions, and square. The first room has a circle within the square and another in the centre, the space between the two being divided into four compartments, in each of which is an animal with a female figure riding on its back ; one may be Spring on a fawn ; the next, holding a bird, perhaps a peacock, rides on a panther ; the third seems to hold a stem or branch, and rides upon a bull ; while the fourth is mounted on a goat. The last two figures are clothed from top to toe ; the first two are naked to below the waist. In the centre is Apollo playing on the lyre, which he holds on left knee.

[1] Gibson's *Camden*, p. 607, figured at 697.
[2] *Proceedings of Society of Antiquaries*, June 16, 1881.
[3] *Archæologia*, viii, p. 97.

22. The larger room contains a square of many geometrical patterns, and a kind of frieze or panel runs along the top and bottom of this square. The top one has a cantharus in centre, and at each side two sea-leopards and two dolphins. The bottom side also has a cantharus, and on each side of it two panthers.[1]

PITMEAD, *near Warminster*.

23. Discovered 1786. Geometrical borders and two centres; one geometrical, the other with draped female figure without head.[2] Sir R. C. Hoare says: "The only fragment now remaining, that of a hare sitting, is preserved at Longleat. These villas remained unnoticed from 1786 to 1800, when Mr. Cunnington employed some workmen in making further investigation of the Roman buildings, and left at his decease the following notes relating to it. The villa is 100 feet in length. Principal entrance by south-west front, leading into a crypto-porticus, 72 feet long by 9 feet wide. At the eastern end of the porticus is a square room of 14 feet, brick flues, painted stucco. The ground was examined again in 1820."[3]

FROXFIELD FARM, *in Parish of Ramsbury*.

24. A pavement found, oblong in shape, divided into three parts, prettily ornamented, but not adorned with any animal figures. Mr. George left a drawing of it.

RUDGE, *on Mr. George's Estate*.

25. Another was found in 1725, of which he took a draught and had it engraved by Vander Gucht.

[1] Will. Fowler's *Twenty-six Plates of Roman Mosaics*, 1796 to 1818.
[2] *Mon. Vet.*, ii, pl. 43.
[3] Hoare's *Mod. Wiltshire*, vols. ii and iii ; *Gentleman's Magazine*, vol. lvii, p. 221 ; *Vetusta Monumenta*, vol. ii, plate 23.

P

BROMHAM, *near Devizes.*

26. Pavement opened at the Congress of the British Archæological Association, at Devizes, in 1880, in a field not far below the surface of the ground. It had been uncovered before at long intervals. There were two pavements slightly different in level, one containing figures of fish and marine monsters, the other a geometrical pattern in black, brown, grey, and red *tesseræ* of chalk and clay; it was much injured.[1]

WEST DEAN, *seven miles from Salisbury.*

27. Square pavement; dimensions not given. Description by Mr. Emanuel Mendez da Costa, Clerk to the Royal Society[2]:—

" Eight rows of bricks and eight of stone surround it, of equal depth with the pavement, of eight inches breadth; each row is 10 feet 8 inches. The stone was common quarry stone, the bricks red, and about one inch thick and long on every way. These rows did not end, but were broken, for the pavement reached only as far as they dug, so that whether it continued further they cannot tell. In three or four fields, called Holly Flower Fields, near the said place where this was dug, which was in Aston Cooper's, a farmer's yard, various such bricks have been cut up by the ploughshare, which lay very shallow, so that undoubtedly there are other pavements and antiquities there. The pavement is divided in the inner circle, excluding the border all round, into twenty-eight quarters or ribs, producing a circle. The middle consists of a four-leaved white flower; the ribs run equal, as the circle admits, and are a kind of tesselated work coloured in arches; in the vacancies at the four

[1] *Brit. Arch. Assoc.*, xxxvii, p. 172.
[2] Winchester vol. *Brit. Arch. Assoc.*; Sir R. C. Hoare, *Mod. Wiltshire.*

corners (the pavement being square and the work circular) were represented a lozenge within a square."

The *tesserœ* are of a quarter to half an inch. In the centre they are black and white; the others are red and brown bricks of one-inch square.

28. Another portion of pavement, in stripes of coarse red and white *tesserœ*, terminating in a square, is also figured in Winchester volume, *Brit. Arch. Assoc.*, p. 241.

29. Another portion, in an apartment 18 feet by 12 feet, was a border in black and white *tesserœ* laid with peculiar care and of great beauty; also figured in same volume at p. 244.

SHROPSHIRE.

WROXETER.

30. Oblong panels of simple pattern about 15 feet wide, and extending the length of a long corridor of 240 feet; the pavement remaining over about half its length. The *tessellœ* are dark grey and cream-coloured, surrounded by a broad field of greenish grey tint of open texture found at the foot of the Wrekin. The dark bluish were probably imported, as they are used sparingly, or may be the finer stones of the lias formation of our own country brought from a distance. The light lime-stone is similar to that known in Italy as *Palombino*, and was probably imported.[1]

31. There is also a fragment of pavement in the bath.[2]

LEE, *near Shrewsbury.*

32. Found in 1793. Geometrical patterns, making up a square within a circle. A cantharus in each spandril.[3]

---

[1] *Brit. Arch. Assoc.*, xvii, p. 100.   [2] *Ibid.*
[3] Will. Fowler's *Twenty-six Plates of Mosaics*, 1796 to 1818.

CHAPTER VIII.

Mosaics in OXFORDSHIRE, LEICESTERSHIRE, NOTTINGHAMSHIRE, and NORTH-AMPTONSHIRE—The Villas and their Situations described by various Authors—Details given of the different Mosaics and of Coins found near them—Authorities quoted.

THE Mosaics to be described in OXFORDSHIRE, LEICES-TERSHIRE, NOTTINGHAMSHIRE, and NORTHAMPTON-SHIRE, if not so numerous as in some other counties, yet the designs upon them are of great interest. In Oxfordshire we have an intelligent guide in the Rev. John Pointer, M.A., Rector of Slapton in Northampton-shire, who wrote an account of the pavement at Stuns-field, situated about a mile and a half from Woodstock Park (and of some others), in 1713. He tells us that "a farmer (one George Hannes) was ploughing his land. His ploughshare happened to hit upon some founda-tion stones, amongst which he turned up an urn, which made the farmer have the curiosity of searching further, whereupon he discovered a large and entire ancient tesse-lated Roman pavement, the superficies of it smooth and level, and composed of little square pieces of brick and stone about the size of dice, generally speaking, but some larger and some smaller. This pavement, by its equal division into different sorts of work, should seem to have served for two different rooms; but, be that as it will, I choose to consider it at present, as it is now, but one entire pavement. That part of the field where it was discovered is called Chest-Hill, and sometimes Chest-Hill Acre, in some old leases of this land, being a rising ground about half a furlong from the old Roman road, and about three furlongs off Stunsfield town. Several pieces of painted plaistering were found inside the foundation walls, and a great many slates were amongst the rubbish, mixed with pieces of burnt timber, mortar, and nails ; and that there were other rooms contiguous to this chief room, one may guess from the foundation walls discovered all round it."

As to the quantity of black, whole, and dried corn which lay so thick upon it, and was of one quality only, that is wheat, the author quoted was inclined to believe that it was dried and laid on for no other end and purpose but to preserve the pavement and keep it dry. With due deference to the rector's opinion, it seems to me more probable that when the chamber was disused, the corn was placed there to be kept dry, Roman pavements being so well adapted by their construction for resisting damp, that they made excellent granaries. As to the urn, the writer says:—
" What should have induced the farmer, as soon as he found it, to leave his man and horses in the field and run off home with it, unless it had contained some coins ? How could he distinguish between a sepulchral urn and a flower-pot or money-pot ? However, he showed his cunning in concealing it, because coin did, by the ancient Statute of Treasure-Trove, belong to the queen or else the lord of the manor ; for so we are told by the Rev. Dr. Wood, in ·his *New Institute of the Imperial or Civil Law*, p. 89."

The same author has a curious remark upon the number of Roman coins often found buried. He considers them to have been purposely left behind, as so many "incontestable memorials of the once Roman greatness, which custom has been practised by our own as well as other warlike nations, as France and Spain and other countries in Europe can witness ; and not only so, but another quarter of the world too, of which I shall produce but one single instance, still fresh in some people's memories, and that is Tangiers, in Africa. When King Charles II demolished this strong place in the year 1682, he caused a great deal of our English coin to be buried there, as an undoubted testimony to future ages of the English prowess, as I am informed by the Honourable Captain Bertie of Chesterton in Oxfordshire, who was himself in that action."

As to the work of the pavement in question, this writer admired it as the most elaborate piece of Roman workmanship of this sort, and one of the finest of the " tesselated pavements that had been hitherto found in all Britain. Upon a nice view of it may be observed such an exact symmetry and due proportion in all its parts, but more especially in the human and animal figures, where the very shades that give life to all figures are visible (as on the right leg of the man and the right side of the circle that encompasses these figures), insomuch that one cannot forbear commending the perfect beauty of the whole. The various authors of antiquity do all agree in the general description of Bacchus and his Panther,—that he was represented as youthful, beardless, and naked ; that he was crowned with ivy ; that he had his cantharus or cup in one hand, and his thyrsus in the other, which was a spear adorned with vine-branches and ivy ; and the panther was dedicated to him as being a lover of wine ; and lastly, that he was the first that showed his subjects the magnificence and solemnity of a triumph. Bacchus was called in Greek Θρίαμβος, which by a little alteration is made triumphus." (See Horace, Ode IV, 2.)

Further examination of this villa took place in 1779, and many beautiful specimens of tesseræ were at this time discovered, of which drawings were made by W. Lewington of Woodstock. These drawings are in the possession of the Society of Antiquaries in London.

Pursuing the investigation of this villa in 1812 and 1813, the Rev. Walter Brown and Henry Hakewill, Esq., in searching the neighbourhood, came upon the remains of the Roman villa at North Leigh, which then engaged all their attention, and the result is given in a letter addressed to the Society of Antiquaries by Henry Hakewill (published in Skelton's *Oxfordshire*). He says, that " in the autumn of 1813 several fragments of bricks and tiles of a peculiar form and substance were accidentally observed by the Rev. Walter Brown on the surface of a field near the banks of the river Evenlode, in the parish of North Leigh, in the county of Oxford, at the distance of about half a mile to the south of the Roman road, called the Akeman Street, which runs along the northern boundary of this parish. The ground in that part of the field where they were found was considerably higher than the natural level of the soil, and had the appearance of four wide ridges enclosing an extensive area. It therefore seemed probable, on the first view, that these ridges had been raised by the ruins of a quadrangular building. Foundation walls were soon afterwards discovered on each side of the supposed quadrangle ; and as in tracing these walls many *tesserae* of different sizes and colours were turned up by the workmen, it was concluded that the building was of Roman origin, and that some of the rooms in it had been decorated with tesselated pavements.

· " It was found on subsequent inquiry that the field had been long known by the name of the Roman piece, and that these ruins are noticed in Warton's *History of Kiddington*, 2nd edition, 1783, p. 59. In September 1815 the north side of the quadrangle was examined, and a suite of rooms found, connected by an interior gallery or cryptoporticus, which was about 170 feet long and 10 feet wide. These rooms were then successively laid open, and from

time to time the remains of a hypocaust, a very curious
bath, several rooms with coarse tesselated floors, and a
small one with a pavement of much finer materials, were
found ; and in the month of October the investigation was
rewarded by the discovery of the large room (No. 30), containing a very beautiful mosaic pavement, 28 feet long
by 22 feet wide.

" The western side was now the chief object of attention,
and a series of rooms, not inferior to those on the north side
either in size or interest, were discovered, with a crypto-
porticus to the east, which was nearly of the same width as
the former, but extending in length to 184 feet; and at
the south-western angle a most interesting room, with its
hypocaust and flues in the best state of preservation.
Room No. 1 seems to have been buried at an earlier period
than the last described, under the ruins of its vaulted roof,
and to have been thereby secured from further injury.

" The situation of this villa was well chosen, for the little
valley in which it was placed, and the scenery round it,
are remarkably beautiful. The ground falls gently from the
site of the villa to the river, but round the south-west
angle of the building it rises abruptly to the brow of the
hill which skirts the valley on the south. Standing in the
western porticus, and looking eastward, you have the river
before you (within the distance of 180 yards), which, after
winding below a rocky bank to the left and passing by the
front of the villa, turns suddenly to the east, close under
a hanging wood, on the steep side of the hill before mentioned. This wood, in the form of an amphitheatre, covers
the right bank of the river during its course through the
valley. On the left bank there is a level meadow, varying
in breadth, but everywhere soon rising into a pleasing
irregularity of ground, till the prospect is terminated by a
high ridge, on which, in front of the villa, stands the village

of Combe, and on the left the woods in the vicinity of Blenheim Park."

I have reproduced Mr. Hakewill's ground plan, which is a good typical example of the Romano-British Roman villa, and shows by its irregular quadrature how it has been altered from its original plan by later occupiers ; and this is also proved by a section of the soil beneath it to the depth of seven or eight feet, the measurement of each layer being given in Mr. Hakewill's drawing.

There have been other such pavements ploughed up some years ago at Great Tew and Steeple-Aston, in the same county of Oxford, as we are informed by Dr. Plot, in his *Natural History of Oxfordshire*, p. 335.

In Leicestershire, a mosaic work is recorded in *Philosophical Transactions*, p. 324, found in digging a cellar, in about 1673, over against the elm-trees near All Saints' Church, Leicester, about a yard and a half under the surface of the earth. It is generally supposed to describe the story of Actæon.

Two plates of a pavement found at Leicester in 1830, about a hundred yards north-west of the Roman wall called Jewry Wall, in excavating for the foundations of a cellar, were published in 1850 by Mr. H. Ecroyd Smith, Saffron Walden. Mr. C. Roach Smith remarks upon them, by saying that the first, Plate IV, is " one of the most beautiful pavements preserved in this country". The design, he says, is " as rich and gorgeous as it is chaste and classical ; it comprises nine octagonal compartments, enclosing quadrilateral and triangular figures, interlaced by a rich guilloche of various colours. It appears to have been about twenty-four feet square. The second, Plate V, is more curious than beautiful, representing a group of three figures, one of which is a female ; the second, Cupid drawing his bow ; the third, a stag."[1]

[1] *Journal Brit. Arch. Assoc.*, vi, p. 160.

Q

In Nottinghamshire, the villa at Mansfield Woodhouse
has been described by Mr. H. Rooke, in *Archæologia*,
vol. viii, who, after pointing out the elegant mosaic pavement in the centre room, described hereafter, says the
walls in the other rooms of his plan were painted, but had
not tesselated pavements; the floors were stucco, which
appeared to be made of lime, pounded brick, and clay.
Ashes, and other appearances of there having been fires,
were visible towards the centre of these rooms. The
entrance of this villa seems to have been on the east front,
into a narrow porticus, or rather crypto-porticus, about fifty-
four feet in length and eight wide, with painted walls
and a tesselated pavement; the cubes, nearly an inch square,
of light stone colour, formed a border of about two feet
round the room, within which were squares of about a foot,
of the same sized cubes, but of a greyish colour. On the
right-hand half of this floor, as you enter, the squares
appear rather larger, but not easily distinguishable. A
limekiln, placed not many years ago, has destroyed great
part of this pavement. At one end of the crypto-porticus
is a small room 16 ft. 8 in. by 12 ft. At the other is a
hypocaust, the flues 1 ft. wide and 14 in. deep; at the
end of one flue was a kind of tile about 15 in. high and
12 in. broad. This seems intended to lift up occasionally
to let in the heat conveyed through an arch under the
wall from the other side, where the fire was made, and a
quantity of ashes found; no remains of a wall appeared
round it.

The best specimens in Northamptonshire are the mosaics
at Castor, the Durobrivæ of the Romans. The church
there, with its fine Norman tower, stands on an elevation at some distance from the river Nen, in the centre of
a cluster of Roman buildings which have yielded many
tesselated pavements; these have been figured in a series

of plates by Mr. Artis (London, 1828, folio), but without letterpress description. The list of them in their order is given below, as well as of those found at Mill Hill, a spur of the table-land on which Castor stands, and overlooking the valley of the Nen.

Mr. Morton, in his *Natural History of Northampton-shire*, tells of several Roman pavements found in his county, particularly at Castor, where, he says, "in digging a little way beneath the new surface, they frequently meet with small square bricks or tiles such as the Romans were wont to make their chequered pavements of, and particularly in the place which is now the churchyard, and on the north side of the town. In digging into that part of the hill which the church stands upon they find these little bricks almost everywhere, sometimes single and loose, sometimes set together, and fixed or inlaid in a very hard cement or mortar. The loose ones appear to have been laid in the same manner as those which are now found in entire or unbroken pavements."

He calls the pavement at Nether-Heyford, in the same county, "a noble piece of art. It lay under ground, covered with mould and rubbish, in a part of the meadow which is every year overflowed with land floods; and yet when it was first uncovered it was so close and firm as to bear walking upon as well as a stone floor would do. But leaving it awhile exposed to the night dews, the cement became relaxed, and the squares easily separable. It appears to have been the floor of a square room in some house or other structure of a circular figure, and about twenty yards diameter.

"The room that had this curious floor was in the southern part of the said structure. In the western and northern part of it were several lesser rooms or cellars about ten feet in length and four broad. That there really were such little rooms is plain enough from the partition walls, the bottoms whereof have been discovered in digging there. The borders or sides of the floors were painted with three straight and parallel lines or stripes of three different colours—red, yellow, and green. The floors were all upon the same level. Upon one of these floors were found three urns."

OXFORDSHIRE.

STUNSFIELD, *one mile and a half west of Woodstock Park.*[1]

Pavement 35 ft. by 20 ft., of six different colours—blue, red, yellow, ash-colour, milk-white, and dark brown—on a bed of mortar about a foot in thickness, supported by ribbed arch work underneath.

1.—A labyrinth fret border surrounds the outside, then a braided guilloche, and the space inside this is divided into two squares, with elaborate panels between. Each square has within it a circle, and in this again is another square ; and in the spandrils are two *canthari* and two heart-shaped ornaments. The other large square has within it a series of concentric circles of elaborate design, and inside is a figure standing on one leg and resting against a panther. In right hand he holds a cantharus ; in his left a stem with leaves ; a crown of leaves on his head. In the spandrils are four birds. The whole pavement was covered with black dried wheat above half a foot, and in some places nearly a foot deep.

No coins ; but an urn was found and carried off, which was supposed to have contained some.

---

[1] Wm. Fowler's *Twenty-six Plates of Mosaics. Stunsfield,* by Rev. John Pointer, M.A., Oxford, 1713.

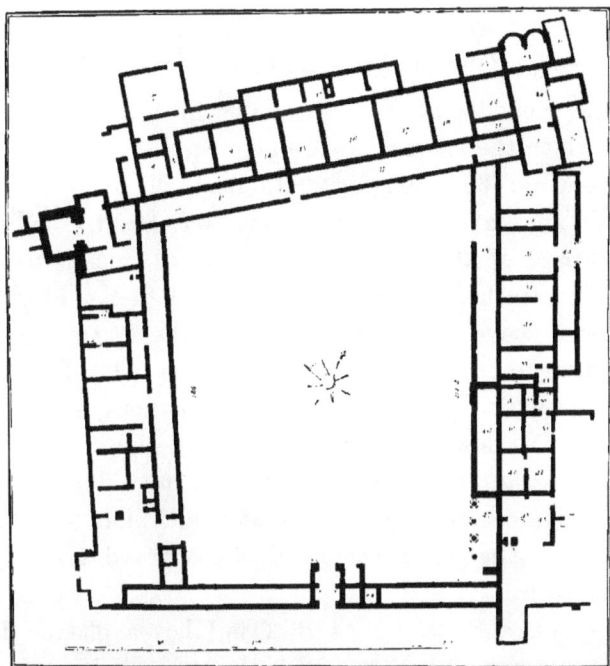

PLAN of ROMAN VILLA at NORTH LEIGH
OXFORDSHIRE.

North Leigh, *half a mile south of Roman Road, the Akeman Street; the Stunsfield Villa, a little north of said road.*[1]

The ground plan from Mr. Hakewill's work is annexed, upon which the apartments are numbered.

2.—No. 1 (33 ft. long by 20 ft. broad), discovered in June 1816. The pavement of this room was about 4 ft. below the surface of the ground. The walls (which are more than 3 ft. thick) were in most part sound to the height of 3 ft. 6 in. above the pavement, and at the south end rose so high as to be scarcely covered with the soil. The tesselated pavement was, with a few exceptions, sound and perfect. No description is given of the design.

3.—No. 2 (30 ft. long by 10 ft. 3 in. wide) seems to have been an ante-room to that which has just been described. The floor is composed of coarse red *tesseræ*, and is very perfect.

4.—No. 3 (9 ft. by 14 ft. 6 in.) has a plaster floor. The stucco was quite sound upon the wall adjoining No. 1, and was coloured of an Etruscan yellow. The skirting was red.

5.—No. 5 was a passage of communication. The floor had been tesselated, but so small a part of it remained that the pattern could scarcely be traced.

6.—No. 8 (discovered Sept. 14, 1816). This room is 19 ft. long by 16 ft. 6 in. wide. The greater part of the pavement had been destroyed; enough remained, however, to show the general design of it. This pavement has stone flues under it, similar to those in the north division of the room No. 1, but there were no remains of funnels against the walls.

7.—No. 9 is 19 ft. long by 16 ft. 6 in. wide. The pave-

---

[1] Both Roman Remains described by H. Hakewill, London, 8vo., 1836; and Skelton's *Oxfordshire*.

ment was much broken, and laid upon flues like No. 8.
The colours and workmanship of both these are very good,
and the cement firm.

8.—No. 10 is part of the crypto-porticus in the east
front of this side of the quadrangle. At the south end
there is a tesselated pavement composed of interesting
circles 2 ft. 4 in. in diameter, and extending 25 ft. 6 in. ;
it was then much broken, and its termination could not be
easily ascertained ; but it probably ceased nearly at that
point, as a pavement of a different design, upon a level 8 in.
lower, was discovered. It was found to go under this pavement ; and it continued to a considerable distance to the
northward. It is evident that great alterations must have
been made on this side of the quadrangle, both from the
irregularity which is perceived in this part of it, and from
the bottom of the bath which remains at the north end of
this crypto-porticus in the rooms Nos. 19 and 20.

9.—No. 11 is a continuation of the crypto-porticus ; it
has a similar tesselated pavement to the lower part of
No. 10.

No. 16, partially examined, and the borders of a tesselated pavement discovered.

10.—No. 17. A trench has been dug across this room.
The floor is of plaster, and was covered in many places
with wheat and lentils—black, as if burnt. The form of the
grain, however, is distinctly preserved.

No. 18, not perfectly examined. The floor is of plaster
laid upon stone flues.

11.—No. 19 is a division at the end of the crypto-
porticus. The floor in several places is paved with coarse,
white *tesseræ*, but not in compartments. At the north end
the bottom of a semi-circular bath was discovered, which is
below the level of the floor, and passes into the adjoining
room. No. 20. This must necessarily have belonged to a

former building, as the partition wall between this room and No. 20 is built across it.

12.—No. 24. This room is 21 ft. long by 17 ft. broad, and has two nearly semi-circular recesses on the western side. The pavement in the north division of this room was in much confusion, having been broken into numberless pieces either by the decay or removal of the pillars in the hypocaust; but by a careful and patient examination of the dimensions and position of the large fragments, the design was very satisfactorily made out.

13.—No. 25. This room is 27 ft. 6 in. by 18 ft. The floor has been tesselated, but there is reason to fear that the pavement is destroyed. At present, however, the room has been only partially opened.

14.—No. 26 (13 ft. long by 11 ft. 6 in. wide). The floor has been tesselated, and where it has been opened, guilloche borders remain very perfect.

No. 29 (28 ft. 6 in. long by 8 ft. wide) has a plain, coarse, red, tesselated pavement.

15.—No. 30. This room is 28 ft. 6 in. long by 22 ft. 9 in. wide. When first discovered, in September 1815, the pavement was entire, except a small part in the south-east corner, and a circular compartment in the middle of the room; but such was the eager curiosity of the country people, who, on the Sunday following the discovery, flocked in crowds to the spot, that, before any precautions could be adopted, the pavement was much injured. What remains will, it is hoped, be protected from further injury, a building having been erected over the room.

16.—No. 31 (28 ft. 6 in. long by 9 ft. 3 in. wide). It has a coarse, red, tesselated pavement.

17.—No. 33 (28 ft. 6 in. long by 13 ft. wide). It has a coarse, red, tesselated pavement. A fire had been made upon the floor, and the ashes were remaining.

18.—No. 35 (19 ft. long by 3 ft. 3 in. wide). This passage had a pavement of small red, blue, and white *tesserœ*. The wall upon the eastern side appears to have been built across the floor; but no traces of the pavement were found in the adjoining room eastward. The stucco adhered to the wall on the western side of the passage, and had been coloured red, with stripes of black. The remains of the pavement were entirely carried away on the Sunday after it was discovered.

19.—No. 44. A crypto-porticus, 80 ft. long by 8 ft. 6 in. wide, paved with coarse red *tesserœ* at the east and west ends; in the middle, for a space of 10 ft. 6 in., the pavement is composed of small red and white squares, chequered. This space of 10 ft. 6 in. corresponds with an opening between two columns, of which the bases and part of the shafts remain very perfect. The columns are 2 ft. in diameter.

20.—No. 45. A crypto-porticus, 105 ft. long and 10 ft. wide, paved with red *tesserœ*.

21.—No. 46. A continuation of the crypto-porticus, separated from the former by a wall or step. This had been tesselated, but very little of the pavement remained. It is 53 ft. long and 10 ft. wide.

More than one hundred Roman coins, chiefly of small brass, have been found in different parts of the building; many of them are entirely effaced, but most of the following are very perfect:—1 Claudius II; 2 Carausius; 1 Allectus; 9 Constantinus; 3 Crispus; 2 Constans; 4 Constantius; 2 Magnentius; 1 Julianus (silver); 2 Helena; 7 Valens; 2 Valentinianus; 3 Arcadius.

LEICESTERSHIRE.

LEICESTER, *near All Saints' Church.*[1]

22.—Found in about 1673. An octagon enclosed within a guilloche border. On it is represented a naked figure with cloak thrown over one shoulder. A stag stands by, and a winged boy is shooting an arrow, apparently at the figure.

NOTTINGHAMSHIRE.

MANSFIELD, *Woodhouse.*[2]

23.—Several fragments from two villas, but one is of beautiful geometrical design, in a room 20 ft. 5 in. by 19 ft. Colours of *tesserœ*—red, blue, white, and pale stone colour. Three coins of Constantine, very perfect; also of Claudius Gothicus and Salonina.

NORTHAMPTONSHIRE.

COTTERSTOCK, *near Oundle.*[3]

24.—A mosaic 12 ft. square, elaborate and diversified in colour and design, having a square centre within which is a diamond and flower. The borders are guilloches, Greek frets and lines.[4]

25.—Shows a mosaic which is probably the same as that described in the next paragraph, though the descriptions differ.[5] This is an oblong figure, with square centre containing a cantharus marked out with blue lines; a heart of four colours is on the bowl, and flowing down from the rim

---

[1] Wm. Fowler's *Twenty-six Plates of Mosaics.*
[2] *Archæologia,* viii, p. 363, with plate (1786).
[3] Artis's *Plates,* 1828, fol.   [4] Plate LX.   [5] Plate LIX.

R

are two stalks ending in heart-shaped leaves. Above and below the square are two borders formed by axe-heads placed in different directions.

A pavement was found here in 1736, with small and simple oblong centre, in which is represented a cantharus. Grey, plain *tesseræ* fill up the outside.[1]

HARPOLE, *in field between Northampton and Weedon.*[2]

26.—A mosaic measuring 22 ft. by 10 ft. was discovered in 1846, and covered up again. *Tesseræ* and other relics were found to a considerable extent beyond the spot. The foundations have not been hit upon, so that a rich mine is left to explore. It was uncovered again in 1849, and a drawing made, which is figured in the *Brit. Arch. Assoc. Journal*, vol. vi, p. 126. Mr. Morton gives a plan and description of a mosaic found here in 1699, that is, in Horestone Meadow.

NETHER HEYFORD.[3]

27.—A pavement was discovered here in 1699, in Horseshoe Meadow, about half-a-mile from Watling Street. It showed four colours, white, yellow, red, and blue, disposed into various regular figures. It measured about 15 ft. in length from east to west. The extent from north to south was not ascertained.

BOROUGH HILL, *half a mile south-east of Daventry.*[4]

28.—Mr. George Baker describes the camp of Borough Hill, and says that in the year 1823 a spot was explored

[1] *Vet. Mon.*, Pl. XLVIII; Wm. Fowler's *Twenty-six Plates of Mosaics.*

[2] Morton's *Nat. History of Northampton* (London, 1712), pp. 527-8. *Journal of the Brit. Arch. Assoc.*, ii, p. 364; v, 376; vi, 126, with plate.

[3] Morton's *Nat. Hist. of Northampton.*

[4] *Hist. and Antiquities of the County of Northampton* (1822-30), vol. i. By Geo. Baker.

on the west side of the enclosure, where were the walls of a building. A room was discovered the floor of which was broken up, but there were decided indications of the entrance. At the north-west corner of the room the fragment of two sides of a tesselated pavement was found, composed of blue, yellow, red, and white *tesseræ*, half an inch square, forming an outer border of the foliated Vitruvian scroll, and an inner one of the simple guilloche, within which was a small ornamented circle, evidently the commencement of a central pattern.

29.—Another room, from its diminutive size, and being considerably below the level of the adjoining apartments, is presumed to have been a bath. The walls had been painted in fresco of various colours; some small portions still adhered to them, as well as to the base, which was finished with a narrow sloped border or moulding. Several large coarse *tesseræ*, of the common stone of the neighbourhood, an inch square, surrounded an elegant square mosaic pavement, partly destroyed, but sufficiently preserved to develop the leading design. The exterior arrangement consisted of five borders; the first white, the second dark blue, the third white and dark blue vandykes transposed, the fourth white, and the fifth a simple guilloche of red, white, and dark blue *tesseræ*. The same ornament was introduced in the central compartment, and disposed into a circle with two intersecting squares. The wall (L) must have been sub-sequently added to form a passage, for it stands on the pavement and interrupts the pattern, which was continued and completed south of it. The room (o) was floored with a composition of pounded brick, lime, and sand. Upon it were considerable quantities of loose ridge and other tiles, apparently the effect of a fallen roof.

30.—The room (P) presented part of a tesselated pavement about 6 ft. wide, principally of the larger *tesseræ*; the remainder had probably been dispersed by the plough, not being more than three or four inches from the present surface. The room (Q) had a similar floor to (O). The whole space excavated was 144 ft. long by 67 ft. wide, without reaching the exterior of the building.

Roman coins have been frequently found here, but a denarius of Constantine was the only one brought to light on the present occasion.

CASTOR.[1]

31.—In the churchyard to the north was found a fragment of mosaic work on which were three oblong figures, one placed lengthwise, and the other two having the narrower sides downwards. The figures were formed of stripes of yellow, blue, and white. This was opened and examined on December 22, 1827.[2]

32.—South-west of the church was found a mosaic 8 ft. square, having a square centre of 4½ ft., in which is a circle round the inner circumference, on which are described sixteen half circles, having a semi-diameter of about 4 in.[3] Within are placed around, in a circle, eight heart-shaped figures; and within these again, to fill up the centre, is a small circle surrounded by petal-shaped figures. In the spandrils formed by the square and centre are two figures at the opposite corners, formed of volutes and petals, and the two others are fronds springing from vases. The border between the central square and the exterior is filled by a square at each corner, containing on the opposite corners a fusil surrounding an elaborate pattern of petals and hearts, and small circle containing a cross in the centre. The other corners have each a fusil with guilloche knot in a circle, and two hearts with flowery figures outside. The colours, to judge from Mr. Artis's plates, are very well toned down

---

[1] Artis's *Plates*, 1828, fol.   [2] Plate VII.   [3] Plate XII.

and harmonised. The intervening spaces are filled by fusils, one within the other, set off by a white border, and containing within these a guilloche border of apparently five colours. This pavement has been relaid in the ante-room to the dairy at Milton.

33.—To the east of the church a fragment of a pavement was discovered on April 9, 1821.[1]

34.—And another pavement is referred to found on the north-east, 10 ft. long and apparently 9 ft. wide, if completed, with 15 in. of plain tiles outside it. The guilloche twist is carried over all the surface, with the exception of an oblong centre formed by black and white stripes.

MILL HILL, *Castor Field*.[2]

35.—A mosaic was discovered here on March 25, 1822, of beautiful design, square, and having a square centre, in the middle of which is an octagon surrounded with plain guilloche frame, and containing as a central ornament a cantharus of many colours. The design of the whole is elaborate, and made up of guilloche knots, oblong figures, petals, and triangles. A kind of axe-head ornament is enclosed in a square or oblong alternately, with an elaborate guilloche knot in smaller frame, and the intervening border is filled up with chequers of black, white, and red alternately. The outside of the pavement is filled up with squares of two colours, alternately set off with double lines of red *tessellæ*.

36.—Another pavement, also found at Mill Hill, is of plain geometrical design, in red brick *tessellæ* upon a white ground.[3]

37.—Another discovered in April 1822 is also figured.[4]

38.—Other fragments.[5]

[1] Plates III and IV.   [2] Plate XIX.   [3] Plate XXI.
[4] Plate XX.   [5] Plate XXII.

39.—A pavement was discovered on December 11, 1827, in one of the fields on the south side of Helpstone, called Pail Grounds, adjoining Oxey Wood and Wood Lane. It is of elegant square design; the centre is a kind of flower-shaped figure, surrounded by a guilloche border. Outside this is a square formed by a scroll pattern, the several lines of blue and white alternating; then a border composed of figures of the shape of arrow-heads in alternate colours, blue and red; then several more stripes of blue and red, and the outside is filled in with plain *tessellæ*.[1]

40.—A pavement found at Water Newton.[2]

41.—Another in Sutton Field.[3]

[1] Plate xxiv.   [2] Plate xxxiv.   [3] Plate xxxv.

CHAPTER IX.

Mosaics in LINCOLNSHIRE and YORKSHIRE—Roman Remains at Barton-on-
Humber described, as well as those at Aldborough, and some account
of the situation of these and of other localities where Mosaics have
been found—The "Corbridge Lanx" and its interpretation—Particular
descriptions of the Mosaics and Coins found near them, and reference
to the authorities.

THE mosaics in Lincolnshire, separated by a long
distance from the gems of Roman art heretofore
described in the south-western counties, yet tell a good
story of themselves, and are amongst the best examples.
It will be seen, by inspecting the Map and Itinerary in the
Appendix at the end of this volume, that though the main
road to York from Lincoln tended a little westward through
Doncaster, yet another route would have been very con-
venient for places on and towards the east coast, if a line
of road were made from Lincoln to Barton-on-Humber,
whence a ferry across that estuary would conduct the
traveller northwards into the line between Patrington and
York. Accordingly, a line has been traced tending to
Barton-on-Humber by a direct course from Lincoln, and at
the former place ancient earthworks are seen to protect a
position which it was as necessary to defend as any other
along the northern roads. An account of these works has
been given by W. S. Hesleden, in the Winchester volume
of the *Brit. Arch. Association*, p. 221. He says, " The
town of Barton is most pleasantly situated upon a gentle
declivity, at the foot of the northern extremity of that
range of chalky hills which, running across the eastern part

of the county of Lincoln, give to it the appellation of the
Lincolnshire Wolds, and is an open, airy, and healthy place
of residence. It is 167 miles distant from London, and
is much noted for its ferry or passage across the river
Humber, being the last town on the great road leading
across the country to Beverley, Hull, and Scarborough ;
and being thickly studded with good dwelling houses and
pleasant gardens and orchards, it happily combines the
pleasing characteristics of a country village with the more
solid comforts and conveniences of a market town. It
contains within its precincts two large and ancient churches
with lofty towers, which are not only conspicuous but
picturesque objects, from whichever quarter you approach
the place ; and from the grounds above the town you have,
from every point, commanding and magnificent views of
the river Humber. From some parts of the lordship,
indeed, the course of the river may be seen for many miles
together, both to the east and to the west ; and at particular times of the tide, the glassy surface of the water is
so studded with vessels that it presents to the eye a wonderfully pleasing and moving panorama, which to a stranger
is a source of equal surprise and delight.

"In the Doomsday survey Barton is called Berton-
super-Humber, to distinguish it from Broughton, a village
about twelve miles distant, once a port or station on the
great Ermin Street or Roman road, and which, in the same
survey, is called Berton, which seems to show that both
names had one common origin, and had reference to some
defensive or protecting positions or ports of the Romans :
it being evident that a military station might be as necessary at Barton to defend or command the passage of the
Humber, as such stations were for protection in the line of
the Ermin Street itself.

" Having already assumed the town of Barton to have

been a Roman station, our attention is called to any additional indications of a Roman origin in or near the place. Taking the direction of the turnpike road, we pass, at the distance of three miles from the town, an old plantation of stunted elms, which has long been known by the name of Beaumont Cote, and which, according to tradition, was planted for the guidance of travellers on their way over the wolds. This tradition serves to give it some object of protection, and it was, no doubt, a Roman camp of an agrarian character. Its form is that of a square, each side measuring in length about twenty-five yards. At the distance of a mile from this we come to an ancient encampment in the adjoining lordship of Burnham, of much larger dimensions, having the form of a parallelogram, and being of the length of 200 yards from east to west, and 100 yards from north to south. It is situated at some little distance to the east of the parish boundary line before noticed, and at about the same distance from the boundary fence of the lordship of Barton. It has been matter of great surprise that this encampment should have been so little noticed."

This information is given as an introduction to the neighbourhood of Horkstow Park, Lincolnshire, where, and at Winterton in the vicinity, the beautiful pavements hereafter described were found. The great Roman road called the High Street, or Old Street, leading from Lincoln to the Humber, passes within four miles of this place. Several Roman mosaic pavements and other antiquities have been found at Winterton and Roxby, each about four miles from Horkstow Hall.

The capital city of YORKSHIRE, *Eboracum*, has been eclipsed as to mosaic pavements by *Isurium*, the ancient city of the Brigantes. Aldborough, on its site, from being a place of importance in Saxon times, and even in our own,

s

having sent two members to Parliament up to the Reform
Bill of 1832, has now degenerated into a mere village.
Isurium lay between York, seventeen Roman miles to the
south-east of it, and Cataracton, twenty-four Roman miles
to the north-west. The ancient Isurium was a town encircled by a massive stone wall, which for centuries provided
the country round with building materials ; and all the walls
between this and Borough Bridge are more or less composed
of the spoils. The upper portion of the fragment of the
city wall, which still exists on the south-west side,
measures ten feet in thickness, but lower down, where the
foundations were opened up in 1794, it showed a breadth
of fifteen feet. In some places the regular courses of
masonry in this wall have been found still to rise above
six feet, though here the average is less.

The numerous buildings within the enclosure have
been described in Mr. Henry Ecroyd Smith's *Reliquiæ
Isurianæ* (London, 1852) ; and among the numerous plates
in that work, to which reference is made hereafter, Plate
XIV may be especially noticed, representing a lengthened
corridor, the extent of which at each extremity has yet to
be determined. This pavement, with the wall two feet
thick remaining upon each side to about its level, lies two
feet below some apartments devoted to the receipt of the
antiquities of Isurium (forming a varied and valuable collection), whence the best fragments, now carefully preserved, can be seen through the trap-doors.

Of the six square compartments of the pattern upon
the mosaics of the corridor, the one at the northern end is
remarkable for the dark-coloured design upon a white
ground. This design resembles the blades of the ancient
Amazonian battle-axe, and is so arranged that the points
meet in fours, whilst that part where, in the weapon, the
socket for a handle would be, is terminated by a small cross
of three red *tesseræ*.

Farther north we miss the tesselated pavements and villas of the Romans; castles and military works rather than decorated floors were more necessary there for securing the occupation of the country near the northern frontier; dedication stones, centurial stones, and other Roman antiquities, being also very abundant. But as these do not form the subject of this work, I will only refer to one object found at Corbridge (Corstopitum), near Newcastle-on-Tyne, because it has a pictorial interest, and is another of those historical dishes of which two other examples have been given in Chap. v. I refer to the famous Corbridge *Lanx*, or dish of silver, which is, however, not circular, as are the others. It is thus described by Mr. Jno. Yonge Akerman, F.S.A., in his *Archæological Index*, p. 116:—

" Among the Roman remains discovered in Britain is the remarkable object represented in the plate accompanying this description. It is shaped like a modern tea-board, weighs 148 ounces, and is about twenty inches long by fifteen broad. It was found in a boggy place near Newcastle, by some children at play, and by them taken to a smith's shop; the smith sold it to a goldsmith in the town, and it finally became the property of the Duke of Northumberland. Without attempting a description of the subject represented on this plate, we may observe that the first three female figures clearly represent Diana, Minerva, and Juno, and the fourth, perhaps, Security. The column surmounted by a globe near this figure will remind the antiquary of the manner in which Security is so often represented on Roman coins, and may, probably, suggest a better interpretation than has yet been offered of the whole group, which, if intended to be symbolical of events in Britain, may typify the security of the province in a state of peace. Such an explanation is suggested by the figure of Security, who alone is seated, while the other divinities stand. We leave

it, however, to the study of more competent judges than
ourselves, and refer those who would learn what has been
said of this very perfect example of Roman art to the
explanations of Gale, Horsley, and Hodgson."

As many interpretations have been offered, I venture
upon another. Diana, in tunic not reaching to the knee,
and chlamys over left arm, holding a bow in left hand
and an arrow in the right, is seen moving to the right
towards another upright figure, apparently Minerva, helmeted, and with a large shield, ægis, and spear leaning on
left arm. Between them is a tree, perhaps a fig-tree, with
birds in its branches, one of which is probably the oracular
crow of Apollo; and on the left side of the tree is a square
cippus with ball on the top, which has some similarity to
one of the astronomical instruments on the mosaic pavement at Morton, Isle of Wight. Behind Minerva, to the
right, stands a dignified draped figure, holding in left hand
what appears to be a spear, or the *hasta pura*, without a
point. This, as described by Mr. Akerman, is Juno, and
perhaps one of the empresses, who, from coins, may appear
to have paid special devotion to the queen of heaven ; and
herself might have been flattered under the form of the
goddess. On her right, again, is seated a figure draped and
veiled, looking round towards Apollo, who stands behind
her under a temple of two columns and pointed roof. He
extends his right hand towards her, holding in it a branch
of some tree. His left hand is raised up in air, and holds the
bow, which is recurved at both ends. His lyre rests against
the foot of one of the columns of the temple. The seated
figure has in her right hand what may be a distaff—though,
according to the usual representation of Fortuna Redux on
coins, it should be an ear of corn—and is raising her left as
if conversing with Apollo. In the back-ground behind her
is a tall, thick column with a globe on the top, which may

be taken for the Umbilicus Romæ, or Milliarium Aureum at Rome, to which the roads tend from the provinces.

Beneath the above figures the following emblematic objects are ranged in line from the left. A *dolium*, or cask, is placed among rock-work, from which a stream of water issues, emblematic of a river, probably the Tiber; then a dog; two wings, or *petasus*, fastened on an upright post. A stag, fallen on its haunches and fore-legs in the air, looks towards a winged griffin to the right, with head turned backwards (*regardant*); between them is an altar on which fire is burning; then a plant with three branches.

I would suggest the seated figure to be Fortuna Redux, that is, "Fortune who brings her votaries home again." Behind her, the great milestone at Rome, and, not far off, the religious fig-tree in the Forum, characterise the goal which it is desired to reach. Under this figure is the altar with the fire, representing, perhaps, the sacred fire of Vesta at Rome.

Apollo, represented here under a shrine, such as used to be dedicated to him at the doors of houses in the city, was probably intended for Apollo Ἀγυιεύς or Ἀγυιάτης, patron of the streets and squares, and seems to be holding out the olive-branch of peace to Fortuna Redux, advocating the safe return of the Empress on the pacification of Britain. Under Apollo is the griffin, a special emblem of the Hyperborean or Northern Apollo. The stream of water is emblematic of the Tiber; the stag and dog have all reference to Diana; the *petasus* represents the wings of speed for the journey home. Apollo's bird in the tree is a happy augury; and Fortuna Redux holds in her hand the ear of corn, one of the attributes of Ceres, to symbolise plenty at home after the return of the Empress. Fortuna Redux is represented on coins as a seated figure, holding an ear of corn, and the anxiety at Rome for the safe return of the Empress

is often expressed by this type. Around the whole is a
graceful border of the vine ; between the alternating waves
of the stalk is a leaf and a bunch of grapes, suggesting,
perhaps, the cultivation of the vine in our northern latitude
of Britain. Wisdom, Sport, Law, and Order may have
reference, by a graceful compliment, to the prophetic intelli-
gence of the Empress introducing them on the occasion of
her visit to the island. Eumenes, in the beginning of the
fourth century, speaks of vines in the territory of Autun as
an old introduction, these being already decayed through
age, and the first plantation of which was totally unknown
to the then generation; and there is some reason to believe
that the vineyards of Burgundy are as old as the age of
the Antonines.[1]

The Empress celebrated in the design of this dish might
be Sabina, who came over to Britain with her husband, the
Emperor Hadrian, and whose coins are, like many other
empresses', sometimes dedicated on the reverse JUNONI
REGINÆ, though she stayed but a short time in Britain; or
it might be Faustina the elder, wife of Antoninus Pius; or
Julia Domna, wife of Septimius Severus; or Mammæa,
mother of Alexander Severus, who took a prominent part
in the government. Of all these, the most probable seems to
be Julia, the wife of Septimius Severus, because she was a
long time in Britain ; her husband died here, and her
countrywomen were especially indebted to her for rebuilding
the Temple and College of Vesta in the Forum at Rome,
which had been burnt during the reign of Commodus, when
the Palladium, or sacred image, originally brought from
Troy, and never seen by anyone in later times except the
Vestal Virgins, its custodians, was snatched from its resting-
place and found shelter in the palace of the Emperors.

Several coins of Julia Pia have "Vesta Mater" on the

---

[1] Gibbon, *Decline and Fall*, i, 58, London, 1809.

reverse, and she has the credit of having brought plenty to Rome under the form of Ceres. Her husband, Septimius Severus, was so thoughtful in making provision of corn for Rome, that at his death there was found a store equivalent to ten years' supply.[1]

The excavations lately made in the house of the Vestals, near the Forum at Rome, have yielded no less than sixteen marble statues and eight pedestals of statues dedicated to Vestal Virgins who had attained the dignity of *Maximæ*, or Superiors. The inscriptions upon these and others previously found from time to time, and recorded in the *Corpus Inscriptionum Latinarum*, yield a long list of the names of grand Vestals during the third century, A.D., and one of them, dated in the consulship of the dedicator, which is equivalent to the seventeenth year of the reign of Septimius Severus, or A.D. 209, is dedicated to TERENTIA FLAVOLA, his sister, "most holy vestal superior", by G. LOLLIANUS, son of QUINTUS POLLIO PLAUTIUS AVITUS, CONSUL, AUGUR, etc., with CLAUDIA SESTIA COCCEIA SEVERIANA, his wife, and LOLLIANA PLAUTIA SESTIA SERVILIA, his daughter. This lady, Terentia Flavola, was apparently of the Emperor's family, and her connection with Julia Pia, the Empress, may give some additional support to the interpretations I have given of the scene embossed upon the Corbridge *Lanx*.

LINCOLNSHIRE.

WINTERTON.

Three beautiful pavements were found here in 1747 near the Trent and Humber.[2]

1.—No. i. Central octagon; contains the delineation of

---

[1] Spartianus.

[2] *Vetusta Monumenta*, vol. ii, p. 9; Wm. Fowler's *Plates of Twenty-six Mosaics*.

Orpheus, with Phrygian cap, and lyre on knee. Eight compartments around contain eight beasts—lion, stag, hippopotamus, boar, horse, dog, elephant, and fox, surrounded by a
circular guilloche border. The spandrils at the corners
contain a cantharus in each.

No. 2. Female head with ears of corn, supposed to be
Ceres. Heart-shaped ornaments in corners.

No. 3. Defective. A stag in one corner.

HORKSTOW, *Barton-upon-Humber.*[1]

2.—A magnificent pavement was discovered in the park
in 1796. It is divided into three panels, which are described and figured in the beautiful plates of Lysons. Plate
III shows one of the panels or compartments, Plate IV,
the central compartment of the same, and Plate V, the
remaining panel. On Plate VI is given the design of the
whole pavement, restored by Robert Smirke, Esq., R.A.;
and the excellent description of each of the plates by Mr.
Lysons is given below.

The red ground of the picture on Plate IV is remarkable;
the serpents forming the extremities of the Tritons are of
ferocious aspect as to fangs and crests, which are red ; the
bodies, variegated brown and white. Of the three medallions the ground is black, which produces an effective contrast. The subjects seem to be Theseus and Ariadne in
two scenes, in one of which she stands erect, undraped ;
from her right hand a crown is suspended, and she holds
one end of a thread or tape, while Theseus holds the other,
having reference to the story of the labyrinth. In the
second scene he is placing a crown upon the head of
Ariadne, who is seated. The third scene represents two
dancing Mænades or Bacchantes. A four-braided guilloche

Brit. Arch. Assoc., Worcester volume, p. 26 ; Lysons' *Reliquiæ Brit.
Romanæ*, vol. i.

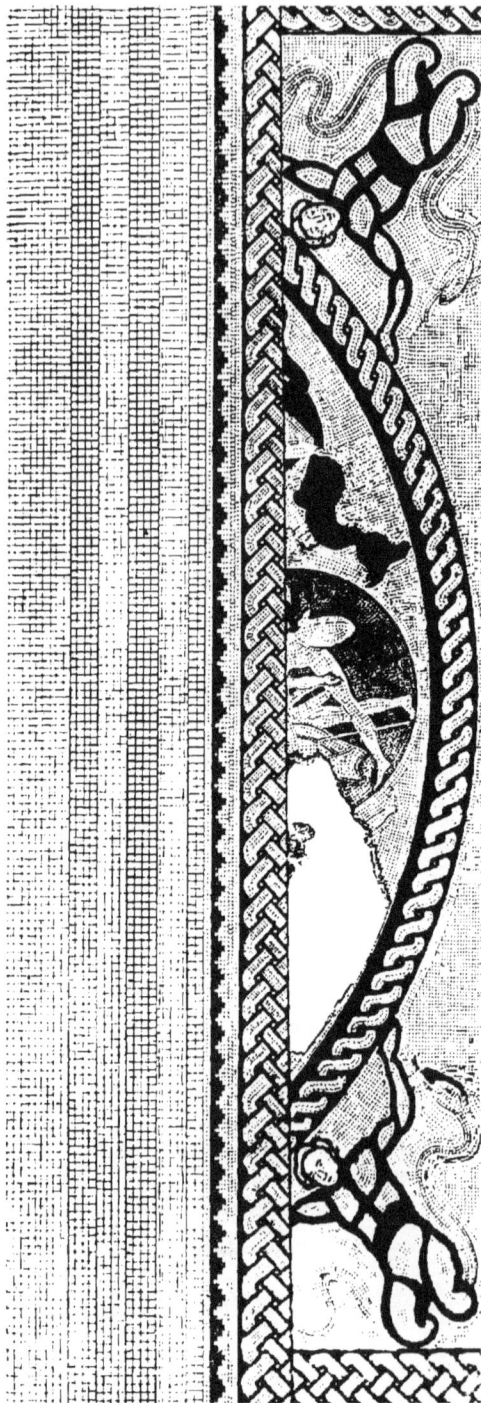

MOSAIC DISCOVERED AT HARKSTOW

border surrounds the whole. The borders are very harmonious and effective.

Mr. Lysons described them as follows :—

Plate III. "The west end of the pavement has been originally a circle 18 ft. 6 in. diameter, divided into eight smaller compartments by radii proceeding from a smaller circle in centre. Small circle contains Orpheus, Phrygian bonnet on head, playing on a lyre and attended by animals. In the smaller compartments, of which two only remain entire, are various birds and beasts. The circles and radii are formed by single twisted guilloches of three colours, bluish grey, red, and white. The large circle, enclosed within a square border of zigzag pattern of bluish grey and white. Each of its spandrils appears to have been filled with a large head having a red cross on each side. Only one of these heads remains. Among the figures of animals which are preserved are an elephant, a bear, and fragments of a boar. *Tessellæ* of about half an inch, of red, white, bluish grey, dark blue, and several shades of brown ; the red, the dark blue, and the brown are of a composition; the grey and white are natural productions, the former being a kind of slate, and the latter of a hard calcareous substance called calk, found near the spot. They are laid in mortar on a stratum of terras about six inches thick, beneath which is a stratum of coarse rubbish."

Plate IV. "Central compartment here figured consists of a circle 15 ft. 3 in. diameter, enclosed within a braided border of four colours, dark grey, red, light brown, and white. Four spandrils are filled by Tritons, whose lower extremities end in serpents, and whose arms support the circle. This circle, and the radii by which it is divided into four equal parts, are formed by a single twisted guilloche. In the centre of these four compartments are small circles containing Bacchanalian figures on a dark blue ground, on

T

either side of which are Tritons, Nereids, Cupids, and
marine monsters on a red ground. On a sea-horse rides a
man backwards, with a girdle round his loins and holding
his hand over his eyes. Facing him on the horse is a female
figure holding a Stemma, and on the tail of the animal
stands a winged Cupid. Figures of genii are seen dancing
round a basket of flowers. The centre is destroyed."

Plate v. "East end of pavement is more entire than
any part of the work. The subject is a chariot race by four
bigæ, which appear to be driven round a platform in the
centre, at the extremities of which are the *metæ*. The
chariots are attended by two horsemen, one of whom has
dismounted to assist the driver, who has lost a wheel, and is
falling backwards. The saddle of the dismounted horseman
has a high peak in front, a fashion prevailing in the time of
the Lower Empire."

" On Plate VII is shown a fragment of a smaller pavement close to the large one, and a third was discovered near,
but of a coarser kind, the *tessellæ* being cubes of an inch,
with no other pattern than stripes of red and white."[1]

LINCOLN.[2]

3.—A pavement was found here 13 ft. 6 in. by 11 ft. 6
in., including the border of coarse red *tesseræ*. Two designs
in geometrical patterns; the colours are blue produced
in slate, white, brownish yellow, and brick red. Spandrils
ornamented with vases, and centre filled with ornaments in
shape of hearts. Another was square, surrounded with
guilloche border, and outside this another of the labyrinth
pattern. Compartments of half circles within the square,
one against each side, formed by guilloche borders, and a

---

[1] Wm. Fowler's *Twenty-six Plates of Mosaics.*
Brit. Arch. Assoc. Journal, ii, p. 186.

whole circle in the centre, and inside it a geometrical pattern in form of a star. The half circles contain each a dolphin, and the quarter circles at corners a heart with double heart within it.

4.—A fragment of another pavement was found forty yards east from the centre of road leading to Newport Gate.

DENTON, *near Grantham*.[1]

5.—Pavement discovered in February 1727 in the lordship of Denton, near Grantham, geometrical pattern.

6.—Another in same lordship, geometrical pattern.

ROXBY, *near the Humber*.[2]

7.—Near the Humber at Roxby, a mosaic of beautiful geometrical design and stripes outside.

WINTERTON.[3]

8.—Another piece of mosaic discovered here in 1797.

SCAMPTON, *near Lincoln*.[4]

9.—A piece discovered here in 1795.

STORTON.[5]

10.—A mosaic of a scale pattern discovered in 1816.

11.—Another, at same place, in 1817.

LACEBY.[6]

12.—A mosaic found here of plain geometrical pattern in a villa, several chambers of which were traced, as well as a hypocaust.

[1] Wm. Fowler's *Twenty-six Plates of Mosaics*.
[2] *Ibid.*   [3] *Ibid.*   [4] *Ibid.*   [5] *Ibid.*   [6] *Ibid.*

YORKSHIRE.

ALDBOROUGH, *the ancient Isurium*

13.—Some forty yards within the rampart of Isurium a portion of mosaic of a long corridor, geometrical pattern.[1]

14.—Traces of two smaller corridors in close proximity, but a foot higher, and other fragments.[2]

15.—A few yards to the south-east, at the back of the "Globe" ale-house, a large paved floor 14½ feet square, geometrical pattern, colours red, slate, and brown.[3]

16.—Eastward from this last, a mosaic in corridor of a large building, opened out for about thirty feet, and now beneath a museum, from which it is seen through trap-doors, geometrical pattern.[4]

17.—Beautiful pavement discovered in 1832 near the "Aldborough Arms"; the apartment enclosed by its broken walls measuring 13 ft. by 11 ft. 6 in., its floor being completely inlaid with mosaic work. Square centre, on which is depicted a tree, and, beneath, some huge animal reposing, part of the head and fore-paws, with small portion of the tail, only remaining. The ground-work of the picture is white, and the colours of the two objects are red, yellow, brown, black, and lilac, the last a very unusual and peculiar colour. The various borders in squares are tastefully arranged.[5]

18.—Mosaic found in 1848. Square centre contains a star. The variation in the Greek fret in one of the borders is a peculiarity.[6]

19.—In 1846 were found remains of an extensive tesselated floor in building, supposed to have been a basilica, from the apsidal form of the western end. Mosaics chiefly

---

[1] H. E. Smith, *Reliq. Isurianæ*, 1852.
[2] *Ibid.*, Plate XII.   [3] *Ibid.*, Plate XIII.   [4] *Ibid.*, Plate XIV.
[5] *Ibid.*, Plate XVI.   [6] *Ibid.*, Plate XVII.

composed of borders, but in the apse are compartments
separated by black borders, in two of which are seen
remains of human figures ; one, the lower part of a draped
female figure, and beneath the elbow, worked in small
tesseræ of blue glass, are the Greek letters $^{EAH}_{EΩN}$; the other,
remains of a head uncertain of interpretation.[1]

20.—Early in last century several pieces of mosaic were
disinterred at Borough Hill, and are figured in *Drake's
York*, p. 24 ; now destroyed.[2]

Small brass coins of the Tetrici and of the Constantine
family, so common here that they are known as Aldborough
halfpennies. Many good coins of the earlier emperors are
preserved in the cabinet of Andrew Lawson, Esq.[3]

21.—"Mr. H. Ecroyd Smith has recently (1868) prepared, from a photograph, a coloured lithograph of a tesselated pavement which was not included in his work. It will
be welcomed by all who possess copies of the *Reliquiæ
Isurianæ*, or collections of tesselated pavements, as it is
singularly curious, and is represented with the most accurate
fidelity, every *tessera* being shown in its proper colour.
The subject is Romulus and Remus suckled by the wolf,
enclosed in a border of elongated lozenges or diamonds, each
containing others, in white, black, and red *tesseræ*. As a
work of art this design is extremely rude ; the wolf and
twins are beneath the traditional fig-tree, but are so rudely
drawn as almost to approach the grotesque ; this does not,
however, lessen its interest. It probably belongs to a very
late period of the days of Roman Aldborough."[4]

22.—John Walker of Malton, under date 9th June 1836,
announces in *Archæologia*, xxvii, p 404, the discovery at

[1] *Reliq. Isur.*, Plate xviii.
[2] *Ibid.*, Plate xix.
[3] *Ibid.*, Plate xxxiv.
[4] C. Roach Smith, *Collect. Antiq.*, vol vi, p. 259.

Hovingham, near Malton, of a Roman pavement, a bath, and coins.

23.—At Mosley Bank, only one mile from Malton, of a Roman pavement, urns, and coins.

He announced also the finding of a Roman altar and coins at Patrington, near the church.

143

CHAPTER X.

Mosaics in BERKSHIRE, ESSEX, and KENT—Reference to the situations of various Roman Villas in these Counties where Remains have been found—The Mosaics separately described and the Coins dug up near them—Authorities quoted.

THE mosaics in BERKSHIRE, ESSEX, and KENT are not so numerous or so interesting as might be expected. This may be attributed to the fact that these centres of Roman civilisation were more effectually purged of all traces of heathenism, which the pictured mosaics displayed, than were the remoter parts of the country. At Silchester, in Berkshire, a villa has been excavated, and described in *Archæologia*, xlvi, p. 329, which is most interesting, both from its magnitude and from the alterations which have been successively made in it at different epochs; which villa, in the language of the author in the volume above referred to, " rose above the earth in the early days of Calleva in the time of the first Claudius, stretching eastward in the reigns of Antoninus Pius and Commodus, its third alteration contemporary with Gallienus, Victorinus, and Claudius Gothicus; whilst its fourth period, the one nearest the surface, yielded coins of Diocletian, Maximinianus, Carausius, Constantine, Theodosius, and Honorius ; and now, fourteen hundred years after its burial, it silently records its consecutive occupation by the Roman, from the earliest days of the Christian era to the last days of his waning power in 410. Taking into consideration the position it occupied in relation to the *Forum* and the *Basilica*, its

great size, the growing importance attached to it throughout three consecutive centuries. and the attention given to
its alterations and additions, we may assume it was not
unlikely to have been an official residence, and, probably,
was the actual home of one of the Duumviri of Silchester.
This is the only building in which any hoard of coins was
discovered. In the room to the west of the *triclinium* a
number of bronze coins were found on the floor about
2 ft. 6 in. distant from the wall ; they appear to have been
thrust into a hole in the wall of the house, probably in a
leathern pouch. In the falling of the wall they came down
with the *débris* of clay and flint, and were found under
roof-tiles and plaster, lying in a little heap on the white
tesseræ, which were stained beneath them a deep bronze
colour. The peculiarities of these *folles* were that the
greater part of them were coins of former emperors, re-
struck by Carausius. This, taken in connection with the
finding of a somewhat rare coin struck at Trèves in commemoration of peace between the three emperors, Diocletian, Maximinianus, and Carausius, and some types of
coins of his reign not often found, has led to a supposition
that this emperor at one time made his headquarters at
Silchester. These coins, doing duty to the memory of past
dominion, and the tardily acknowledged power of the successful usurper, are of various dates. In some, the head of
Carausius is hardly more apparent than that of Postumus,
Gallienus, Maximinianus ; in others, the legend belongs to
Carausius ; whilst the head of Postumus still asserts its
primary origin. In many, irrespective of the reverse having
at an earlier date carried a legend of different sentiments,
PAX is stamped upon the coin. Out of the forty-two coins
found in this group, thirty-one bear the impress of Carausius. Amongst others, one found on the north side of this
house appears to have been struck by Carausius, and pur-

posely circulated by him, bearing the head of Maximinianus
to publish to his subjects the establishment of peace between
the three emperors. The coin is in the most perfect condition possible, and can hardly have been in circulation at
all; it bears in the exergue MLXX. Reverse, Peace standing to left with olive-branch in left hand, and sceptre.
Transverse, PAX AVGGG. Carausius and his successor Allectus appear to have used the London Mint, which was
probably established about that date, with little or no
intermission.

"A coin of Carausius, helmeted, has been found in the
adjacent house; it is an excellent specimen; and there is
also a very beautiful coin with its reverse exactly similar
to the 'Adventus' of Aurelian, a soldier on horseback, and
below the horse's foreleg a small bird; whilst a coin, not
apparently described in any published list, has on its reverse
a capricorn to left with a trifid tail. A great number of
the ordinary types of the coins of Carausius have been
found and chronicled in the journal of the excavations.
The tiles found were throughout of remarkable size and
thickness; one of these bears upon it a record of daily life.
It has part of an inscription on its surface,—not, however,
a name stamped into it, but a word written with great
freedom and clearness with some sharp-pointed tool whilst
the clay was moist. Some Roman lover was thinking of
the maid he worshipped whilst preparing his tiles for the
kiln, and, with a lover's ardour, he scribbled on one of
them some sentence about the maiden, more indelible than
the passion it expressed, of which the last word '*puellam*'
alone is left to record to a distant age the Roman's love."

Mr. Roach Smith has described a pavement at Basildon,
near Pangbourne, discovered in excavating for the Great
Western Railway in 1839: "It lay about twelve or fourteen inches below the surface of the ground, and this, like

l·

all the Roman pavements hitherto (1839) laid open by the
cutting of railways, has been destroyed. A few only have
been drawn and published." Mr. Smith has given a
coloured photograph of this in his *Collectanea Antiqua*,
vol. i.

In Essex it is very remarkable that the remains are
so few. or at least those which have been discovered;
but Colchester was especially associated with Constantine
the Great and Helena. The early converts to Christianity,
in their zeal to extend Christian influence, would, probably, as far as they were able, mutilate or destroy
objects of mythological reference without waiting for the
edict of Theodosius by which they would be compelled to
do so.

The same reasoning will apply to Kent and Middlesex.
In the former county two fine pieces of mosaic work have
recently been discovered at Wingham, near the Roman
road connecting Richborough with Canterbury; but, at
present, Mr. G. Dowker, who has superintended the excavations, has only met with buildings connected with the
bath, and these not of a large size; and it is impossible to
say what may prove to be the extent of the villa, as
neither the entrance nor the atrium or crypto-porticus have
been discovered. In the words of Mr. Dowker, "Traces
of walls some yards to the south are indicated by the trial
probe of iron, and foundations of walls are discernible in
the arable field some hundred yards or more south-east of
the present excavation. The bath with tesselated sides,
and the two tesselated-floored rooms adjoining, bespeak a
villa of the better sort. The situation is that usually
selected by the Romans: a spot sheltered from the east
and north winds, and open to the south-west. A beautiful
spring of water, that of Wingham Wells, runs close by,
and turns a water-mill beyond. At Ickham, the adjoining

parish, and almost within sight of this spot, another Roman villa exists. It is hoped that sufficient funds will be found to make a thorough exploration of this villa."

Mr. Geo. Payne, junr., of Sittingbourne, in describing the discovery of a Roman leaden coffin in May 1878, at Chatham,[1] refers to the walls of two Roman villas in the neighbourhood, and he says, "It would seem that each had its private burying-ground." It was hoped that that indefatigable antiquary might be able fully to explore their extent, and, perhaps, come upon some rooms paved with mosaic work. He has since described an interesting discovery of a Roman villa and pavements near Lower Halstow, at Boxted, where, having found the ground thickly strewn with broken tiles and mortar rubbish, he "cautioned the brickmakers to exercise care in case of their coming upon walls or pavements". The caution was given none too soon, for within a few days (9th February 1882) the wall of a room was exposed, and a small portion of a tesselated floor remained *in situ*, paved with sandstone cubes. The *tesserœ* were fixed by means of a white cement, and firmly set in a three-quarter inch bedding of concrete made of lime, sand, and pounded tile; the whole being laid upon a base levelled with fine gravel. The original size of the apartment could not be ascertained, as it had been torn up by the plough. Two or three gallons of sandstone and hard chalk *tesserœ* were found upon the spot, together with fragments of pottery, a spindle-whorl of bone, and a middle brass coin of Vespasian. About thirty yards to the south-west a well was met with filled up with Roman materials. Some of the *débris* were cleared out, among which were found a bronze finger-ring and a hairpin. Within a hundred yards of the well coins of Domitian, Antoninus Pius, M. Aurelius, and Lucilla were exhumed. In September

[1] *Archæologia Cantiana*, xiii, p. 168.

1882 the ground was opened, and a wall discovered at a depth of fourteen inches.

BERKSHIRE.

SILCHESTER.[1]

A villa was excavated not quite 120 yards from the quoin of the Forum at its north-west corner, and in this same space stood also a temple, certainly an altar and a precinct, to Hercules of the Segontiaci.

1.—Two figured mosaics were found, one of which, 16 feet square, is figured in *Archæologia*, xlvi. The ground-work of this is of grey and white *tesseræ*. In the centre is a circle formed by an elegant braided guilloche. This surrounds a cantharus, highly ornamented in stripes and arches of coloured *tessellæ*. The space outside the circle up to the square is ornamented as follows, in black and grey lines : at each corner of the square is a small square enclosing a guilloche knot; in the centre of the north and south of the outer squares is an oblong panel containing a guilloche braid; and on east and west sides are oblong figures, each containing a guilloche twist. The interstices between these various panels and the inner circle are filled with geometrical figures in double lines of *tessellæ*, forming triangles, and parallelograms. In two of the triangular compartments is the axe-head figure. This mosaic is now preserved at Strathfieldsaye.

BASILDON, *two miles to the north of Pangbourne on the Thames, in a field called Church Field.*

2.—" A square pavement, with three borders of zigzag plain white and guilloche patterns, including an octagon which comprises two intersecting squares with the guilloche

[1] *Archæologia*, xlvi, p. 329.

border, the octagonal compartments being filled alternately with diamonds and Gordian knots. The four corners formed by the octagon with the square are filled with figures of the lotus. The *tesseræ* are white, red, blue, and grey, arranged with admirable skill to produce a pleasing effect.

3.—"Another pavement adjoining was a parallelogram, formed by the addition of three rows of *tesseræ* to two sides of a square which comprised five others, gradually decreasing in diameter towards the centre ; the line of demarcation between each being made by a streak of deeper red. The monotonous effect of the red colour was relieved by the introduction of twenty-four *tesseræ* of blue brick, placed at equal distances round the outer square ; twenty arranged in like manner round the next, and decreasing similarly towards the centre. The design was chaste, simple, and unlike any that I am acquainted with."[1]

UFFINGTON WOOLSTON, *in the Vale of the White Horse.*

4.—This pavement is to be deposited at the Ashmolean Museum, Oxford. No description yet published. Mr. Arthur J. Evans, Keeper of the Ashmolean Museum, who saw it *in situ,* says, " It is evidently a part of a much larger pavement which has been destroyed, and is a fair specimen of mosaic work. It is divided by a coil pattern into various compartments, and contains the usual conventional rose ornament, but no figures. Mr. James Parker made an accurate drawing of it."

5.—A second pavement in the same villa is referred to in *Illustrated London News* for July 5, 1884. And further excavations are being proceeded with.

[1] C. Roach Smith, *Collect. Antiq.,* vol. i, p. 65.

ESSEX.

STANWAY PARISH, *Gosbeck Farm.*

6.—An important building, with hypocaust; *tesserœ* scattered about, of various colours. Thirty coins found; among them Titus of 2nd brass; Helena, 3rd brass; Carausius, in fine preservation—reverse, PAX AVGGG.[1]

COLCHESTER.

7.—Across the yard of the "Red Lion", in a house dating from about Henry VII, about eighteen inches of a pavement was uncovered. White and black *tesserœ* of half-inch cubes.[2]

8.—In Angel Lane, just below the Moot Hall, was found a rude and coarse pavement of brick *tesserœ*. No design. A quantity of wheat was found under the pavement.[3]

KENT.

THE MOUNT, *near the Medway.*

9.—Extensive walls and rude pavement found, but effect as rich as that of a Turkey carpet. Two coins, one of Gordianus III, much corroded; the other a mere lump of oxide.[4]

SOUTHWARK.[5]

10.—A pavement was discovered by Gwilt to the south of St. Saviour's Church, in the churchyard. It is now laid down within the building.

" In the operations for forming the Southwark approach of the new bridge, was found in the middle of the Borough

[1] *Brit. Arch. Assoc.*, vol. ii, p. 45.   [2] *Ibid.*, vol. v, p. 87.
[3] *Archæologia*, ii, p. 286.   [4] *Brit. Arch. Assoc.*, vol. ii, p. 87.
[5] C. Roach Smith, in *Archæologia*, xxix.

High Street a Roman pavement of coarse *tesseræ*, a plain proof that that could not have been the line of road to the Roman *trajectus* over the Thames. While, in making some alterations last month (May 1831) in the pavement of the choir of St. Saviour's Church, stone foundations were discovered crossing the church from north-east to south-west; and there is known to be a narrow line of tesselated pavement in the churchyard, perhaps the floor of the crypto-porticus of a Roman house, running in the same direction. Let a line be drawn from Kent Street, a portion of the old Roman way from Dover to London, across the Borough Market, and it will be seen that the buildings in the Roman suburb in Southwark, in conformity with the road, must have taken a north-westerly direction,—nay, the very point of the Roman *trajectus* may by this method be nearly ascertained."[1]

WINGHAM, *half-way between Richborough and Canterbury, in a field called the Vineyard.*

Hasted mentions traces of Roman stones, in 1710, behind Wingham Court; and Mr. Sheppard and Mr. Akerman had seen Roman tiles and coins in the same field called the Vineyard.

11.—A discovery was made by Mr. G. Dowker on 22 July 1881 of Roman buildings, of which a plan is given with his account. He first came upon "a bath with foundation of concrete, the walls covered with a tesselated mosaic, the upper part white, the lower half of a slate colour. The bottom had likewise had a tesselated floor of similar material, but had been broken up, and a small portion next the sides alone remained. The wall of this bath was of Roman tile, and eighteen inches thick. The slate-coloured *tesseræ* of the lower portion of the walls extended

---

[1] Alfred Jno. Kempe, in *Archæologia*, xxiv, p. 198.

fifteen inches from the bottom. They are cubes of some half-inch. This bath is numbered 1 on the plan, and steps from it lead up to a room, No. 2, due north of it. On this northern side of the bath-room, east and west of the steps, was a projection 18 inches wide, 17 inches deep, and 9 inches high ; the inner surface being tesselated with a continuation of the *tesseræ* of the east side of the bath, and rounded off at each corner.

12.—" Room No. 2, 9 ft. 9 in. east to west ; 10 ft. 10 in. north to south, with a floor 13 in. higher than the bottom of No. 1, and tesselated with a pattern of alternate large diamonds and small squares, with a banded border in dark grey and white *tesseræ*. The south and west walls had each a projecting cornice of red concrete at base next the floor, and the sides of the wall were covered with the same ; it had a remarkably smooth surface, as if to receive colour. A recess in the south wall had white *tesseræ* on it. Towards the north-west corner of this apartment was a doorway through the wall, paved with white *tesseræ* leading into a room to the west, No. 4, which was a hypocaust, with all its arrangements. The tesselated floor of room No. 2 was tolerably perfect, excepting towards the south-east, where a portion had been destroyed.

13.—" Room No. 3 is again to the north of No. 2, and has a tesselated floor of a different pattern, consisting of a central portion of fret labyrinth, with three bands of alternate black and white, forming a margin. The south-east and north-west corners are broken up. This room is 11 ft. 4 in. by 11 ft. 11 in. The entrance to it was probably from the north-east of room No. 2, where the wall is broken. The level of this room is 15 in. higher than that of No. 2.

" Excavations outside the walls showed no appearance of there having existed any rooms either north, east, or west of this. It appeared as if the tesselated floor of room No. 2 had been continued into the hypocaust No. 4. Most of the suspended floor had fallen in, and was found in the *débris* at the bottom."[1]

Roman coins found in the Wingham Bath were as follows :—

1.—ANTONINUS PIUS, large brass, with the common reverse of a standing female. This coin was perforated for suspension as an ornament.

2.—CONSTANTINE THE GREAT, the *reverse* is of the altar type, BEATA TRANQVILLITAS. The mint mark STR shows that it was struck at Trèves.

3.—*Obv.* IMP. CONSTANTINUS MAX. AUG. Head and bust in armour. *Rev.* VICTORIÆ LÆTÆ N. PRINCIPIS, two-winged figures hold a shield ; upon a cippus is VOT. PR.

4.—VICTORINUS.

5.—TETRICUS.

6, 7, 8, of the CONSTANTINE family.

9.—*Obv.* MAGNENT(ius) NOB. C. E. *Rev.* VICTORIÆ D.D. NN. AVG ET CÆS. Two winged genii hold a wreath, within which is VOT. V. M.X.

CANTERBURY, *in cellar of house next the "King's Head".*

14.—Pavement discovered on 20 June 1758, at three feet under the surface of the soil. A drawing was taken of this relic, which was once in the possession of a Mr. Edward Jacob, of Faversham.[2]

The above drawing is reproduced by Mr. C. Roach Smith in *Archæologia Cantiana*, xv, p. 127.

[1] G. Dowker, F.G.S., in *Archæologia Cantiana*, xiv, p. 134 ; and xv, p. 351.

[2] John Brent, "Canterbury in the Olden Time", *Gentleman's Magazine*, Jan. 1808.

BURGATE STREET.

15.—Specimens of these mosaics are preserved in the Canterbury Museum.

JEWRY LANE.[1]

16.—Pavement discovered in 1739.

Cellar in St. Margaret's Parish[2]; St. Martin's Parish, opposite the "Fountain" Inn.[3]

17, 18, 19.—The whole of these were portions only of dwelling-houses, probably of considerable extent. That in St. Martin's parish must have belonged to a villa beyond the city wall. They cannot be said to afford a fair example of the tesselated decorations of the houses in Roman Canterbury, for they occupied but a trifling portion of the extensive area of the city.

BOXTED, *Newington.*

The following villas should be named, though not productive of pavements hitherto. A suite of apartments occupied the centre of the plan, making a total length of 193 ft. 3 in., and width of 23 ft.; the whole being unpaved. The walls averaged 22 in. in thickness, and, where tested, gave a foundation of 3 ft. They were chiefly constructed of flint, sandstone, or rag and tufa roughly set in mortar. The outer or eastern wall being almost entirely built of tufa.[4]

HARTLIP, *near Place House.*

This neighbourhood is near the famous Upchurch Potteries, described in vol. vi of same work.

---

[1] Hasted's *Hist. of Kent.*   [2] Somner.
[3] C. R. Smith in *Archæologia Cantiana*, xv, p. 127.
[4] C. Roach Smith, *Collect. Antiq.*, ii.

ROMAN PAVEMENT

as now found at

CANTERBURY.

Tesseræ shewn Black are dark Blue
dotted are Yellow.
lined are of Red Brick.
plain are White.

CHAPTER XI.

LONDON.

OF the busy crowds who throng the broad-paved streets, or are carried, underground, by carriages of steam, beneath girders of iron, through modern London, how few ever give a thought to the fact that they are treading over and among the wrecks of a city of the dead, buried some eighteen feet below the present surface!—yet 1,500 years ago or more, amidst the "fumum et opes strepitumque" of this locality, an enterprising population lived and moved in Roman London, whose works are still to be seen and admired by those who care to seek them out. Who, too, it may be asked, in treading upon the new tesselated pavements which adorn the portals of the palatial buildings dedicated to banking, insurance, and other business, or which cover with their variegated patterns the inviting entrance-halls to a modern eating-house, will stay to consider that deep in the ground beneath his feet may lie the ancient proto-types which have suggested the geometrical designs, the fret and guilloche borders, which have been revived and adopted by modern art, unable to invent any patterns more beautiful or in colours more harmonious than the ancient? Yet such is the case, and let us endeavour to awaken more public interest in these relics of a far-off past.

Among the specimens of modern art, the pavements in

the Western Branch of the Bank of England, in Burlington
Street, the numerous tesselated floors in the Holborn
Restaurant, and those designed to adorn the premises of
Messrs. Burroughs, Wellcome, and Co., on Snow Hill, are
by no means the least worthy of the nineteenth century,
and the last-named, designed by Mr. Wellcome, and
executed by Signor Capello, as having a pictured meaning
upon it, shall be figured by way of a comparison of the new
world with the old. The proprietors have kindly furnished
a drawing of the pavement to which reference has been
made. Mercury, upon this mosaic, is brought up again
after an interval of fifteen centuries or more, to personify
the astute and far-seeing merchant of commerce; and four
panels, representing the appropriation of the forces of
nature, through the ingenuity of man, to the four great
mainsprings of modern commerce, viz., the electric tele-
graph, the printing press, the railway engine, and the
steam ship, complete the picture.

If the Metropolis has not yielded up Roman pavements
of pictorial designs in such numbers as some of the western
counties, still many of the fragments found have been
excellent, and in some respects unrivalled; and their distribution over a large area, and the direction of the walls of
houses in which they were placed, have been of the utmost
value in determining the course of streets and buildings in
ancient London. Upon the extent of the Roman city at
different epochs much has been written, and without any
very definite conclusion. The configuration of the great
wall, supposing it to have been built upon Roman foundations throughout its whole circuit, affords certain data
which, as well as the position of the mosaic pavements, may
establish some facts with confidence, but the deductions
from them hazarded in the following pages must be taken
with some hesitation and reserve.

Sir Wm. Tite considered, from the diagonal position of the walls of a house he exhumed on the site of the old East India House, in Leadenhall Street, that the direction of a Roman street must have been towards Bishopsgate, between the house he discovered and that with mosaics in Cullum Street. Now to adopt this view, if a straight line be drawn from the corner of Camomile Street and Bishopsgate, where pavements were found, to between the before-named two sites, the road will cross the site of the church of St. Ethelburga, over St. Helen's Place, and Great St. Helen's, passing Crosby Square, which would lie to the west of it; then, passing eastward of the Roman buildings lately found at Leadenhall Market, and of important character, it would pass over the site of the mediæval chapel there, and crossing Lime Street Passage and the site of the church of St. Dionis, it would follow the course of Philpot Lane, Botolph Lane, and to Botolph Wharf. As to this locality on the Thames, Mr. John E. Price gives the following information.

" The situation of London Bridge has varied at different periods. It is tolerably clear that the most ancient bridge, of which we have any record, was further eastward than the present one, viz., towards Botolph Wharf at Billingsgate, which was doubtless the Roman harbour or landing-place. The immense quantities of piling discovered some thirty years since, at this spot, was evidence of this, as well as of the existence of historic testimony to the circumstances of the head of the first bridge being at St. Botolph's Wharf."[1]

At about a hundred yards further east than the supposed road referred to, and near the river, were the baths discovered in 1848, on the site of the Coal Exchange. Mr. Price,

---

[1] "*Roman Antiquities*, illustrated by remains recently discovered on the site of the National Safe Deposit Company's Premises, Mansion House." By Jno. E. Price, F.S.A., London, 1873, p. 18.

in the work before referred to, has traced the course of the
Walbrook from north to south, and this seems at one time to
have been the western boundary of the Roman City. It
sprang from the marshy country beyond Moorgate, and fell
into the Thames somewhere near Dowgate or the Water
Gate. Mr. Price gives some interesting particulars about
the finding of this southern part of the stream, one of the
Roman terminal marks (*arca finalis*), and coins not later
that Antoninus Pius. Here its course is circuitous and uncertain. Mr. Price says that " in the sewerage excavations,
made some years ago at Tower Royal, Little St. Thomas
Apostle, and Cloak Lane, the channel was observed to be
no less than 248 feet in width, filled with made earth and
mud placed in horizontal layers, and contained a quantity
of black timber, of small scantling. The form of the banks
could be distinctly traced, covered with rank grass and
weeds."

He then speaks of the London stone, which "tradition
has always asserted to be a limitary stone". He says, that
" in defining the line followed by the stream we shall
observe that the stone, prior to its removal in 1742, from
one side of the road-way to the other, was situate much
nearer to the embankment, though it is impossible at this
spot to define where would be the actual limit of dry land."
" The stone would thus be near the end of Cannon Street,
and adjoin the way across the stream which ran westward
through Watling Street, and really occupied such a situation as would be selected by the *agrimensor*." These facts
being established, and supposing the city bounded on the
north and east by the London wall, on the west by the
Walbrook, and on the south by the river Thames, a nearly
square camp is marked out, having the Prætorian gate,
which faced the enemy, in the wall at Bishopsgate, and the
via principalis bisecting it in a straight line down to

Botolph Wharf, where would be the Decuman gate, or gate in the rear, through which the commissariat operations were conducted, and communications were kept up. This camp would have measured about 3,000 feet from north to south, and about the same distance from the angle of the wall at Aldgate on the east to the brook on the west. A much smaller area northward than this has been given by many antiquaries to the first Roman settlement; but an important city and seat of government to which no less than eight out of the fifteen roads, laid down in the Itinerary of Antoninus, conducted, would require space for a large garrison and population. The perimeter of the walls of Calleva (Silchester), according to the latest survey, was 8,010 feet (*Archæologia*, xlvi, p. 345); and for the perimeter of a capital city like London 12,408 feet would certainly not be excessive, nor the extension, when raised to 16,280 feet (my measurements of Roman London are calculated on the Ordnance map of 5 feet to the statute mile, or 1 inch to 88 feet), falling very far short of the perimeter of Ancient Rome, which within the walls of Servius was estimated by Pliny at what would equal in English feet 30,690;[1] but the circuit in the time of Vespasian was more than doubled, that is to 13,200 Roman paces (*passus*) of five Roman feet each.

Before Christianity reared its first shrine, as is supposed, on Ludgate Hill, which sloped down to the Thames on the south, and to the then broad river of Fleet on the west, an old Roman wall seems to have come down in a straight line from the bastion forming the north-west corner of London Wall in the churchyard of St. Giles', Cripplegate, and to have formed a continuation southward of that wall which turned off, in later times, to the west at the back of the Castle and Falcon Hotel. A straight line would have crossed

[1] Burgess, *Topography and Antiquity of Rome*, vol. i, p. 458.

Paternoster Row at the eastern end, where remains of the wall have been seen, as well as in Queen Victoria Street. A continuation of this would bring it diagonally across the the site of the present choir of St Paul's, skirting the southern porch of the cathedral on the east ; and thence, passing to the west of St. Benet's Church, the wall would enter the premises of the Carron Iron Company to the Thames, where it was flanked by the Castle of Baynard, or an older one on the same site, known as the Palatine Tower, which defended the city on the west, as did the Tower of London on the east.

This suggestion of a wall here in Roman times is rendered probable by the fact of many sepulchral remains having been found outside of it, and notably the collection of urns and glass vessels dug up in Warwick Lane, on the premises of the Messrs. Tylor, and now in the British Museum. There would be ample space for a large necropolis between this wall and the Fleet river ; and it is probable that the road to and from London passed through it from Ludgate and up to the bridge which crossed the Fleet into Holborn. Such an arrangement would, in the course of time, suggest the opening of the Newgate on a spot nearly opposite the bridge, and the building of another wall still farther westward of the old one, by which the boundaries of the city might be further extended.

The addition to the camp by the extension westward to the first wall at Paternoster Row and Aldersgate Street would extend it in this direction about 1,750 feet beyond the Walbrook ; its dimensions would then be about 4,750 feet by 3,000 feet. This seems to suggest, if the usual construction of camps were followed, that the conditions as to attack and defence might have been altered. The *via principalis* would now run from Aldgate, where would be the Prætorian gate against the enemy, and the Decuman gate might be somewhere near the eastern end of St. Paul's, in a line with Ludgate Hill. The course would be by Leadenhall Street, and the line south of Cornhill and Cheapside, but parallel to them, as a portion of a road, was seen by Sir Christopher Wren below the foundations of Bow Church. Another road to the said Decuman gate might have led from the Thames at Dowgate, by the London Stone, up Budge Row, between the towers of St. Antholin and St. Mary Aldermary churches, and through Watling Street.

According to Stowe, "a water-gate of old time called *Eb-gate*, and now Old Swan, was a common stair on the Thames", and was probably a passage across the river at low tide. Ebb-gate Lane is a boundary between the wards of Dowgate and Bridge, and also between the parishes of St. Laurence Poultney and St. Martin Ongars ; and this Dwr-gate or Water-gate was in a quarter of the town known by the significant name of Cold Harbour. "Under this name it was a separate precinct or liberty, until it was incorporated with the City of London by a charter of James I. Coldharbour is mentioned in the reign of Edward II as a capital messuage. It was the site of a magnificent house built or occupied by Sir John Poultney, in the reign of Edward III, and afterwards conveyed by him as his whole tenement, called 'Cold Herberghe', to Bohun, Earl of Hereford. It was granted by Henry IV to his son the Prince of Wales, by the title of 'Quoddam hospitium sive plateam vocatam le Coldherberghe'; and again by Richard III to the College of Heralds as a messuage with appurtenances called Poultney's Inn or Cold Herbore."[1]

Another *porta sinistra* would have been required, to which a road probably led up Aldersgate Street, parallel with the wall and at no great distance from it. It has occurred to me as a fact worth remarking, that at the end

[1] *Archæologia*, xxxiii, p. 401.

Y

of the four most ancient approaches to Roman London
there is a church dedicated to Saint Botolph—that is, at
the site of the earliest bridge, at Aldgate, at Bishopsgate,
and at Aldersgate.

The southern or river frontage was probably guarded by
a wall, if not continuous, at least strong enough for defence,
and necessary because the banks were then less steep than
they have since become, and could be reached in parts by
fords at low water. Mr. C. Roach Smith, F.S.A., in his
numerous works on Roman London, has given evidence
that remains of such a wall have been found; and some
valuable facts connected with the wall of London are
given by him in a paper read before the London
and Middlesex Archæological Society, and printed in the
Builder, vol. xlviii, p. 231. Now, as to the history of
the wall, we have no actual account of it by the Roman
classical writers, and in the fifth century it fell into the
penumbra of the eclipse of history which prevailed, more or
less, for seven hundred years, and we must therefore fall
back upon the foundation stones of the wall itself to obtain
a clue to the first builders. As to the documentary evidence,
Fitz-Stephen, in the reign of Henry II, is said to be the
first writer who mentions the wall.

The city of London is conspicuous by its absence from
history during many centuries. The theory hitherto
adopted has been, that because Boadicea burned London
it could not have had walls in the times of Claudius
and Nero; and because the Franks made an easy entry
into it after the murder of Allectus, it must have been
an open town in his time; and because Theodosius, when
he restored tranquillity to Britain, left the camps and
forts in a good state of defence, therefore he probably
first fortified London with a stone wall, about A.D. 379.
It is further argued that, at the earlier periods, it was

rather in the interest of the Romans to leave London open for the encouragement of free trade, and procuring by this means abundant supplies for their armies ; while it is maintained that at the latter period it was necessary to make a strong fort of London against the continued attacks of the Saxon invaders and native chiefs. These arguments seem to me invalid ; and it may be replied that if under Claudius and Nero the vallum and ditch were the only fortification to the camp, yet, when the whole country was subdued under Vespasian, and the north and west pacified, it is very unlikely that the usual scientific rules would have been neglected for the permanent defence and occupation of so important a military position as that of London city, which at this time would have been thoroughly taken possession of and occupied by Roman official personages and others. Even at the earlier period, Tacitus says London was *maxime celebre* from the number of its merchants and its traffic; and because Suetonius Paulinus abandoned it to Boadicea, it does not follow that it was not walled and fortified, but the Roman general feared that there were not soldiers enough to man so extensive a place, though he had 10,000 regular troops with him at the time, but he judged their safety to be the first consideration after the recent fatal experience of Petilius. (Tacitus, *Annales*, xiv, 33.)

As this passage in Tacitus has often been quoted to prove that London in A.D. 61 was an undefended British town without walls, it may not be amiss for the reader to refer to the passage itself, in which there appears nothing to warrant such a theory, unless it be the use of the single word *oppidum* applied to it, which certainly ought not to be restricted to the sense of a British town without walls, as described by C. J. Cæsar, for it was used by Latin writers to denote their own garrisoned towns, occupied alike by citizens and soldiers. Livy has even applied the word *oppidum* to

Rome itself. The passage in Tacitus may be thus rendered
in English :—"Suetonius, surrounded by enemies, with
wonderful firmness ruled over London, a place not indeed
by the cognomen of a (Roman) *colonia* illustrious, but,
beyond measure, renowned for the multitude of its
merchants and for its commerce ; there, doubtful whether
he should select that as the seat of war, yet seeing the scar-
city of troops, and by sufficiently severe examples knowing
how the temerity of Petilius had been checked, he came to
the determination of preserving all by the sacrifice of one
town (*oppidi*). Nor is he turned, by the wailing and tears
of those imploring his help, from his determination to give
the signal for departure, and to receive those who would
accompany his party. If the weaker sex, or the debility
of old age, or the attractions of the spot, held some back,
these were killed by the enemy. There was a similar
slaughter at Verolamium, because the barbarians, passing
by the castles and military forts, made for what was richest
to the spoiler and what was incapable of defence, rejoicing
over the plunder, and caring for nothing else. In the
places which I have named it is estimated that about
70,000 citizens and allies fell. Nor was it a question of
making prisoners or selling into slavery, or other of the
practices of war, but of slaughter, of the gallows, of fire and
executions, as if they were eager to take revenge in advance
for punishment they had themselves to suffer in the future."

I must not conclude these opinions and suggestions
about Roman London and its extensions without referring
to two important discoveries made of late years ; first, those
on the site of Newgate, described by Mr. E. P. Loftus
Brock, F.S.A., in the *Journal of the British Archæological
Association*, vols. xxxi, p. 76, and xxxii, p. 385. These
excavations disclosed a part of the machinery for an extensive system of water-supply in Roman times, according to

the opinions set forth by myself in vol. xxxii of the said *Journal*, p. 388 ; and this leads me to quote a passage by Sir W. Tite as to the discovery of a large pond or lake existing in the time of the Romans in front of the Royal Exchange, which agrees very well with descriptions of such reservoirs supplied by artificial means for the use of cattle and for extinguishing fires, the devouring flames appearing to have been as frequently destructive in London as they were in Rome. The distinguished architect of the Royal Exchange, Sir W. Tite, writes as follows, in *Archæologia*, xxxvi, in Feb. 1854 :—

" When the works were commenced for the erection of the new Royal Exchange, as it was always anticipated that some important antiquarian discoveries might be made in excavating the foundations, every care was taken that they should be properly developed and preserved. About the beginning of April 1841, when the workmen began to break up the substructure of the western side of the merchants' area of the old edifice, it was found that the wall had been hastily erected on some small but interest-ing remains of a Roman building, which were evidently still standing *in situ* and resting on the native gravel. They consisted of a piece of wall, with a kind of pedestal built obliquely across the ground, inclining to the north-west, the pedestal being covered with stucco, and moulded and painted in distemper, with a sort of volute in yellow on a red ground. At this part of the excavations it was found that the small remains of Roman work ceased to afford support to the old walls ; and, therefore, that oaken piles had been driven down into some construction older, with sleepers laid above them. The whole of this more ancient work was subsequently found to have been erected over a very large pit or pond, which went down 13 feet lower through the gravel to the clay. The pit was

irregular in shape, but it measured above 50 feet from north
to south, and 34 from east to west, and it was filled with
hardened mud, in which were considerable quantities of
animal and vegetable remains. There were also found in it
numerous fragments of the common red Roman pottery
called Samian ware, pieces of glass vessels, broken terra-
cotta lamps, and the necks and other parts of Roman
amphoræ, mortaria, and other articles made of earth. In
this mass likewise occurred a number of imperial coins,
several bronze and iron styles, parts of wooden writing-
tablets, a bather's *strigil*, tools of artificers, and a large
quantity of remains of leather, such as *caliga* soles and
sandals. All these mutilated *reliques*, which are full of
interest and curiosity, and available for the illustration of
ancient manners, were evidently the discarded refuse of the
inhabitants of the vicinity ; and were broken, old, or worn
out before they were thrown into the forgotten receptacle
where they were found. That excavation was certainly not
closed before the third century, the time of the Emperor
Septimius Severus, as one of his coins was found in the pit
from 20 to 30 feet in depth. It might, however, have been
in circulation after his time ; and another small coin of
Gratianus was also preserved there, which can be positively
assigned to A.D. 374, and probably more accurately indicates
the closing of the pit."

The second discovery to which attention has been drawn
is that on the site of the ancient Leaden Hall, described
by Mr. E. P. Loftus Brock, F.S.A. in the *Journal of the
Brit. Arch. Assoc.*, vol. xxxvii, p. 90. This is particularly
interesting as exposing the Roman remains and the Leaden
Hall, a building famous in mediæval times, and on a likely
spot for the site of the ancient *prætorium* of the first camp
of London. He has described wall paintings on the stucco
found in great quantities, with numberless *tessellæ* of various

colours, but no pavement *in situ* which could be distinguished. The Roman tiles found here, from the letters stamped upon them, seem to suggest that here was the house of the Prefecture, or palace of the Prefect of Roman London, and it would have been on the highway, or *Via Principalis*, to which reference has been already made. On the 2nd March 1881, Mr. Brock described further discoveries at Leadenhall, showing the great extent of the Roman building, and the thickness of walling. He also exhibited fragments of fresco-paintings, with ornamental patterns of green foliage of a flowing style, on a dull red ground, of the plaster-work of the walls. The building appears to have had the form of a basilica in some respects, with eastern apse, western nave, and two chambers like transepts on the south side.

It seems unaccountable that no large bathing establishment of the Romans should up to this time have been discovered in London—for that in Thames Street and another in the Strand, have the dimensions only of private baths—when we consider that Septimius Severus and his two sons, Bassianus (*Caracalla*) and Geta, who resided in Britain, were known for their public works of this kind. Geta had the government of the south-western provinces, and a supposed equestrian statue of him (according to Wm. Musgrave, F.S.A., in his *Dissertation*, published at Exeter in 1714) was dug up at Bath, then the social capital of the western provinces. The coins of Geta, as Princeps Juventutis and others, on which he is represented as taking part on horseback, with other young men, in the "Game of Troy", show him to have been at the head of the rank and fashion of the time, and spending his time at Aquæ Solis. He became so popular as the young Cæsar, and afterwards Augustus, that his brother Bassianus caused him to be murdered soon after their father's death.

The Thermæ at Bath, recently uncovered, may have been, under the rule of Geta, a reflex of the magnificent works of his brother Caracalla, at Rome, though the baths of Sul-Minerva at Bath have been ascribed to an earlier period, that is, to so far back as the first century of our era, which would have been 100 years before Geta's time; yet he may have extended and decorated them, or at all events we may conclude that they were in full and daily occupation in his time.

A few words shall be quoted, first on the Thermæ of Caracalla at Rome, from the Rev. John Chetwode Eustace, and then on the recently discovered baths at Aquæ Solis (Bath), which may help to stimulate the researches for a similar establishment in London, where lately some very large and bold cornices and other portions of buildings have been discovered in Castle Street, Houndsditch, near the Roman wall; others of a similar character were also found, in 1852, against the lower part of the wall near the Postern-gate adjoining the Tower moat, and some of which are now to be seen in the British Museum [1]

" The length of the Thermæ of Caracalla was 1,840 feet; the breadth of the building 1,476. At each end were two temples, one to Apollo and another to Œsculapius, as the *"genii tutelares"* of a place sacred to the improvement of the mind and to the care of the body. The two other temples were dedicated to the two protecting divinities of the Antonine family, Hercules and Bacchus. In the principal building were, in the first place, a grand circular vestibule with four halls on each side for cold, tepid, warm, and steam baths; in the centre was an immense square for exercise when the weather was unfavourable to it in the open air; beyond it a great hall, where 1,600 marble seats were placed for the convenience of the bathers; at each

[1] *Journal of the Brit. Arch. Assoc.*, viii, p. 240.

end of this hall were libraries. This building terminated on both sides in a court surrounded with porticos, with an *odeum* for music, and in the middle a capacious basin for swimming. Round this edifice were walks, shaded by rows of trees, particularly the plane; and in its front extended a gymnasium for running and wrestling in fine weather. The whole was bounded by a vast portico opening into *exhedræ* or spacious halls, where poets declaimed and philosophers gave lectures."[1]

Dean Merivale remarks on the baths of the Romans that they were " presented to the populace without charge, for even the payment of the smallest copper coin which had been required under the republic was remitted under the empire; no tax whatever was put on the full enjoyment of their attractions. The private lodging of Caius or Titius might be a single gloomy chamber, propped against a temple or a noble mansion, in which he slept in contented celibacy; but while the sun was in the heavens he lounged in the halls of the Castle of Indolence; or if he wandered from them to the circus, the theatre, or the campus, he returned again from every place of occasional entertainment to take his ease at the baths."[2]

The Thermæ of Bath, even supposing they extend as far again underground as the parts of the building which have been thus far uncovered, would still be scarcely one-fifth of the size of those of Caracalla at Rome, yet do they give a grand idea of Roman civilisation and architectural skill in the provinces. In the centre of the town, where the four roads from the four gates met, stood the *forum*, extending over the area whereon the Abbey Church now stands, and it is probable that the whole southern face of this was occupied by the baths, which have proved by the

---

[1] *Classical Tour through Italy in* 1802, vol. i, pp. 385-6.
[2] *History of the Romans*, vol. vii, p. 35.

recent excavations to be much larger than was formerly supposed when, in 1755, one of the baths, quite at the eastern end of the large bath lately uncovered, was described by Dr. Lucas,[1] and was again written upon by Dr. Sutherland in 1763.[2] This bath extended from north to south, being 34 feet long by 15 feet wide, contained in a hall 43 feet long by 34 feet wide, originally arched and decorated by pilasters, similar to those recently discovered. At the north and south ends were semi-circular recesses similarly pilastered and arcaded, which are supposed by Mr. Davis to have been cold water baths, or so constructed that artificially heated or cold water might be turned on at will, to give the bather an opportunity of a change of temperature. A great part of the Roman work was removed at that time, and the Kingston Buildings and Baths were erected on the site.

The next important discovery was made upon the erection of the Pump Room, in the last ten years of the last century. Various portions of worked stones were then discovered, being parts of a temple, and a piece of sculpture of the tympanum of a pediment, the subject being "a large clypeus, or shield, supported by two flying figures of Victory; in the centre is a mask, with moustache and flowing locks, developing into snakes, with wings springing from behind the ears. The head, the personification of the celebrated hot spring itself; the abundant curls pertain to the flowing streams; the wings relate to the fleeting nature of the Bath waters." This was the interpretation of Mr. G. Scharf, in his paper upon it read before the Society of Antiquaries in 1855,[3] and of Rev. H. M. Scarth in *Journal of Brit. Arch. Assoc.*, xiii, p. 268.

---

[1] *An Essay on Waters*, Part III, p. 222.

[2] *Attempt to Revive Ancient Medical Doctrines*, 1763; and see *Gentleman's Magazine*, Aug. 18, 1755.

[3] *Archæologia*, xxxvi, p. 190; and Warner's *Guide through Bath*.

From these various fragments, which are preserved in the Museum of the Bath Royal Literary and Scientific Institution, Mr. James T. Irvine was enabled to make two restorations on paper of a temple, and of the front of the entrance hall to the baths, which have been engraved in the *Journal of the Brit. Arch. Assoc.*, vol. xxix, plates 13 and 14, with a full description of the fragments, and of their discovery, p. 379.

The first announcement of the discovery of the large bath was made to the British Archæological Association by Mr. Richard Mann, contractor for the Mayor and Corporation of Bath, on 2nd December 1879, and by the Rev. Preb. Scarth (author of *Aquæ-Solis*), on 7th January 1880. The excavations were then systematically proceeded with by Mr. Charles E. Davis, F.S.A., architect to the Corporation of Bath ; and at a depth of 20 feet from the surface the excavators came upon the steps of the great Roman bath on the northern side of it, and then drained off the old water into a Roman culvert which had been opened to the length of over 120 feet. Mr. Davis described the remains in an address to the Bristol and Gloucester Archæological Society, which has formed the substance of a "Guide to the Ruins", from which I will extract some interesting particulars.[1] He mentions having sunk a shaft in 1871 in Abbey Passage, and came down upon the north-west corner of what is now called the great Roman bath. In 1878 he opened and restored the Roman culvert, and came upon a very fine Roman arch formed with stone and a few tiles. In continuing these explorations the excavators came upon a work of surprising grandeur, the

---

[1] *Guide to the Roman Baths of Bath, with a Plan of the Present and Former Discoveries.* By Charles E. Davis, F.S.A., Hon. Local Secretary of Soc. Antiq., London ; and author of *Bathes of Bathes Ayde in the Reign of Charles II.* 8th edition.

Roman enclosure of the hot springs, built to unite the
various sources of the springs in one irregular octagon
50 feet in length from east to west, and 40 feet wide.
This octagon is beneath the King's Bath, and forms now, as
formerly, the great well of the springs. The octagon is
built of large masonry 3 ft. thick, and 6 ft. 6 in. to 7 ft.
high, exclusive of foundations, and was found cased on the
inside in great part with lead, 30 lbs. to the square foot,
which was also folded beneath a border of tiles and concrete that went round the well. Near these springs was
found a small tablet of lead, having on it an inscription to
bear testimony to the visit of a family party to bathe in
the waters. Among the names, two probably belonged to
the class of *libertini*, a class to which the courtly Horace in
his day was not ashamed of belonging, though he admits
that all had a peck at him as being the son of a freedman.

"Me rodunt omnes libertino patre natum."—*Sat. I*, vi, 46.

The frequent mention at this period of the *libertini* in history, or the slaves who obtained their manumission either
by the saving up of money, or by their special talent, or by
the liberality of their masters, confirms the fact of the
wealth and influence they had acquired; and could we but
read the history of the times we should probably find that
many of this class were owners of the fine villas with their
tesselated pavements of which we have been treating.

The great bath laid open was contained in a hall 111 ft.
4 in. long by 68 ft. 6 in. wide. It runs from east to west,
and in the north and south sides are three recesses or
exhedræ, the central one being rectangular, and the others
circular. In these recesses were seats; in the circular ones
were stone seats called *stibadia*; but in the rectangular
recess the seats appear to have been of wood, and the
clothing of the bathers appears to have been hung up there,

as in one of the pilasters is a mortice-hole for the rail, and in another the slob to admit the other end. The platform that surrounded the bath is 14 feet wide, within a few inches more or less, measuring in the top step as if the *scholæ* were perfect ; and six steps formed of very massive masonry led down to the bath, the bottom being coated with lead in sheets of about 10 ft. by 5 ft. square, laid on a layer of brick concrete placed on solid masonry, one foot in thickness. The lead probably covered the steps also.

On the length of this bath six piers on either side formed clustered pilasters. The hall consisted of three aisles. The centre one, being the width of the bath, was roofed in by a dome springing from a cornice, rising 48 ft. 2 in. from the floor of the bath, exceeding by 14 ft. the height of the Pump-room. The sides, or aisles, were arched also. The arches of the centre and aisles, except when the abutment was sufficient, where they were of stone or flat tiles, were formed of brick boxes, open at two sides, and wedge-shaped, 1 ft. long, $4\frac{3}{4}$ in. thick, and $7\frac{3}{4}$ in. at the wider end, set in usual Roman mortar, a mixture of broken brick and lime, roofed (as in the case of the larger arch) on the upper side with the roll and flat tile known to this day as the Italian tile, and over the smaller arches with hexagonal stone tiles. The bath was filled at its north-west angle with hot water by a rectangular lead pipe 1 ft. 9 in. wide by 7 in. deep, sunk in the lower floor of the *scholæ*, direct from the great octagon well, which was distant 38 feet ; 25 feet of this pipe have been removed.

In the centre of the northern *scholæ* was a pedestal of stone and some sculpture, and beneath this are indenta-tions in the steps, and a plinth, on which, perhaps, stood a bronze or stone sarcophagus, which received the water as it flowed from an aperture in the sculpture from which the pipe has been removed, but a considerable length of which

(25 feet) still remains some few feet distant. This pipe
did not convey mineral water, as was at first supposed (as
there is but little deposit from it), but cold water. The
pipe was carried on farther along the platform on the north,
branching off on the west and south to supply the semi-
circular baths already described as having been discovered
in 1755. The platform, or *scholæ*, was formed by a layer
of large freestone 9 to 10 in. thick, laid on the level of the
top step but one, on a bed of concrete. Very little of this
paving remains, and even where it does it is very much
worn and fractured. The approach to the great bath was
by two large doorways in the west; and there were, probably, three entrances at the other end from the eastern
wing discovered in 1755. The fragments found lead to the
belief that the buildings were of the purest Roman taste,
with considerable Greek feeling, and decorated with sculpture.

The portion of the bathing establishment which thus
far has been opened presents us with the several varieties
of baths used by the Romans; that is, the Great Bath, with
the boiling water coming up from the ground at the temperature of 116 deg. Fahrenheit; then the same water conveyed to the eastern bath, opened in 1755, which would
thus be of a cooler temperature; and the cold baths in the
same hall in the apsides at each end of it, as suggested by
Mr. Davis; then sweating baths, to judge by the hypocausts for warming them, and doubtless each had a *laconi-
cum*, or apsidal termination, for the regulation of the temperature. Though the portion discovered is, to a certain
extent, complete in itself, yet, from what Mr. Davis has
said, it may be inferred that a portion only, and perhaps
not more than half of the whole buildings, has yet been
uncovered, and beyond all this there would be gardens,
palæstra, and peristyles, so that the establishment would

have been no unworthy example of public baths in a Roman provincial town. Mr. Richard Mann considers that "collateral evidence of the early period at which the baths were built is afforded by the entire absence of any tesselated floors, except a small one of very primitive arrangement found in 1756. This evidence is still further strengthened when we take into consideration the fact that the first, or original floor, had sustained a very considerable amount of wear, so much so, that we find a second flooring of pennant laid upon it; and yet at the end of the long period which must have elapsed between the erection of the building and the laying of the second flooring, it would seem to have been anterior to the tesselated floor period. But in the buildings around, in Abbeygate Street, the sites of both Hospitals and the Blue Coat School, we meet with tesselated floors of somewhat ornate character, thus giving us a guide to the sequence of the erection of the respective buildings."[1]

Ἄριστον μὲν ὕδωρ (*water is best*), are words well selected as a motto for modern Bath; the continuation of the quotation might have been applied to ancient London—ὁ δὲ χρυσὸς αἰθομενον πῦρ[2] (*but gold is a blazing fire*), for the wealth of the city and its importance are shown by the mintage here of gold coin in Roman times, an example of which is shown in the plates hereafter described in Chap. xix.

---

[1] Richard Mann, from his letter to the *Bath Chronicle*, November 26, 1884.

[2] Pindari, *Olymp. I*, ver. 1-2.

CHAPTER XII.

MIDDLESEX—Mosaics in London, particularised and described—Coins found near them and authorities quoted.

LONDON.

HOLBORN.

IN 1681 was found "a piece of mosaic-work deep under ground in Holborn, near St. Andrew's Church, inlaid with black, white, and red stones in squares". This fragment was originally preserved in the museum of the Royal Society in Fleet Street.[1]

BUSH LANE.

2.—"Soon after the Great Fire", writes Harrison, "the workmen digging the foundation of houses in Scot's Yard, Bush Lane, Cannon Street, discovered a tesselated pavement with the remains of a large building or hall, the former supposed to have belonged to the Roman governor's palace, and the latter to have been the basilica or court of justice." This is, presumably, the same referred to by Stow, who says: "In Canning Street, nigh Bush Lane, was found pretty deep in the earth a large pavement of Roman mosaic work. Dr. Hooke gave a piece of it to the repository in Gresham College."[2]

[1] Stow's *Survey*, Strype's edition, 1721.
[2] J. E. Price, *Bucklersbury Pavement*, p. 17.

CAMOMILE STREET, *Bishopsgate*.

3.—In April 1707 divers Roman antiquities were found in digging by the (City) Wall in Bishopsgate Within. Mr. Joseph Miller, an apothecary living very near the place, while the labourers were digging for foundations and cellars for some new houses in Camomile Street, first discovered several of these antiquities, which he communicated to Dr. John Woodward, of Gresham College, who gave this narrative of them in a letter to Sir Christopher Wren, which he courteously let me peruse :—" About four feet underground was discovered a pavement, consisting of dried bricks, the most red, but some black and others yellow, each somewhat above an inch in thickness. The extent of this pavement in length was uncertain, it running from Bishop's Gate for 60 feet quite under the foundation of some houses, not yet pulled down. Its breadth was about ten feet, terminating on that side at the distance of three feet and a half from the wall."[1]

———

SHERBOURNE AND BIRCHIN LANES.

4.—" In the great discovery of Roman remains during the autumn and winter of 1785 and 1786, while digging a new sewer beneath Lombard Street and Birchin Lane, a pavement was found 12 feet below the surface near Sherbourne Lane, 20 feet broad from east to west, the length of which was not ascertained. It was composed of small irregular bricks, measuring two inches by one and a half, principally red, but some few were black and white, strongly cemented together with a yellowish mortar, and laid in a thick bed of coarse mortar and stones. Near it was a wall built with Roman bricks of the smaller size ; and further

———

[1] Stow's *Survey*, Strype's edition, 1721.

A A

on, opposite to the Post Office, was another wall of common Roman masonry, and two other pavements.

5.—" One of them was found nine feet below the surface, and was made of thin flat tiles, each $17\frac{4}{16}$ in. in length, $12\frac{1}{16}$ in. broad, and about $1\frac{1}{16}$ in. in thickness.

6.—" Beyond it, about a foot lower, was another pavement much decayed, chiefly composed of red bricks about an inch square, with a few black bricks and some white stones irregularly intermixed. This pavement, as well as most of the rest, was laid on three distinct beds of mortar ; the lowest was about three inches thick, very coarse, and mixed with large pebbles ; the second was of fine mortar, very hard and reddish in colour, from having been mixed with powdered brick, and about one inch in thickness ; and upon this the coloured bricks were embedded in a fine cement. Other fragments of walls and pavements were discovered in the course of the same excavations in Birchin Lane, and especially one angle of a fine tesselated border composed of black, green, and white squares, about a quarter of an inch in size. As this pavement appeared to pass under the adjacent footway and houses, the complete extent and character of it were not ascertained."[1]

7.—Mr. J. E. Price says that "other discoveries of a kindred character are recorded as being made in this locality by Charles Combe, M.D., and Mr. Jackson, of Clement's Lane,—among other things, many coins in gold, silver, and brass of the Higher Empire, associated with foundations of extensive buildings, pottery, charred wood, and other evidences of conflagrations."[2] Portions of borderings are now in the Guildhall Museum.

[1] *Archæologia*, xxxix, by W. Tite, F.R.S., F.S.A.; and *Ibid.*, viii, pp. 116-132.
[2] *Bucklersbury Pavement*, p. 18.

CRUTCHED FRIARS.

8.—In 1787 some remains of a tesselated pavement were found in Crutched Friars, now in the Museum of the Society of Antiquaries.[1]

WINCHESTER or POULETT HOUSE.

9.—In 1792 the excavations for a sewer from the church of St. Peter Le Poor, in Old Broad Street, to Threadneedle Street, brought to light a large circular pavement, behind the old Navy Pay Office, better known as Winchester or Poulett House. A quantity of burned corn or charcoal was found laid upon it, with vessels of earthenware and some coins.[2]

OLD INDIA HOUSE, in Leadenhall Street

10.—Perhaps the most beautiful, if not the most perfect, of the mosaic pavements found in London was that discovered in December 1803, at the depth of 9 feet 6 inches below the carriage way, as it then existed in Leadenhall Street, in constructing a sewer opposite to the easternmost columns of the portico of the late East India House.[3] It was a part only of this fine work which was then discovered, for the eastern side of it appeared to have been cut away at the time of making the sewer, and the remainder formed about two-thirds of the floor of an apartment of uncertain dimensions, but evidently more than twenty feet square. The centre compartment appeared to have been a square of about eleven feet; and though it was

[1] Allen's *Hist. of London*, vol. i, p. 29.
[2] C. R. Smith's *Roman London*.
[3] W. Tite, in *Archæologia*, vol. xxxix, p. 491. T. Fisher, *Description and Plate*, 1804 ; also *Gentleman's Magazine*, May 1807, vol. lxxvii, p. 415. C. R. Smith's *Roman London*, p. 57, Plate XII.

not quite perfect, it contained a series of circles, enclosing a figure of Bacchus reclining on the back of a panther, holding the thyrsus, and having an empty drinking-cup in his right hand. Round the brows of the figure is a wreath of vine-leaves, and his mantle falls down from his right shoulder and is gathered up over his leg and right thigh, showing the long sandal boot laced in front. This design was surrounded by three broad circles filled with elegant ornaments enclosed within two broad squares, forming rich borders ; and of the spandrils produced by these figures, two were occupied with representations of large Roman drinking-cups, and two with figures of leaves and flowers. The colours employed in this tesselation were a blue-grey, purple-green, black, yellow, red, and white ; and it is stated by Thomas Fisher, who made a very careful drawing of it and described it while it was in its original condition, that the *tesseræ* of it comprised about twenty separate tints. They were of different sizes, and for the most part of baked earth, but the purple and green employed in the drapery were of glass.

The central picture of this pavement, which was about four feet square, was taken up complete, and the remainder in separate pieces, in which state it was at first deposited in the library of the East India House. Some years after it was removed into the open air, and the *tesseræ* became loosened by the action of the atmosphere, which destroyed all the work excepting the centre. Professor H. H. Wilson caused this fragment to be carefully mounted on a slab of slate and replaced in the Museum of the India House. This is now preserved in the Romano-British Room at the British Museum.

It will be noticed that the spandrils between the circle and square of the centre are filled in with two *canthari* and two floral patterns issuing out of axe-heads. " The

ROMAN TESSELATED PAVEMENT (DESIGN IN ENGRAVING, SIZE, LARGE PICTURE 1897)

blue, purple, and green colours", says Mr. Roach Smith, "are formed of glass, the others of natural stones and coloured argillaceous earths"; and the treatment of the subject closely resembles that on the pavement at Thruxton, near Weyhill, in Hampshire.

BANK OF ENGLAND, *in Threadneedle Street.*

11.—"At the close of 1805 a beautiful pavement, though consisting only of a floriated cross and ornaments, was found within the area of the Bank, under the northwest angle of the building, about twenty feet to the west of the west gate opening into Lothbury, and at the depth of twelve feet below the street. The whole of the floor formed a square of eleven feet. This *relique* is in a very fine state of preservation at the British Museum. Its ornamental centre was about four feet square ; within the circle is a foliated cross, the limbs of which terminate in flowers and tendrils, surrounded by a square guilloche pattern with flowers in the angles. The white ground is studded with dark stones." Upon the same level, about the year 1835, a pavement was uncovered opposite Founder's Court, near to the church of St. Margaret, Lothbury.[1]

ST. CLEMENT'S CHURCH.[2]

12.—Adjoining St. Clement's Church, at about twelve feet beneath the present level, ran a tesselated pavement composed of pieces of red brick of about 1 in. or 1¼ in. long, and ¾ in. wide, corresponding with fragments lately discovered in Eastcheap, at about an equal depth, connected probably with some public building or dwelling-house of the

---

[1] W. Tite, in *Archæologia*, xxxix. C. R. Smith's *Roman London*, p. 57, Plate XI. John E. Price, *Bucklersbury*, p. 21.

[2] C. R. Smith, in *Archæologia*, xxvii, p. 141.

better class on or near the site of St. Clement's Church. A precisely similar pavement occurred in Lothbury, which may with like reason be supposed to branch off from a building that occupies the position of the Bank of England.

<hr>

CROSBY SQUARE.

13.—On 14th April 1836 Alfred Burgess exhibited a small portion of a Roman pavement, discovered by some labourers during the previous month, while digging for a drain in a house, No. 3, Crosby Square. The width of it did not exceed five feet; the depth from the surface was about thirteen feet from the foot-paving in the square. The pavement had been of a scroll pattern, with a border round the margin; the colours used appeared to be red, yellow, white, and black; the first two evidently of brick and the other two of stone. The site of Crosby Square was at one time attached to the priory of St. Helen's, and afterwards occupied by the mansion of Sir John Crosby, of which the only remains are the splendid hall and some vaults now attached to the adjoining houses. By the discovery of this pavement we are led to suppose that upon this very spot a building, perhaps a forum, was erected by the Romans during the time they were masters of this country, of which this beautiful specimen of their taste and workmanship formed the floor.[1]

<hr>

101, BISHOPSGATE STREET WITHIN.

14.—Pavement found in October 1839, beneath cellar of No. 101, Bishopsgate Within, fifty-three feet from street, and fifteen feet from Excise Yard, part of one compartment of a floor; black and white *tesseræ*, arranged in squares and diamonds.[2]

[1] C. R. Smith, in *Archæologia*, xxvii, p. 397.
[2] *Archæologia*, xxix, p. 155, by C. R. Smith, figured. p. 166.

HALL OF COMMERCE, *Threadneedle Street.*

15.—"In the spring of 1841 two fine examples were excavated from the foundations of the French Protestant Church in Threadneedle Street, removed for the erection of the Hall of Commerce. One had apparently belonged to a passage only ; it measured six feet by five feet, and comprised rows of red *tessellæ*, an inch square, which enclosed squares and lozenges, the latter arranged lengthways and transversely, the spandrils being the halves of lozenges similarly disposed. The squares were filled alternately with rosettes of eight and four leaves, frets, and wheels or whorls ; the lozenges were filled with a labyrinthine pattern. The *tessellæ* were white, black, and slate colour, a dull green formed from natural stones, and red and yellow artificial ; the green was apparently a native marble, much worn by time and weather."

16.—The building to which this belonged must have been an important one, and of some extent, for numerous evidences of other floorings were observed. Fragments composed of the large red and yellow *tessellæ* were met with ; and at about ten feet from the preceding discovery was seen "about two feet of another pavement similar, but in which the monotony of the red was relieved by an occasional insertion of white *tessellæ*. These were deposited, at the suggestion of Mr. Roach Smith, F.S.A., by the late Mr. Moxhay, proprietor of the premises where the discovery was made, in the British Museum.[1]

---

[1] Jno. E. Price, *Bucklersbury*, p. 21. C. R. Smith's *Roman London*, p. 55. *Gentleman's Magazine*, June 1841, p. 637. *Archæologia*, xxix, p. 400.

THREADNEEDLE STREET.

17.—Two months later, at about 6½ ft. from the former find, there occurred another pavement ; this was 13½ ft. long, but the full extent of the outer border was not ascertained. It was composed of variegated *tessellæ*, the red greatly predominating. This is also figured and described by Mr. Smith, and it is preserved in the National Collection. The design upon it represents a central flower or rosette of elaborate character. " It has eight leaves, from behind which the points of eight others are visible; each of the eight upper leaves has in its centre a trefoil, and these are connected by a band of two rows of red *tessellæ.*" Around it are rows of grey or bluish *tessellæ*, composed of Petworth marble, and a small white border of four rows, in another of white *tessellæ* half a foot wide, and, towards the centre, bounded by a kind of embattled fret in yellow and red.

In April 1844 portions of a mosaic pavement were discovered in Threadneedle Street, not far distant from Merchant Taylors' Hall, at a depth of about twelve feet from the surface.[1]

PATERNOSTER ROW.

18 —Mr. Smith records the discovery of a fine example in Paternoster Row. It was very extensive and superb ; its length was no less than forty feet, and it possessed a border composed of the guilloche ornament, enclosing rosettes. Towards the centre were compartments in which were depicted birds and beasts ; in one division was an object resembling a star fish.[2]

---

[1] Jno. E. Price, *Bucklersbury*, p. 22.   [2] *Ibid.*

CHEAPSIDE and ST. PAUL'S.

19.—A pavement was also found, at a depth of eighteen feet, at a site near the junction of St. Paul's Churchyard with Cheapside, and was connected with Roman walls; it was, unfortunately, destroyed soon after discovery. The design was a rosette pattern, in red, grey, white, yellow, and black *tessellæ*; a hypocaust was below it, with its rows of tile-pillars or columns, averaging from fifteen to twenty tiles to each column. Associated with the remains were coins of Constans, Constantine, Magnentius, Decentius, and Valens: indicating that, like the discovery in Paternoster Row, which was above an interment in a tile-tomb, it really belonged to the closing period of the Roman occupation.[1]

Proceeding up Cheapside, as far as Foster Lane, sewerage excavations revealed further discoveries of like character. In the lane itself a pavement was found, accompanied by quantities of glass and pottery.

At Wood Street, at the corner by St. Michael's Church, large quantities of white pavement were exhumed in 1843; this was at the north side of the building; and that it extended entirely below it was evident from the fact that it was seen again during excavations in Huggin Lane, which runs along the south side of the church. And again, in 1847, at about forty feet from the above site, similar remains were seen, with large blocks composed of *tessellæ* of a grey colour, in addition to the white. These are all indications that on the site of St. Michael's Church an important edifice existed during Roman times.[2]

20.—This was also the case at the site of St. Gabriel, which formerly stood in Fenchurch Street.[3] At the depth of twelve feet a tesselated floor was seen in 1833, and

---

[1] Jno. E. Price, *Bucklersbury*, p. 22.   [2] *Ibid.*
[3] *Gentleman's Magazine*, 1834, p. 157.

between Rood and Mincing Lanes a large and perfect red
brick floor was also found.

LOWER THAMES STREET.

21.—Baths or villa discovered in 1848, on the site now
occupied by the Coal Exchange, under which it is preserved, and where it can be seen. During the early part of
the year 1859 another portion adjoining was inspected by
Mr. T. Gunston, who has given a plan of the whole building,
and described the remains in the *Journal of the British
Archæological Association.* He mentions one room measuring
about 23 ft. square, surrounded by a wall 3 ft. in thickness,
constructed entirely of red and yellow bricks or tiles 18 in.
by 12 in. and 1½ in. thick, remaining in parts to the height
of 6 ft., and lined in the interior with stucco.[1]

The original floor was paved with inch-square *tesseræ*,
but the room appears at a subsequent period to have
been newly floored; for in parts above this floor was
a very thick layer of coarse concrete, upon which lay a
covering of very hard red cement three inches in thickness.
Within this apartment was found a quantity of window
glass, an iron key, several jet hair-pins, a large bone pin
for securing the dress, some bone needles, an earthen lamp
bearing a tragic mask and the maker's name, EVCARIS, and
a second brass coin of the Emperor Nero.

22.—North of this room was another, 19 ft. in length
by 12 ft. in width, with semicircular ends projecting
towards the east, the walls being two feet thick, and composed of all flat tiles; the floor, of plain red and yellow
tesseræ, was supported by the pillars of the hypocaust,
thirty-one in number, regularly disposed.

23.—Northward, but adjoining, were the remains of a

---

[1] *Brit. Arch. Assoc. Journal,* iv, 38-45; xxiv, p. 295.

third room, measuring 20 ft. by 12 ft. The walls existed only to the floor, which was coarsely tesselated. Within this apartment was found the capital of an oolitic stone column, fragments of stone cornice, besides brass coins of the Roman emperors Antoninus Pius and Marcus Aurelius. Further eastward, and indeed in nearly all parts of the excavation, traces of subordinate rooms and other specimens of architecture were met with ; but the outer wall was of extraordinary solidity, and entirely formed of Kentish ragstone. Scattered about were fragments of culinary and drinking vessels, roofing-tiles, and red coralline pottery, some highly embossed, and others bearing the impress ALBYCI ATILIANI and MARTI, besides a perfect patera and urn of Upchurch ware ; also remains of the boar, stag, sheep, and ox, and shells of the oyster, mussel, and edible snail. All these remains, except the portion under the Coal Exchange, have been covered up and built over.

EXCISE OFFICE, *between Broad Street and Bishopsgate Street.*

24.—An account is given by Sir William Tite of the discovery of a tesselated pavement under the vaults of the south-eastern area of the late Excise Office on 10th Feb. 1854. The modern foundations ceased at a "depth of twelve or thirteen feet from the level of Bishopsgate Street. In this ground first appeared traces of Roman remains, in very imperfect fragments, of pottery and glass, of doubtful origin, with a few coins, and fragments of Roman mortar and concrete. Nothing, however, was discovered, excepting a silver coin of Hadrian, until the morning of 10th Feb. 1854, when one of the workmen, in digging a hole deeper than the other excavations, for a scaffold pole, came upon a fragment of this tesselated pavement."[1]

[1] *Archæologia*, xxxvi, p. 203, by Wm. Tite, F.R.S., F.S.A.

After describing the careful manner in which it was cleared, Sir William Tite goes on to say : " The pavement itself was constructed in the following manner. The earth having been cleared away and levelled down to the natural clay and gravel, a bed of coarse concrete was laid, about six inches thick. The concrete was composed of river ballast and lime, with occasional pieces of broken and pounded brick, and on this coarse substratum a bed of very hard mortar or cement was laid, about an inch in thickness and perfectly level. I should suppose that this mortar was composed of about two parts of clean, sharp sand, one part of pounded bricks or tiles, and one part of lime ; the whole mass of which must have been well beaten together and consolidated. This formed the bed for the *tesseræ*, which were generally of a uniform thickness, of the usual dimensions of about half an inch square, and set in fine mortar. The pavement thus discovered constituted the floor of a room twenty-eight feet square. On the side there were some traces of wall plastering ; but though we searched with the greatest care, there was not any trace, *in situ*, nor near it, of any walls, flues, or Roman bricks. Every fragment had disappeared, and even this trace of wall plastering had nothing behind it but loamy earth.

" The only additional fact requiring to be noticed, con‐ nected with the construction of the pavement itself, is one which is of equal interest and rarity, namely, that in some places it had evidently been mended in Roman times, but by an inferior hand ; and the *tesseræ* introduced in those places were whiter, and in general colour did not coincide with the older work. The pattern, however, had been care‐ fully preserved and restored. I think it probable that we shall find further traces of pavements as we proceed north‐ wards ; for there is a tradition in the neighbourhood that in digging a well under a house in Bishopsgate Street in that direction, at about thirteen feet from the surface, some remains of a pavement were found."

The account is continued at a later date—that is, March 1855—when he says : " This expectation has been partly realised, because northwards of this pavement we have found the floor of a room paved with dark red *tesseræ*. The pavement was about twelve feet square ; the *tesseræ*, uniform in size, being about seventeen inches square. I still expect to find further remains to the north-east, but the old buildings cannot at present be removed." ·

He then makes the following observations. " A work so finished as this pavement evidently points out a period of security and comparative wealth in the inhabitants ; and such a period may doubtless be found in the reign of Hadrian, to which the silver coin found on this floor also belongs. Hadrian began to reign in A.D. 117, and died in A.D. 138. This interval of tranquillity appears also to have continued for many years afterwards, certainly until the middle of the reign of Marcus Aurelius, about A.D. 170, and it was doubtless during this period that the mansion, or merchant's house, was erected which stood on the site now under consideration. The nature of the site is very peculiar. In passing from Bishopsgate Street to Broad Street, through the late Excise Office, there was a descent of twenty steps, giving a difference of level of about ten feet between the two streets. This difference of level was no doubt always greatest at this particular point ; but the same general features may still be traced in the continuing high level of Bishopsgate and the comparative low level of Old and New Broad Streets, Throgmorton Street, and Lothbury, down to the line of the Wall Brook, which at that point was thirty feet below the present level of the ground.[1]

[1] This is shown in a section of the Wall Brook in my possession, made by Mr. Richard Kelsey, the late Surveyor of Sewers of the City of London.

"This Roman house, therefore, in my opinion, stood on a
gravelly bank; and the pavement was itself level with the
ground at the back. In the front of the house the ground
was probably considerably higher, and was the Roman
causeway that passed through the City Wall, about 330
yards to the north, and then through the Roman cemetery,
which we know to have existed at Spitalfields. The road
was then continued in a direct line to the fords over the
Lea between Stratford and Ilford, and about the spot which
is regarded as the Roman station *Durolitum*, five miles
from London. This road, as in the Appian Way at Rome
and the street of the Tombs at Pompeii, was probably lined
with the tombs of the Roman and British residents of
London.

"It now only remains for me to add that the design
or pattern of this pavement is elegant, and differs in detail
from others; but in principle and in material it resembles
most of the Romano-British pavements. The nearest resemblance to it which has occurred to me is an example
published by Hearne, found at Stunsfield, two miles from
Woodstock,[1] in which there is a group in the centre somewhat resembling the figures in the middle compartment
of that at the Excise Office. It is represented in a
very careful and elaborate engraving executed in 1712
by Michael Burghers; but I am inclined to think that
the descriptive text by Hearne mistakes the central figure
in supposing it to be Apollo, since it should be certainly
regarded rather as the young Bacchus (the Egyptian or
beardless Bacchus), crowned with vine leaves, and holding
horizontally in his hand an empty *cyathus*, and in his
left the *thyrsus* upright. The animal in the background
is there indisputably a tiger, as Hearne says 'some
have conjectured'; though he himself was inclined to think

[1] Leland's *Itin.*, vol. viii.

it was intended for a griffin without wings. But without any regard to the possibility of this figure being a griffin destitute of wings, not only the human effigy represented with the animal, and all its accessories, seem to prove it to be Bacchus (Dionysus) and his tiger, but the very pavement now found at the Excise Office, with the effigy of Ariadne and her panther, seems to corroborate the truth of the interpretation. As the figure of Ariadne in the Excise Office pavement was upright when seen from the north-east, the couches of the *triclinium* and the table enclosed by them probably looked towards the west, and the garden of the edifice would thus perhaps be situated behind towards Bishopsgate, or nearer to the extremity of Roman London. The pavement was taken up with great care by Mr. Minton, under the direction of Owen Jones, and has been removed to the Crystal Palace at Sydenham, where he intends to restore it completely and place it in the centre of the nave. By the judicious means taken by Mr. Clifton, the resident architect, and Mr. Owen Jones, I believe that not a single fragment of it has been lost."

<hr>

FENCHURCH STREET.[1]

25.—"The next discovery seems to be that made in 1859, opposite Cullum Street in Fenchurch Street, at a depth of 11 ft. 6 in. The dimensions are about three feet each way. Upon a white ground appears a bird, possibly a peacock, though, owing to portions being lost, the tail feathers are not very clearly defined. The *tessellæ* composing the breast and neck of the bird are of a bright azure glass, with a slight admixture of green of the same material; the wing is of red, white, and yellow *tessellæ*. On the same ground is a vase in red, white, and yellow, with a centre of

[1] Jno. E. Price, *Bucklersbury*, p. 24.

green glass.   In the perfect state of the pavement another
peacock probably occupied the opposite side of the vase.
Around the subject is a guilloche border of white, yellow,
and red ; the white being heightened in effect by numerous
bands of black coarse *tessellæ*.   It has been beautifully
engraved in the Catalogue of the Works of Art and Antiquities, exhibited at Ironmongers' Hall."

OLD EAST INDIA HOUSE.[1]

26.—" In 1863, a little beyond the portico, westward
and opposite the spot whereon the former pavement was
found, important ancient remains were discovered *in situ*.
An apartment containing a mosaic floor is shown upon a
plan.   The pavement is of red *tesseræ*, neatly laid in the
usual bed of Roman cement ; and the walls are of Kentish
rubble and chalk, with bonding courses of Roman bricks
inserted in two thicknesses, one at the bottom in the
earth and another two feet higher up.   All the bricks are
well made, and the mortar and rubble-work are so hard
that they cannot be separated from the general mass.   The
walls of the apartment had been plastered and coloured in
fresco in lines.   On the western side, which no doubt contained the doorway, the wall has been destroyed ; but a
few traces have been found there of a passage five feet
wide, paved and constructed as the other remains.

" In my former paper, on the pavement discovered at
the Excise Office, I stated what I believed to have been the
real line of the Roman way crossing the city from the south,
and its union with the great road leading to Chelmsford
and Colchester on the north-east, and I am inclined to
think that this ancient house stood on the side of that
original road-way.   I consider also that the *tesselated pave-*

---

[1] Wm. Tite, in *Archæologia*, vol. xxxix.

ment found at this place in 1803 once formed the floor of the *atrium* of that dwelling, and that the apartment now discovered was one of the small domestic offices on the side of the centre court, approached by the passage indicated on the plan. It might, no doubt, have been a lower story ; but the difference between the depth of 9 ft. and 19 ft. 6 in. does not, I think, present any difficulty to this conjecture ; the latter is the general depth of the rubbish in Rome, and my own experience in London has convinced me that the average accumulation above the native soil must be estimated at least at eighteen feet."

27.—" In 1864 a further discovery was made in front of the portico of the India House and under the pavement of the street. About 9 ft. 6 in. below the ground one of the division walls of a cellar had been built across a tesselated pavement of a somewhat elegant pattern, and forming no doubt the floor of a small room. The floor had been a good deal crushed, but with care the pavement was taken up tolerably complete, and is now in the British Museum. This, no doubt, was a continuation of the great pavement found in the year 1803, and described and engraved by Mr. Fisher. The depth of 9 ft. 6 in. coincides with that given by Mr. Fisher, and therefore this house must have had two floors, or at all events floors at different levels, one ten feet below the other."[1]

St. Mildred's Court, *Poultry.*

28.—" In 1867, in the foundation of the New Union Bank of London, at the corner of St. Mildred's Court, a pavement was discovered, of which a notice appeared in Part IX of the *Transactions* of the London and Middlesex Archæological Society. At that time, from the fragmentary

[1] Wm. Tite, in *Archæologia*, xxxix.

condition of the pavement, the nature of the design could
not be ascertained with accuracy; but, as far as has been
possible, the pieces found, though but a small portion of
the whole, have been appropriated to their several positions;
and from a drawing of them, communicated by Mr. G. Pluck-
nett, F.S.A., to Mr. Jno. E. Price, it is shown to have been
a mosaic of good execution, both in design and treatment,
and as a work of art very similar to that lately found on the
opposite side of the course of the Walbrook. It comprised
a square enclosing a circle; the central ornament was a
vase of the same character and type as that so often seen;
the *tessellæ* composing it were formed of brown, white, red,
and black materials, with the addition of bright green glass;
around the vase there appeared portions of a tree with
foliage; also an object resembling an archway, with embattled figures and other objects, the meaning and inten-
tion of which it is difficult to describe without an illustration. Around the whole were two simple bands of black
tessellæ, separating the circle from an elaborate scroll of
foliage and flowers analogous in character to that on one of
the pavements at Bignor. At each corner was a rose or
other flower, showing eight petals in stones of white, black,
and varied colours. From the centre of each flower there
spring in opposite directions two branches, which unite
with a leaf, possibly that of the lotus, and of analogous
form to that observed within the scroll. The entire design
is bordered by the guilloche, elegantly worked in seven
intertwining bands of black, red, brown, and white *tessellæ*.
The pavement was laid upon the well-known concrete, and
apparently on the soil, there being no evidence of any
hypocaust or substructure. Its depth was about eighteen
feet from the surface, corresponding in this respect with
other remains from this locality."[1]

[1] Jno. E. Price, *Bucklersbury.*

BUCKLERSBURY.

29.—At no great distance from the last-described
pavement, though on the opposite bank of the Walbrook, was found a pavement in Bucklersbury, "situated
19 ft. from the level of the roadway, at a very short
distance from the course of the stream and parallel there-
with. In form it is a parallelogram, 13 ft. wide and 12 ft.
6 in. long, exclusive of a semicircular portion at its northern
end of 7 ft. 3 in. diameter, making its total length about
20 ft. It was enclosed by walls of brick and tile, with
blocks of chalk and ragstone about 18 in. thick. These
rested upon a chalk foundation laid on square wooden piles,
pointed at the end, and from 3 ft. to 4 ft. long ; they were
firmly driven into the clay. But little more than the
foundation of the walls remained, and around the semicircular end these were principally of chalk, but in some other
places indications of ' herring-bone' brickwork appeared.
At the line of the floor ran a neatly-turned plaster moulding, which had evidently gone round the building, and
formed the base of the stucco covering of the walls. In
many places this skirting was of a green shade, caused by
the chemical action of the colouring matter used in the
decoration of the walls, and fragments of a bright blue and
red stucco painting of the usual kind were observed. In
the wall surrounding the recess there were, at intervals,
upright flues connected below with the hypocaust, the
whole being the arrangement for warming the apartment.

"The semicircular recess is by no means unusual, yet
it at the same time is, so far as London is concerned, of
especial value, as it gives to us *in situ* the prevailing form
of one of the principal chambers in a Roman house. It is one
that is invariably met with in villas throughout England;
one room at least usually has this peculiarity, sometimes

more. The most perfect example of the kind is perhaps
that at Lymne, in Kent, where there was discovered a
complete ground-plan of a detached house, which is to a
great extent typical of others.

"On referring to some of the finest villas exhumed at
Pompeii, we find much that will illustrate and explain
analogous remains in Britain. In the house of Diomedes,
and in one of the principal apartments, there was a recess
of the form described, and among the *débris* occurred the
rings that had been employed in the suspension of the
curtain drawn across the front. These recesses appear to
have continued in use after the Roman occupation, and
were perhaps represented by the oriel windows of the
Middle Ages.

"The elaborate design of the decorative portion of this
pavement shows at a glance the amount of skill and labour
which has been bestowed upon the work, the taste and
genius displayed in its conception, and the spirited and
artistic way in which it has been carried out. For boldness
of design, harmony in colour, and the effect of gradations of
light and shade in the tints selected, this pavement, with
the exception perhaps of that from Leadenhall Street, sur-
passes anything of the kind previously found in the metropolis. The end south of the projecting piers has a bordering
in large *tessellæ* of red brick, with occasionally some of a
yellow tint; this at the south end is 3 ft. wide, and on
either side 2 ft. 7 in. It encloses a panel eight feet square,
formed by an elegant guilloche border in five rows of small
cubes of coloured *tessellæ*. This surrounds the two interlacing squares. One square is worked in colours, the other
tastefully relieving it with the soft tint produced by *tessellæ*
of white or bluish-grey and black. In the centre is a simple
floral ornament of four heart-shaped petals; the upper
portion worked in colours of grey and yellow; the lower

half, defined by a line across the centre of each leaf, is continued downwards in small *tessellæ* of red brick, presenting the appearance of a cross. Around the central figure are two rows of black *tessellæ*, and a third one surrounding it is in an undulating or serpentine form ; the space produced by the bends is filled by stones of grey and blue. Around this is a double circle containing twenty-six divisions, each parted by a line of black representing diagonal forms. These are in blue, grey, red, and yellow stones. Surrounding this is the braided guilloche, in the same tints as the external border. In the four angles of the interlacing squares are fanciful objects, each two being similar in a diagonal direction.

"Above the panelling, and between the projecting piers, are the most beautiful features of the design, viz., a spirited scroll of flowers and leaves, on either side a centre ornament of. flowers, apparently lilies. The beauty of this design will at once be recognised as a style of decoration familiar on cornices of Grecian art. Above this are two rows of black *tessellæ*, making a dividing line between it and a guilloche ornament which runs above it and entirely round the apse. This elegant border encloses a beautiful scale or leaf-like pattern, formed in parti-coloured sun-like rays, extending from what would be the centre of the circle. This is in twenty-six divisions, every two of which are taken up in the elaboration of the figure. This thatch-like pattern is worked in small *tesseræ* of red and yellow brick, alternating with others in blue and black.

" This latter ornamentation may be considered unique as regards London, though similar figures, especially the under portion or fan-like part of the design, have been seen in Wiltshire. The scale-like pattern is purely classical in its character. A similar figure is sculptured on a marble tomb, discovered at the island of Rhenea in the cemetery of Delos.

It also appears on the choragic monument of Lysicrates, commonly known as the lanthorn of Demosthenes at Athens, and elsewhere. Around the whole design are three rows of small white *tessellæ*, which relieve the ornamental pattern from the sombre heaviness of the external border, formed of large *tessellæ* of red and yellow brick, the small ones being of coloured stone or marble. Some of the latter have been shown to Professor Tennant, who considers them probably not all of native stone. The black ones are of marble, possibly procured from Wales, where similar material is obtained, and was doubtless well known to and quarried by the Romans, who always utilised native products ; the white are of a light-coloured, compact limestone of the kind usually known as 'lithographic'; the blue or grey is probably a stone of foreign origin. It is probable, there-fore, that the stone employed in pavements of a high class was often brought from abroad ; especially might this be the case in London, where, with the exception of clay, there would be no indigenous materials that could be applied."[1]

Besides the above description of the Bucklersbury pavement, Mr. Jno. E. Price, in his work on the subject, has given many interesting particulars of Roman London, and to which the reader is referred, particularly to his description of the carpentry work in and about the founda-tions of this pavement, which bears upon the subject of the construction of Roman houses generally ; and he treats of the course of the Walbrook with the villas upon its margin and the antiquities discovered in its bed, with many valuable comparisons between the Bucklersbury remains and those found in other parts of the country.

[1] Jno. E. Price, *Bucklersbury*.

CHAPTER XIII.

Mosaics in Sussex, Surrey, and Dorset—Comments upon the Situations and Characteristics of the Remains of Villas in these Counties—Particular Descriptions of the various Mosaics found in them—Coins taken up in the vicinity—Authorities quoted.

THE mosaics to be described in the counties of Sussex, Surrey, and Dorset comprise those found in the interesting villas of Bignor and Frampton, conspicuous by the beauty of their designs and by the number of figures introduced into them. That of Bignor was first discovered by the plough in the month of July 1811, in a field called the Berry, in the parish of Bignor in Sussex, lying about a quarter of a mile east of the church, belonging to and in the occupation of Mr. George Tupper. The large pavement was arrived at after removing earth to the depth of one or two feet ; the decorations of this pavement consisted of two circular compartments, the one 7 ft. 6 in. in diameter, the other 16 ft. The smaller one contains a representation of the rape of Ganymede, as well executed as the nature of the materials would admit ; the large one is sub-divided into six irregular hexagonal compartments.

This pavement much resembles one which was found about a century ago at Avenches, in Switzerland, and which there is good reason to suppose was executed in the reign of Vespasian or Titus. As in this, so in the Avenches pavement, there was an octagonal cistern in the centre, and these are supposed to have been the only two examples of the kind which have occurred. It appeared that the room to which this pavement belonged had been heated by a hypocaust, some of the flues of which having given way, the surface of the pavement has been rendered uneven. This room, when the walls had been traced, appeared to be an oblong of 19 ft. by 30 ft., with a recess on the north side 20 ft. 10 in. wide, making the whole length of the room from north to south 31 ft. 11 in. The walls on the east, west, and north sides were 2 ft. 6 in. in thickness; that on the south side 3 ft. Between the ornamented part of the pavement and the wall was a considerable space (filled up with a coarse tesselated pavement of red brick *tesseræ*), varying in width on the east and west sides from 4 ft. 6 in. to 5 ft., 4 ft. 10 in. in width on the north, and 1 ft. 10 in. on the south side, producing a good effect, as it serves to relieve and set off the design of the mosaic work.

It seems probable that this room was a grand banqueting-room (*triclinium*), in which the couches might have been so disposed on the red ground as not to have hidden any of the decorations of the pavement; and the recess was well calculated to answer the purpose of the high table in our public halls. The walls had been ornamented with paintings on stucco, many fragments of which were found among the rubbish.

Mr. Lysons concludes his account of the pavements by saying that, " In the year 1708, a mosaic pavement was discovered at Avenches in Switzerland, the *Aventicum Helvetiorum* of Antonine's *Itinerary*, called by Tacitus *Gentis Caput*, which was patronised in a particular manner by the emperors Vespasian and Titus. Of this pavement an account was published by M. de Schmidt, Seigneur de Rossau, in his *Recueil d'Antiquités de la Suisse*, from which it appears so exactly to resemble the large pavement first discovered at Bignor, that there seems good ground for conjecturing that they are the work of the same artist. Each of them has a cistern of about the same size: a cir-

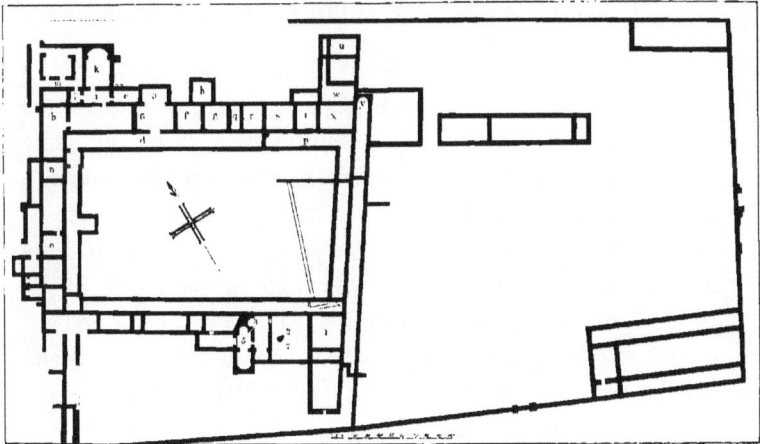

Measured by Williams I.ANo.S   Plan of the Remains of a Roman Villa discovered at Bignor   Published by Hayward July 1811

cumstance which is not known in any other work of the
kind. The pavement at Avenches has figures of Bacchantes
in octagonal compartments, executed exactly in the same
style, and with the same defect of the lower extremities,
being too short, as they appear in the Bignor pavement,
and a blue nimbus round the head of Bacchus, as it here
appears round that of Venus, which is supposed to be
peculiar to these two pavements. There is also a general
agreement between the style of ornament in both of them.
To this may be added that the general style and arrangement of the ornaments, which uniformly prevail in all the
Bignor pavements, differs from any yet discovered in Britain,
and has the appearance of much greater antiquity. The
figures, too, are composed of much better materials, and are
much better drawn and executed than those which appear
in other works of the kind so frequently found in this
island."

The pavements hitherto discovered in Surrey, though
enough to show that Roman villas of a superior class existed
among the scenery of its beautiful hills and woods, yet do
not rival in importance those which have been referred to
in Sussex, nor those which will be described in Dorsetshire.

In the latter county, besides the magnificent one at
Frampton, illustrated by S. Lysons, there was one found at
Tarrant-Hinton, five miles from Blandford, in 1846, in a
villa which has been but imperfectly excavated, and further
discoveries may be made on this spot. Mr. Wm. Shipp, in
describing it, says that " in a field called Barton Field,
some labourers were excavating stones for building and
road-making, and soon came upon an extensive area of old
foundations. The remains of these ancient walls reached,
in various directions, over an extent of nearly twenty acres,
which in several points were dug down upon, and the
dilapidated ruins discovered to the eye of the antiquary

D D

the evident traces of a Roman villa or settlement. The
only opportunity there was of tracing the foundations was
in that of apparently a small house, situated at some
distance from the principal building; they consisted of an
entrance, leading through a passage about four feet long, at
the end of which were two small apartments, about $5\frac{1}{2}$ ft.
square. The passage, which was bounded by a wall of
great thickness, was cased on each side with stucco, the
painted frescoes on which, exhibiting great boldness of
design, were as bright and vivid in colour as the day they
were finished by the artist. The floors of these two apartments were likewise stuccoed, but of a much coarser description, composed principally of small stones, sand, lime, and
ashes. At every part of the field where excavations were
made some monuments of Roman character were brought to
light,—quantities of broken and detached squares of *tesserae*;
fragments of urns used for domestic and other purposes;
one highly finished bronze fibula; two querns; a quantity
of tiles; the neck of a large amphora; one or two beautiful
fragments of Samian ware; several ornamental tiles; three
3rd brass coins of Constantine and one of Constantius;
two circular pipes, used in all probability for conveying
water to the baths; and at the bottom of a well or vault
of nearly thirty feet, the capital of a stone column of the
Doric order.

"The only perfect tesselated floor discovered was a plain
figure compactly cemented together, and composed of only
two coloured squares of *tesserae*, red and white. These
tesserae, particularly in the centre, were much worn, clearly
showing that they had been subject to the tread of the
foot for a number of years."

The extent of the buildings reached 650 ft. by 350 ft.,
of which the mansion proper occupied nearly one-half.[1]

[1] *History of Sussex*, by Mark A. Lower, M.A., 1870.

RAPE OF GANYMEDE (*BIGNOR*).

See chap. xiii, p. 203.

SUSSEX.

Field called the BERRY, *quarter of a mile east of Bignor Church, six miles and a quarter from Arundel, and six miles from Petworth.*

1.—In the large room was found a mosaic pavement; this consisted of two circular compartments, the one 7 ft. 6 in. diameter, the other 16 ft. The smaller one contained a representation of the rape of Ganymede; the eagle is carrying him off, clasping him in his talons; the youth has a red and blue cloak over his shoulder, and holds in his left hand a *stemma* with recurved top. The large circle is subdivided into six irregular hexagonal compartments, within which are figures of dancing nymphs; one of them has been quite destroyed, but enough remains of the other five to indicate the dress and attitude. These figures are well executed, except as regards the lower limbs, which are too short. In the centre of the circular compartment is a hexagonal piscina or cistern of stone, 4 ft. in diameter and 1 ft. 7¾ in. deep, with a step at about half its depth.[1]

2.—About 30 ft. west of this pavement part of another was found, which appeared, when entire, to have been 44 ft. long and 17 ft. wide, and to have consisted of two large square compartments. One portion includes a circle, subdivided into irregular hexagons, with oval compartments in the spandrils of the circle, and ornamented with figures, of which part of a boy, a dolphin, and a pheasant, with a cornucopia, remained, with the letters T R in one of the angular spaces between the hexagons; the second letter seems to have been intended for a combination of E and R. The other compartments appear to have originally contained

[1] *Account of the Villa at Bignor*, by Sam. Lysons; London, 1815. *Archæologia*, xviii, p. 203; and xix. See also *Sussex Arch. Collect.*, viii, p. 292; xi, 132; xviii, 99.

four octagonal divisions, each including a star, formed by
two interlaced squares; within was an octagon. Only one
of these remained entire, indicated, by being enveloped in
clothing, and by the leafless branch which accompanies it,
to be the head of "Winter". The other three divisions
contained, no doubt, the heads of the other seasons.

The *tesseræ* were of various sizes; the larger red ones
for the outside work and the inferior parts of the pavement
were cubes of about an inch, and formed of red brick or of
stone; those of which the ornamental parts were composed
varied in size from cubes of $\frac{1}{2}$ in. down to $\frac{1}{6}$ in.

3.—On the west side of the recess in the great room was
another pavement, 20 ft. by 9 ft. 9 in., quite entire. The
mosaic work consisted of two compartments, each 5 ft. 4 in.
square, with an oblong one between them, 5 ft. 4 in. by
2 ft. 6 in.; the rest of the pavement being filled up with
coarse red *tesseræ*. The design of the oblong compartment
consisted of two scrolls of ivy leaves proceeding from a
goblet, surrounded by a guilloche and a black and white
indented border. One of the square compartments enclosed
an octagon filled with squares and rhombs, in which were
frets and ivy leaves; in the middle was a square enclosing
a large rose. The other square included a sort of star of
twelve points formed of rhombs, within which was a smaller
square, with a guilloche border enclosing a flower. This
pavement was several inches above the level of that first
described, from which it was separated by a wall, and did
not appear to have any communication with it.

On the south side of the great pavement the foundation
walls of a crypto-porticus of great length were discovered;
it was 10 ft. in width, and remains of the walls were traced
to the extent of 150 ft. to the eastward; part of its tesselated pavement, ornamented with a blue labyrinth, and
having a red stripe on each side, was remaining at the west

See chap. xiii, p. 204.

RECEPTION ROOM (*BIGNOR*).

See chap. xiii, p. 204.

HEAD OF WINTER (*BIGNOR*).

end, to the extent of about 65 ft. in length; the rest appeared to have been destroyed.

4.—Another room had a pavement of coarse *tesseræ*, of a light brown colour.

5.—Adjoining this, on north side, was a room in which was a mosaic eight feet square, geometrical pattern.

6.—To the north of the rooms described was found a very fine mosaic pavement, in form of a parallelogram, 22 ft. by 19 ft. 10 in., with a semicircular recess at the north end, 10 ft. in diameter, making the whole length 32 ft. The design of the pavement consisted of a large compartment, 13 ft. 6 in. square, between two narrow oblong ones, with a fourth, approaching to a semicircle, occupying the recess at the north end. The square enclosed an octagon, within which had been eight small oblong compartments, meeting towards the centre, which had been entirely demolished. Each of the small oblong compartments was 2 ft. 9 in. by 16 in.; two of them were entire, containing figures of cupids or genii, dancing in the manner of Bacchantes; and of three others, sufficient remained to show the attitudes of the figures.

The triangular divisions at the four corners of the square were filled with figures of urns, with fruit and foliage and cornucopiæ alternately. The oblong compartment on the north side of the square one is 13 ft. 7 in. long by 2 ft. 6 in. wide; it contains twelve figures of cupids or genii, habited as gladiators, and exhibits a very complete representation of the costume of the *retiarii* and *secutores*. Here also appear the *lanistæ* with wands, instructors and guardians of the gladiators. The subject seems to represent four different scenes, in which the same parties are engaged. In one, they are preparing for the combat; in another, just engaged in it; in a third, the *retiarius* is wounded; in the last, he is fallen, disarmed, and wounded in the thigh.

The semicircular division at the north end of the pavement is surrounded by an elegant scroll of foliage proceeding from a goblet, and enclosing a circular compartment, within which is a female head ornamented with a chaplet of flowers; tresses of hair appear on the shoulders, which are naked. The head is surrounded with a nimbus of light blue colour, few of which appear in any of the remains of ancient art. On each side of the circular compartment are cornucopiæ and festoons of foliage, with two birds, one on each side, which seem to have been designed for pheasants.

7.—On the southern side of the villa, in a room of a distorted square of about twenty-five feet, is a mosaic pavement, the design being a square containing four stars of eight points, each formed by two interlaced squares composed of guilloches differently coloured; within each star was a circle of three borders. In the middle of the pavement was a circle consisting of a guilloche between two indented borders, within which was the head of Medusa. Beyond the mosaic pavement were three rows of black and red tiles, laid chequer-wise, and next to the wall a row of bricks.

SURREY.

WARPLESDON PARISH, *Broad Street Common, two miles and a half from Guildford, eight miles from Farnham, and same from Tuxbury Hill Camp.*

8.—Discovery on 13th July 1829, communicated by Allen Sibthorpe.[1] Small *tesseræ* were first found, in red, white, yellow, and brown. The red were of burnt earth; the white, of chalk; the yellow and brown appeared to be chalk stained with some liquid colours. Several portions of pavement were afterwards developed, forming a suite of apartments. Entire length of building, running north and south,

[1] *Archæologia,* xxiii, p. 398.

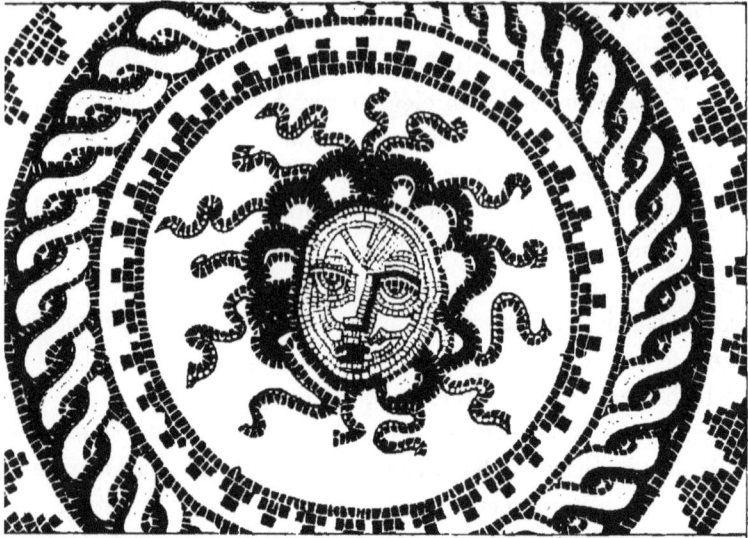

See chap. xiii, p. 226.

HEAD OF MEDUSA AND FRAGMENTS (BIGNOR).

was about 62 ft. within the walls ; the breadth, including a passage, was 23 ft. 3 in.   On each side of the centre apartment is a smaller, 16 ft. by 5 ft. ; and beyond these again, on each side, is the floor of a larger room, 16 ft. by 14 ft. Along the whole western side ran a piece of paving, ornamented on its outer edge with a border formed of very small *tesseræ*, arranged in a double wavy pattern in the centre, red and black.   With the exception of the ornament and border above described, the whole of the pavement is composed of the iron-stone found in great abundance in the sand hills lying to the south of Guildford, particularly at St. Martha's and St. Catherine Hills.   The *tesseræ* are about an inch square, thus giving 144 to each square foot of pavement.

Mr. Kempe, in his account of the Loseley MSS., refers to this pavement on Broad Street Green in similar terms to the above, and refers to the locality in the following words : "Loseley is situated about two miles from Guildford, and from the left or west bank of the Wey. That ancient town is supposed in the early period to have stood on the west side of the river, and by its castle and outworks to have occupied also the site of the present town on the east. This assertion is pretty well confirmed by the curious ancient vaultings still existing under the Angel Inn at Guildford, on the west side of the main street, and by the supposed site of the ancient town being still marked out as the Bury Fields ; and there is great probability that the last-mentioned spot was occupied in the time of the Romans, of whose presence, at least in the neighbourhood, undoubted evidence has been discovered."[1]

---

[1] *The Loseley MSS.*, now first edited, with notes, by Alfred Jno. Kempe, Esq., F.S.A.   London, 1836.

WALTON HEATH.[1]

Walton Heath is part of the high ground forming the southern rim of the chalk basin of London, and of which Banstead and Epsom Downs are parts adjacent.

In the year 1772 Mr. Barnes called the attention of the Society of Antiquaries to Roman antiquities discovered on this heath, consisting of foundations, walls, and some portions of a flue, and a small brass figure of Æsculapius, engraved in the *Archæologia*. Mr. W. W. Pocock says : " My attention was first directed to these vestiges of Roman occupation by my friend, the Rev. Ambrose Hall, in conversation. Having inspected some *tesserœ*, remains of pottery, and other articles he had himself dug up upon the spot, and learning that the remaining foundations were being destroyed for the sake of re-using the materials in a garden wall, a visit was soon arranged, and a very little labour sufficed to uncover a considerable portion of the pavement. At the same time I measured the trenches, from which rough masonry, consisting chiefly of flints, had lately been removed.

" The walls appear to have been little more than a foot in thickness, and the foundation to have been laid about three feet below the present surface, the pavement found being generally a foot below the turf, which distinguishes this site from the thick heath and gorse of the surrounding common. The excavations made extend over a space not more than forty yards square ; but a very slight removal of surface reveals abundant remains of Roman *fictilia*, affording ample scope for enterprising diggers.

" Of the spaces within the walls, several retained a large portion of their pavements, mostly executed in red *tesserœ*,

[1] *Surrey Arch. Collections*, vol. ii, pp. 4-13, 1860.

1½ in. to 2 in. square and 1 in. thick, of a coarse material, and apparently laid without reference to any figure.

9.—" But the only one of an ornamental character yet brought to light is in an apartment towards the middle of the eastern side of the space occupied by the remains, and about twenty-one feet square. The design consists of a central circle, containing an urn, and surrounded by four semicircles and four small squares disposed at the angles, all being included in a larger square, formed by a wide border, of a bold and elegant pattern, consisting of circles and points, the former containing alternately a heart and a figure resembling the seed of the columbine. On the outside of this larger square is a Greek meander, then a band of white; and lastly, the large red *tesseræ*, before described, complete the whole.

"The central urn was executed with great care, and in it I discovered two colours, that I could trace in no other part of the design. One of these was a deep crimson, and the other a purple or violet. The urn was surrounded by a circular border, consisting of a guilloche in three colours, and two bands executed in two colours. This circle was enclosed in a square formed by a double-twisted guilloche. One of the angular spandrils was filled by a heart-shaped ornament, and I believe the others to have been similarly occupied. Each side of this inner square is flanked by a semicircle of equal diameter, and formed by a border of a triple plait and bands, and within this the guilloche and bands first described, and which is continued across the cord as well as round the circumference of the circle. The interiors of these semicircles are filled up with series of small semicircles, and each of the centres is occupied by a flower of three petals. The angles of the general design are occupied by the four smaller squares, formed of the same guilloche, containing an effective and not un-

E E

common border in two colours, the centre being filled by a
double endless knot.

" By far the greater part of the cubes employed in this
floor were only sun-dried clay of a fine texture. Some
were cubes of chalk, and the rest pieces of broken Samian
ware, upon many of which the portions of figures or ornaments of various kinds occur on the under side.

" With the exception of a few found in the urn, the
sun-dried *tessellæ* were of two different colours, one at least
having been tinted with some colouring admixture ; and it
is probable that the firing was omitted with a view of
obviating the red colour that would otherwise have been
imparted to the clay. The general size of the *tessellæ* is
half an inch every way. In general outline it greatly resembles one found in Dyer Street, Cirencester, some eight
years back ; the whole of the interior of which consists of a
circle and parts of circles within a square framework. But
the introduction of the central and corner squares in the
Walton design gives it such an admixture of straight lines
and curves, as produces a force and character that the Dyer
Street pavement does not possess.

" The pavement at Walton was formed on the solid
ground, with but a slight foundation of pounded brick under
it ; and as it was usual to form the floors of their principal
rooms hollow, for the purposes of warming, either this was
not a principal apartment, or the building was not of a very
important character. I adopt the former of these alterna-
tives. Among other remains was found a coin of Vespasian."

DORSET.

DORCHESTER.

" In February 1812, the Rev. Thomas Rackett, M.A., F.S.A., presented to the Society a drawing of a mosaic pavement found at Dorchester.[1] The mosaic was discovered two feet below the surface of the ground, in digging the foundation for a garden wall belonging to the new gaol at Dorchester (formerly the site of the castle), about three years ago. The pattern is very simple, and appears to differ little from that of any tesselated pavement hitherto observed in Britain. It consists of a series of three parallelograms, one within another, each formed by two rows of blue *tesserœ*, on a white ground ; on each side of this is a blue stripe formed by five rows of *tesserœ*.

10.—"About ten feet in length of the pavement have been uncovered, and it is 4½ ft. wide. It appears to be part of a passage; and as Dorchester is so well known as a Roman station, it probably formed a part of a considerable and elegant building. There is, however, but little prospect of future discoveries, as the walls of the gaol stand within a few feet of the eastern extremity of the pavement, and other buildings intercept it towards the west. Not far from this spot, whilst the wall above mentioned was building, several large and coarse *tesserœ* were dug up, and Roman coins are frequently found by the prisoners who are permitted to cultivate the garden."

NUNNERY MEADOW, *quarter of a mile west of Frampton, a village five miles distant from Dorchester.*

11.—These pavements were discovered in 1796. On that at A a variety of elegant ornaments and figures of

[1] *Archæologia*, xvii, p. 330.

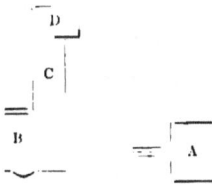

Jupiter, Mars pacifer, Neptune, Apollo, and Bacchus. The head of Mercury is five times repeated. On one side are dogs hunting, most of them indifferently executed. B. On this is a circular compartment in the centre, round which were four squares and as many semicircular ones, alternately, formed by a single guilloche of four colours; the centre much mutilated. A figure of a man on horseback is seen combating a lion with spear. The semicircular compartments were all very imperfect, and not one of the figures once contained in them was to be seen except a fragment of that on the east side, in which was a head of a small fish and tail of another. The figures at the northeast angle were quite obliterated; that at the south-east much mutilated. The other two squares were in better preservation; that at the north-west angle was entire. A young man is seen sitting, with Phrygian bonnet on head and pipe of reeds in his left hand; also a female figure, apparently addressing him. They are coarsely executed.

At the south-west angle is a young man reclining on a piece of drapery, apparently in a dying state, from the female figure who stands by holding an inverted torch, and with her left hand on her breast. Beyond the compartments above described and the guilloche border, is a border of dolphins, in the middle of which, on the south side, is the head of Neptune, with horns, and two dolphins proceeding from his beard. Above this is an inscription running in two lines on both sides of the head—

NEPTVNI VERTEX REGMEN   SCVLTVM CVI CERVLEA EST
SORTITI MOBILE VENTIS   DELFINIS CINCTA DVOBVS

(*Cœrulea barba*)

Below this the sign ℞. The ornaments of this lower part

seem inferior to those of the square, and probably the work
is of a later age. At the eastern extremity of the square
appears the lower part of a human figure ; and on one side
of it an inscription in two lines, the beginning of which is
mutilated, runs thus—

    (*Facinus*)   NVS PERFICIS VLLVM
                CNARE CVPIDO

Tesseræ of these two pavements are mostly of half-inch,
except the figures, in which many of them were smaller.
The colours are five,—red, blue, white, yellow, and dark
brown, of which last the outlines were usually formed. The
white are of a hard kind of pipeclay ; the blue of Cornish
slate ; the yellow of a hard kind of stone, which seems to
be stained by art ; the red and dark brown are of burnt
clay. The mortar in which they were set was inferior to
that at Woodchester and other places.

    12.—There is a smaller pavement to the east of this,
21 ft. by 15 ft. In the middle was a circular compartment,
the border of which was a scroll of foliage between two
guilloches ; in the centre was a leopard, with some remains
of a clothed figure sitting on it. At one end of this pavement was an oblong compartment containing fragments of
group, a man combating a leopard ; and another at the
opposite end, with similar fragment of a man hunting two
wild animals. Several fragments of stucco painted with
stripes were found in the ruins, and a few coins of the Lower
Empire.

    The long piece of pavement is 8 ft. $2\frac{1}{2}$ in. wide and
94 ft. long.

    13.—Plate VII.—Another pavement, more entire than
the others, lay to the north of the long corridor, measuring
19 ft. 4 in. by 12 ft. 8 in. There were five octagonal and
ten hexagonal compartments, formed by a single guilloche.

The central one contained a bearded head (Neptune), and four other heads of Nereids with shells. In the hexagonal compartments were figures of dolphins, and at each end a plain Vitruvian scroll, with spirals to represent water.

14.—The pavement of a passage, 42 ft. by 5 ft., leading from the pavement last described to those first discovered, was ornamented with double fret running down the whole length of it. The mosaic work here was of a coarser kind, and of only two colours, dark brown and white. Under the pavement at A the foundations were found to be as follows : 9 in. of hard terras, with white pebbles and bits of brick ; 1 ft. of large flints laid in mortar, interspersed with bits of burnt wood ; 2 ft. of yellow sand with bits of brick and other substances. Total thickness, 3 ft. 9 in.

BARTON FIELD, *in parish of Tarrant Hinton, five miles from Blandford.*[1]

15.—A small house, the walls in stucco, painted with frescoes ; stuccoed floors in two rooms, and *tessellæ* scattered over the field. Also large ruins in which was one tesselated floor, perfect. Design was plain, consisting of two coloured squares ; the *tesseræ* red and white. Three 3rd brass coins of Constantine and one of Constantius.

PRESTON, *near Weymouth.*[2]

16.—In a field near the church a Roman cemetery and ruins of a temple were found in 1842, a villa or bath in 1844, and in 1852, a pavement, described on the spot by the Rev. Prebendary T. Baker, at the Congress of the British Archæological Association at Weymouth in 1871. An atrium twenty-one feet square was found, and nothing

[1] *Brit. Arch. Assoc. Journal,* Winchester volume, p. 179.
[2] *Ibid.*, xxviii, p. 91.

on the north of it. A room at the south-west, with very rough *tesserœ*, the court paved with stone in the centre ; and a room to the south-east, about 12 ft. square, also roughly paved with *tesserœ*. There was a long wall, 63 ft. 8 in. in length. The white *tesserœ* belonged to the lower chalk, the red being of burnt brick, and the black pieces umber, or, according to Mr. Edward Roberts, of the brown sandstone, of which there was a high cliff at Lulworth.

The pavement was found in excellent preservation, and the surface very slightly damaged. It was about eighteen inches below the soil.

FIFEHEAD NEVILLE.

Mr. Middleton communicated the subjoined notes on the site of a Roman villa, which were illustrated by careful drawings of a pavement and other remains.[1] " The land where these Roman remains have just been discovered is the property of Mr. Wingfield Digby, of Sherborne Castle, but the fact that they have been discovered and exposed to view is owing to the energy and care of Mr. W. W. Connop, of the Manor House at Fifehead Neville.

"The digging up of great quantities of fragments of Roman bricks and worked stones in a field called 'Verlands', about ten or twelve acres in size, led Mr. Connop to have excavations made at a point where these seemed most abundant, and the result has been the following discoveries.

17.—"First, a fine mosaic pavement, about 13 ft. 6 in. by 11 ft. 6 in., as shown in the drawing exhibited. The design consists of a sort of vase in the centre ; next, a ring, round which fishes (something like gurnets) are swimming; next, a larger ring, containing four sea-monsters, rather like dolphins

[1] *Proceedings of Soc. Antiq.*, 16 June 1881.

in shape. This outer band is set in a square, the corners being filled up with a flowing ornament, and the remainder of the surface is filled up by bands of red and white, containing a sort of battlement ornament; round the whole is a broad panel of plain bluish-grey *tesseræ* larger than the rest. The colours and materials used are these :—1, the main part of the ground of hard white clunch ; 2, a bright red, made of terra-cotta ; 3, brown, made of soft argillaceous pebbles, existing in great quantities in a neighbouring stream ; 4, bluish grey, made of Purbeck marble. The *tesseræ* average half an inch square, and a little more in thickness. They are set on a thin bed of cement. The walls round this pavement have been almost entirely dug up and carried away for building purposes ; and this is the case with all the walls of the villa, so that it is impossible now to make out the plan.

"The surface of the mosaic was only from nine to twelve inches below the level of the ground, and consequently some damage has been done to it by ploughs passing over it. The next room contained the hypocaust, and was of the same width as the room with the above-mentioned pavement. The internal walls of the villa appear to have been coated with coloured decoration in blue, white, green, black, and red.

"A considerable quantity of 3rd brasses have been found, chiefly illegible from corrosion. The few that can be deciphered are of Probus, Carinus, Constantine the Great, and his sons ; the latest being of the middle of the fourth century. It appears as if the whole of the large field in which these discoveries have been made was once occupied by Roman buildings."

CHAPTER XIV.

Mosaics in HAMPSHIRE and ISLE OF WIGHT—Accounts of the Situation of the various Roman Villas where Mosaics have been found—Particular descriptions of the latter—Coins found near—Authorities quoted.

THE county of Hampshire, occupied by the Belgians in the time of Julius Cæsar, next claims our attention, their territory extending across to the other sea, that is, to the Bristol Channel. If the Belgians of Gaul were the most warlike and powerful of all the tribes there, so we may presume were the nation of the Belgæ in Hampshire, who were a portion of the same people, according to Julius Cæsar. They were rich in flocks of sheep, as well as in men and in property.[1] If Havant, then, was their chief town, or Venta Belgarum on the south coast, we may well suppose a large trade to have been done there in wool, the chief staple of the country ; and when occupied by the Romans, it is not surprising to find numerous and wealthy settlements at Havant, at *Brige, Sorbiodunum,* and *Vindogladia* and neighbourhood, and villas paved with mosaics, during the period treated of in this work. Two of these, at

[1] The two passages in which reference is made to them are as follows (C. J. Cæsar, *Comm. de B. G.*, 1, i) : " Horum omnium fortissimi sunt Belgæ ...... : proximique sunt Germaniæ qui trans Rhenum incolunt, quibuscum continenter bellum gerunt." And as to the British Belgians, he says (*ib.*, v, 12): " Maritima pars ab iis, qui, prædæ ac belli inferendi causa, ex Belgis transierant, qui omnes fere iis nominibus civitatum appellantur, quibus orti ex civitatibus eo pervenerunt, et bello illato ibi remanserunt, atque agros colere cœperunt. Hominum est infinita multitudo, creberrimaque ædificia, fere Gallicis consimilia ; pecorum magnus numerus."

F F

Thruxton and Bramdean, are especially interesting, both
from their designs and the inscriptions upon them.

In the Salisbury volume of the Royal Archæological
Institute is a coloured engraving of the former, from a
private plate in the possession of Joseph Clarke, Esq., of
Saffron Walden ; and from the description there given, it
appears that the whole building at Thruxton, of which the
tesselated pavement formed a part, " was in length eighty-
five feet and in width fifty feet. Its walls were composed
of large and rough flints embedded in mortar. These had
fallen inwards and buried a chalk floor, in which were
placed two rows of upright stones, five in each row, of a
large size and perfectly smooth on their upper surface, being
of polished freestone. These rows of stones were one-and-
twenty feet apart. Midway between the rows of stones, a
human skeleton was discovered, lying on the floor of the
building, and cross-legged. Near to it, and about twelve
feet from the end wall, a small axe, the head of an arrow,
and several small coins, etc., were found. At the end
another human skeleton was uncovered, but, unfortunately,
destroyed ; and at some distance behind the outer wall was
a third skeleton. The building appears to have been roofed
or covered with slates, as numbers of them were found
among the ruins. The walls, too, and probably the ceilings,
were plastered and painted, as many fragments of plaster,
variously coloured, were found.

" The recent discoveries at Cirencester only serve to
make the pavement at Thruxton doubly interesting. The
figures on the Cirencester pavement are of the highest class
of design, and perhaps stand unrivalled among similar
remains of Roman or of Grecian art; but the architectural
arrangement of the different compartments of the floor
at Thruxton, and the disposition of the embellishments
and enrichments, are, perhaps, inferior to none hitherto

discovered. The inscription also claims our particular attention. QUINTUS NATALIUS NATALINUS ET BODENI is on one line at the top of the pavement, but the line of inscription at the bottom is destroyed, except the two letters v and o."

The author of the above description suggests that by substituting B for an interchangeable letter—v or w—some connection with Woden may be traced ; and this seems more probable than that the word Bodeni can be the name of a tribe or people. The word is perhaps continued in the next line, which no longer exists, and there is nothing to substantiate the conjecture that v and o are parts of the sentence *ex voto*. The same writer refers to a ' Natalis' in the Annals of Tacitus, in the time of Nero. He was of equestrian rank, and in the confidence of Piso, who headed the conspiracy against Nero. It is not improbable that Q. Natalius Natalinus might be descended from the Roman knight who acted so conspicuous a part on this occasion.

We know that the Saxon kings boasted a descent from Woden ; their genealogies from that hero being given in the *Saxon Chronicle*.

The second villa in Hampshire which claims especial attention is that at Bramdean, remarkable for the interest and diversity of its pictured mosaics. The gods and godesses portrayed on them are the divinities presiding over the several days of the week, which has been pointed out by Mr. C. Roach Smith, in his *Collectanea Antiqua*, vol. ii.

At Bramdean, bust of Saturn has been destroyed. This would represent Saturday.

Sol, with radiated crown and whip, Sunday.

Luna, with the crescent moon, Monday.

Mars, with helmet and spear (Fr. *Mardi*), Tuesday.

Mercury, with winged cap and caduceus (*Mercredi*), Wednesday (Woden's day).

Jupiter, with sceptre in form of a trident (*Jeudi*), Thursday (Thor's day).

Venus, with a mirror (*Vendredi*), Friday (or Freya's day).

The eighth head has been destroyed; the design of which, to complete the even number, seems to have been chosen almost at pleasure.

Mr. Smith illustrates this by reference to a votive altar in the museum at Mayence, found at Castel, 3½ ft. high, divided into two parts, the lower being quadrilateral, the upper and smaller being octagonal. On the former are Mercury, Hercules, Minerva, and Juno; and on the latter Saturn, Sol, Luna, Mars, Mercury, Jupiter, and Venus. The eighth is inscribed H D D, *In Honorem Domus Divinæ*. Montfaucon has published an engraving of the seven busts in a boat.

The bronze *forceps*, before referred to in chapter iv, illustrates this subject, and is now in the British Museum. It is surmounted by small heads of Juno and Cybele, crowned with towers. Lions' heads are on each handle, and horses' heads at the point, where was the hinge. Ranged up each shank, beginning from the handle, are diminutive heads, in metal, of Saturn, Sol or Apollo, Diana, Mars; and down the other flange follow in succession Mercury, Jupiter, Venus, and Ceres, to make up the eighth. The two shanks, 11½ in. in length, now separated, together formed a forceps, probably used for securing by the nose the victim about to be sacrificed.

The Romans generally began their week with Saturday, not with Sunday; as did Ausonius in the lines quoted at page 45.

ROMAN PAVEMENT. FOUND AT ITCHEN ABBAS.
NEAR WINCHESTER. MARCH. 1878.

ABOUT 6 FEET SQUARE.

Colours. black white. and red
on both pavements

E COLLIER DEL'

To face p. ..21.

HANTS.

ITCHEN ABBAS, *near Winchester*.[1]

1.—The best design is a square of twelve feet each way. Outside is a braided guilloche border ; next to it a fillet ; then a plain guilloche and another fillet ; then a circular medallion in the centre, formed by a guilloche border on dark ground. In the medallion is a head, wreathed, and from it proceed six stars upon stems,—or are these intended for the ivy-leaves of Bacchus ? In the spandrils between circle and square are two knots of guilloche pattern, and two floral ornaments with tendrils. The colours are black, white, and pale blue.

2.—Others form the flooring of two rooms, measuring 16 ft. by 8 ft. and 6 ft. by 6 ft. The design of one was a central guilloche knot, in the form of a square, and around this a labyrinth pattern at the corners, alternating with a floral panel and a strip of guilloche pattern ; the borders were of red *tesseræ* for about eighteen inches from the walls.

3.—The design of the other was an oblong double-braided guilloche border ; three panels or compartments are divided by a guilloche border. The central square contains within it a circle of geometrical design. The other compartments have a cantharus in each, and scroll pattern. Two coins were found here, one not to be deciphered; the other was of Constantine, with the legend SARMATIA DEVICTA.

THRUXTON, *between Ambresbury and Andover*.[2]

4.—The pavement here has a central medallion, with the figure of Bacchus crowned with leaves; a cup in his right hand and a stem in his left. He sits upon a tiger or leopard,

---

[1] *Brit. Arch. Assoc. Journal*, xxxiv, pp. 231-5, 504.
[2] *R.A.I.*, Salisbury volume, p. 241.

which crouches beneath him ; and four leaves and stems of
the vine (judging from the tendrils) fill up the background.
In the spandrils formed by the outer circle and inner square
border are four female busts, apparently representing the
seasons.

The outer border of this pavement, which is sixteen feet
square, is formed of single red lines on a white ground,
describing geometrical figures, in two of which are two
small crosses. This border surrounds a square of elaborate
design, of which a guilloche border is a distinguishing
feature ; and in a line above this square is the inscription,
very perfect, QVINTVS NATALIVS NATALINVS ET BODENI; below
the square the pavement is very imperfect, and only two
letters, V O, with an interval between wherewith to complete the inscription above. Contained within the square
is the circle, surrounded by a guilloche border within lines
of yellow and red, while another smaller circle forms the
central medallion before referred to, which is also surrounded by a similar border as the larger circle, and the
intervening space between the circles is divided by same
border into eight compartments. Each of these contains a
human head wearing a cap, one of them being in the form
of the Phrygian, and from the necks proceed floral ornaments. The coins found are small brass of Gallienus,
Claudius II, Maximin, Carausius, Constantine the Great,
Crispus, Constantine II, Constans, and Magnentius, A.D.
254 to 360.[1]

———

CRONDALL, *half-way between Farnham and Odiham.*[2]

5.—Square pavement in good preservation. Within two
arabesque borders are six octagon compartments filled with

[1] *Archæologia,* xxii, p. 49 ; *Gentleman's Magazine,* Sept. 1823.
[2] *Archæologia,* xxii, p. 54.

various designs, and in the central one is a cantharus with two handles. The pavement not equal to those at Thruxton and Bramdean.

———

6.—Two of the apartments of villa found here deserve attention, each being decorated with historical subjects. The first has a square pavement with angles cut off, in each of which was the representation of a vase. The central compartment was circular, with two intersecting squares within it, and within those squares was an octagon in which is the head of Medusa. In the space between this circle and the outer square border were eight compartments of this form, in each of which was the head of a deity, of which four only remain perfect, that is, Venus with her glass, Jupiter with a sceptre in form of a trident, Mercury with his caduceus, Mars in armour with his helmet and spear. Parts of two more indicate Diana with her crescent, and Sol with radiated crown and whip.

7.—In same line with the above, but somewhat separated, is another mosaic pavement, of larger dimensions and much richer in its decoration than the former. It was laid on piers, and the flues that warmed the room are still visible underneath. It is composed of four intersecting squares, and in the centre is an octagon compartment containing a design of the story of Hercules and Antæus. In each of the four squares there is a head placed within an octagon; in two of the extreme angles are two vases, and in the others arabesques; and in the centres between the angles are vases and dolphins. Hercules is seen lifting Antæus from the ground, before he touches it to recover his strength in presence of his mother *Terra*. The work-

———

[1] *Archæologia*, xxii, p. 52.

manship is superior, and coins of the Lower Empire have been found.

———

ABBOT'S ANN, *two miles and a quarter S.W. by W. from Andover.*

8.—" This, called in the earliest records the manor of Anna, anciently belonged to Hyde Abbey, Winchester. In a field about a mile south-east of the church were discovered, a few years ago, the remains of a Roman villa."[1] Some pieces of mosaic pavement were removed, and are now placed in the British Museum, in compartments Nos. X, XI, and XII, in the Roman gallery on the ground-floor.

[1] *Topographical Dictionary of England,* by Sam. Lewis. London, 1849.

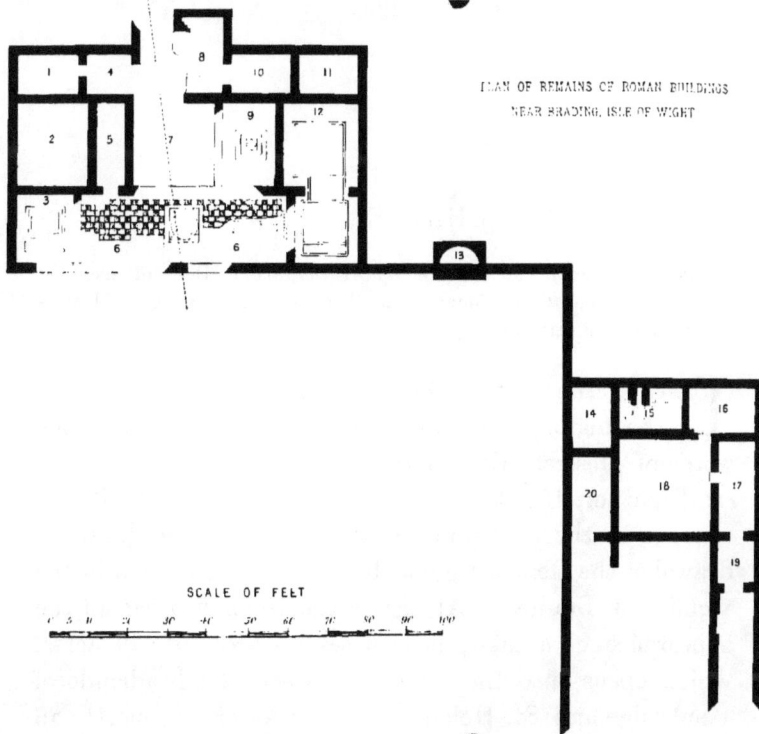

PLAN OF REMAINS OF ROMAN BUILDINGS
NEAR BRADING, ISLE OF WIGHT

SCALE OF FEET

CHAPTER XV.

Mosaics in HAMPSHIRE and ISLE OF WIGHT (*continued*)—Descriptions of the
Mosaics and Coins found near them—Some passages in history
quoted in illustration.

THE position of the villa at Morton, Isle of Wight, and
the history of its discovery, can best be given in the
words of Messrs. Price, in their *Guide to the Roman Villa,
etc.* (Ventnor, 1881). "In few parts of the island will the
changes in the configuration of the land, since the withdrawal of the Roman legions, be more apparent than in the
vicinity of Brading. At high water the haven has all the
appearance of a lake; it encloses an area of 840 acres,
which opens into the Solent, between the headlands of
Bembridge and St. Helen's. At low water it is mostly an
expanse of mud, with a narrow channel through which the
Yar meanders to the sea. Many attempts have been made
to reclaim this valuable tract, but without avail. It is said
that in the course of an attempt to throw an embankment
across the mouth (which the sea quickly washed away) a
well cased with stone was found. It was near to the middle
of the haven, demonstrating that its site had once been dry
land, and that the sea had overflowed it within the historical period. Captain Thorp of Yarbridge, who has throughout our work been an ever-zealous colleague, is under the
impression that he has discovered an ancient ford in the
direction of Yaverland and the shore line. We have
recently come across important indications of a road or
way, the direction of which has yet to be ascertained.

"The site chosen for the erection of the buildings now

G G

in course of excavation is a remarkably fine one; centuries
since it was in one holding, but at the present time these important remains are partly on the property of Lady Oglander of Nunwell, and partly on the property of Mrs. Munns;
indeed, the line of demarcation runs in a direct line through
three of the apartments excavated. The two fields at
Morton are known respectively as 'Seven-Acre Field' on
one side and 'Ten-Acre Field' on the other; they together
form an elevated site which, looking towards the high road
which separates them from the lowlands and marshes, appears
as a gentle slope of cultivated land, which would have at
once commended itself to the attention of Roman architects.
Their text-books on such matters contain many important
hints as to the selection of sites for building operations, and
in this case there is every advantage to be desired. Looking seawards, there is to the left Brading-down and the
bold chalk range of hills terminating in the promontory of
Culver Cliff, while to the right is the growing town of
Sandown, with the picturesque hills and vales leading on-
wards to Shanklin and Ventnor.

"Skirting Brading-down, and marking a boundary line
to the field in which our excavations are situated, is a fosse
way, which as a bridle-path has in turn been used by Celts,
Romans, and Saxons, and runs at the base of the hills by
Arreton to Newport and Carisbrook. The vast tract of
land which separates this position from the sea is at high
tides mostly covered by water, and in olden time it is
probable that the site selected by the Roman colonists was,
as it were, insulated from Bembridge-down and the adjoining heights; but in the indication of buildings discovered at
Brading Haven, and the encroachments of the sea upon
certain portions of the coast, we see how much there is to
be investigated, in a geographical point of view, ere any
opinions can be confidently expressed.

"The present explorations originated in the finding on Mrs. Munns' property such indications of Roman buildings as offered encouragement for further investigation. On this land, walls, roof-tiles, and traces of pavements were discovered by Captain Thorp of Yarbridge, who devoted a considerable amount of energy and zeal to a complete examination of the ground.

"A description of the discoveries then made has been printed by the Rev. S. M. Mayhew, F.S.A., in the *Journal of the British Archæological Association*, vol. xxxvi, and Mr. C. Roach Smith, in his *Collectanea Antiqua*, vol. vii, p. 23. It was subsequently suggested that, in order thoroughly to explore and ascertain the full extent and nature of the buildings, excavations should be started on the adjoining land belonging to Lady Oglander. Upon the introduction of our esteemed colleague, Mr. Roach Smith, himself a native of the island, and his relative, F. Roach, Esq., of Arreton, Lady Oglander most kindly accorded the permission required. The co-operation was also obtained of Mr. Micah Cooper, the present tenant, and arrangements made; the work commencing in August last, was, with brief interruptions, continued to the present time.

"The chambers traced are laid down upon the accompanying ground plan, reduced from an accurate drawing prepared to scale by Mr. W. R. J. Cornewall Jones of Ryde. Their positions indicate how much has yet to be excavated ere any notion of the extent or purpose of the building can be properly obtained ; we have, therefore, abstained from theorising as to the objects of the various chambers, or from allotting any names to them, as it would be premature until further explorations have revealed the whole building. A number has been affixed to each chamber corresponding with the plan. The rooms numbered from 1 to 5, together with parts of 6, 7, and 8, are upon the

property of Mrs. Munns, and are divided from that of Lady.
Oglander by the hedge. These were excavated by Captain
Thorp of Yarbridge, in April last, and we are indebted to
him for the list of antiquities then discovered."

The period indicated by the coins found in this extensive villa recall several passages in Roman history which
bear upon our own. From the time when Septimius
Severus and his wife went up to check the invasions of
Roman Britain by the Caledonii, the lords of the forest,
and the Mæatæ, the dwellers in the plains, to the reign of
Aurelian, and even as late as Constantine, the worship of
the sun under the oriental form of Mithras in a cave, with
its Persian rites and self-denying initiations, seems to have
engaged the minds of men in North Britain as elsewhere ;
and perhaps before this time, as it prevailed in Rome as
early as the reign of Trajan. Mithraic worship was imported into Alexandria under the name of Serapis, where
the magnificent temple to the god was considered one of
the wonders of the world. The same form was introduced,
under the simple name of Helios, into Palmyra, a city
which had been restored by Hadrian, and whose citizens
were proud to call their city after him, Hadrianopolis,[1]
instead of Tadmor in the Desert (the City of Palms). The
same divinity was recognised as Baal at Baalbec, where
that famous Temple of the Sun was erected which gave the
name of Heliopolis to the city situated at the foot of the
Antilibanus, on the road between Tyre and Palmyra. This
latter great city, placed half-way between commercial Tyre,
on the coast of the Levant, and the head of the Persian
Gulf, was enriched by the important traffic of the east with
the western world ; and it was the interest of the Romans
that it should be carried on by this route through Palmyra
rather than by the Black Sea, and through Greece. The

[1] Stephanus Byzantinus.

palm-tree grew luxuriantly in this oasis of the Arabian
Desert, and gave its name to the city whose Corinthian
columns (some standing *in situ*, and others strewing the
ground) recall the favourite architecture of the Romans in
the age of the Antonines. The traveller of the present day
wanders with astonishment amidst the columns, the pedestals, and ruined walls of the Temple of the Sun, which
stand among Christian churches, Turkish mosques, sepul-
chres, and the mud huts of the miserable villagers who now
dwell there.

The historical episode of the reign of Queen Zenobia,
who defied the whole power of Rome from this her capital
city, first in union with her husband, and after his death
on her own responsibility, threw a lustre upon the brief
reign of the Emperor Aurelian, A.D. 270-275. It will
be remembered that he put an end to the Gothic war
by surrendering the Dacian conquests of Trajan north of
the Danube, fixing that river as the boundary southward
of the Gothic kingdom. He chastised and repelled the
Marcomanni, who had invaded Italy; and what is specially interesting to us, he recovered Gaul, Spain, and Britain
out of the hands of Tetricus, whose copper coins are so
numerous in this country. After this, turning his arms to
the east, he set about subduing the determined and powerful Zenobia, and defeated her two armies in the battles of
Emesa and Palmyra. The Queen fled on a dromedary as
far as the river Euphrates, but was captured by the light
cavalry of the Emperor Aurelian. The triumph at Rome
followed, and the captive Zenobia, in fetters of gold, and
the ex-Emperor Tetricus and his son, had to march in the
procession of the exultant conqueror, who rode up to the
Capitol in a chariot drawn by four stags which had belonged
to one of the German kings.

Tetricus had been instigated to assume the purple, and

his son the title of Cæsar in Gaul, by Victoria, mother of the deceased Victorinus ; this lady having been hailed by the soldiery with the Imperial appellation, "Mother of the Camps" (*Mater Castrorum*), but she did not long survive the honour.

Tetricus and his son, after being led captive in triumph, were promoted to high positions by Aurelian, whose conscience smote him for thus ill-treating noble and highly gifted Romans. He not only permitted Tetricus to live, but gave him the governorship of all Italy, calling him often his colleague, sometimes his fellow-soldier, and at others *imperator*. Trebellius Pollio relates that, in his time, the house of the Tetrici, father and son, was still extant on the Cœlian Hill, between the two groves. It was a fine building ; in it Aurelian was depicted, *in mosaic* work, giving to both of them the *prætexta*, a mark of senatorial dignity, and receiving from them a civic crown. At the dedication of this house the two Tetrici are said to have invited Aurelian himself to be their guest.

A new fact of history connected with the Tetrici has lately come to light by the discovery, in May 1879, of an inscribed stone, excavated on the Place Lavalette, within the citadel of Grenoble. It is engraved in bold but not deeply cut letters, on a stone which appears to have formed the pedestal of a statue. The dedication is to Claudius Gothicus, who was proclaimed emperor under the walls of Milan about the 20th March, A.D. 268. On his election he found civil war raging in various parts of the empire. Aureolus had been acknowledged emperor at Milan by the troops, and Tetricus, Governor of Aquitaine, had accepted the sovereignty of Gaul and of Spain, after the death of Marius in 268. soon after the death of Gallienus. Claudius. having defeated the Allemanni on the shores of Lake Garda, marched against Aureolus, who was defeated and killed.

The inscription is referable to the year 269, corresponding to the second year of the Tribuniciate and of the Consulate, and seems connected with an expedition directed against Tetricus. The presence at Grenoble of the prefect of the municipal guards of Rome and of a corps of the Imperial guard show that the troops quartered in the town had been detached from the garrison at Rome.

Claudius, however, had not time to put this project in execution, for the Goths had invaded the empire, notwithstanding their recent defeats. He said, "The war with Tetricus was his own affair; that with the Goths was in the interest of the public, and therefore it was his duty to prefer the latter." The detachment at Grenoble, then under the command of Placidianus, was no doubt stationed there to watch Tetricus and prevent him from throwing himself upon Italy during this war. Grenoble was on the direct road from Vienne to the Cottian Alps.

The inscription shows also that Grenoble and the Narbonnese, or at least a part important enough to be called the Narbonnese Province, obeyed the Emperor Claudius, at a time when Tetricus ruled over the rest of Gaul.

Claudius died in the year 270, at the age of fifty-six years. The inscription is preserved in the epigraphic museum of Grenoble. The text is as follows :

IMP . CAESARI
M . AVR . CLAVDIO
PIO . FELICI . INVICTO
AVG . GERMANICO
MAX . P . M . TRIB . POTES
TATIS . II . COS . PATRI . PA .
TRIAE . PROC . VEXIL .
LATIONES . ADQVE

EQVITES . ITEMQVE
PRAEPOSITI[1] . ET . DVCE
NARI . PROTECT . TEN
DENTES . IN . NARB
PROV . SVB . CVRA . IVL .
PLACIDIANI . V . P . PRAE
FECT . VIGIL . DEVOTI
NVMINI . MAIESTA
TIQVE . EIVS .

[1] The officers of the Prætorian cohorts bore the names of *Centenarii*, *Ducenarii*, and *Trecenarii*, representing the pay of 100,000, 200,000, and 300,000 sesterces, or £800, £1,600, and £2,400 a year.

"To the Emperor Cæsar Marcus Aurelius, Claudius, the dutiful, fortunate, invincible Augustus, Germanicus, Maximus, Pontifex Maximus, the second time invested with the Tribuniciate, Consul, father of his country, Proconsul.[1]

"The detachments and cavalry, as well as their commanders and tribunes of the Prætorian cohorts of 200,000 sesterces quartered in the Narbonnese Province (have erected this statue) under the care of Julius Placidianus, most perfect personage, Præfect of the municipal guards, devoted to the divinity and the majesty of the Emperor."

I am indebted for the whole of this account to the description read by M. Florian Vallentin at the Congress of the Society of French Archæology, held at Vienne in 1879, and the references he has given in the notes.

Another curious inscription found at Grenoble again introduces us to this Julius Placidianus, who had then attained the rank of Prætorian Præfect.

IGNIBVS

AETERNIS . IVL

PLACIDIANVS

V . C . PRAEF . PRAE

TORI

EX VOTO POSVIT[2]

He became Consul in 273, and was the colleague of Tacitus, who was proclaimed Emperor in 275.

Besides the suggestions offered by the coins found in this villa, the Bacchanalian subjects in the large dining-hall call to mind the question of the cultivation of the vine in Britain. Domitian, besides banishing the astronomers, or mathematicians, as they were called, from Rome, though

---

[1] V. Allmer, *Insc. Antiques de Vienne*, p. 384. *Rev. Arch.*, Août 1879, p. 120. *Bull. Mon.*, 1879, pp. 432, 539.

[2] Long, *Antiq. Rom. du Pays des Vocontiens*, p. 183. Florian Vallentin, *Divinités "Indigètes" du Vocontium*, p. 67.

they seem to have been allowed to talk freely enough in the suburban villas, is said to have forbidden the cultivation of the vine in the Ionian provinces, and even to have caused the vineyards already planted to be rooted up.

Dr. Merivale seems to consider the story, reported only on the authority of Philostratus, in his life of Apollonius, as weak in evidence. He says[1] : "It seems more likely that the edict referred to was part of a general measure, such as that indicated by Suetonius, by which the Emperor, alarmed at the increasing dearth of corn and cheapness of wine, prohibited the withdrawal of arable land from the plough in Italy, and restricted the cultivation of the vine throughout the provinces to one-half, at most, of the extent to which it had been developed. The culture of the vine continued, however, to depend on the favour of the Government." Thus we read, at a later period, of the Emperor Probus granting such an indulgence to certain of the northern provinces,[2] to Britain among the number. He also employed the soldiers to plant new vines on the slopes of Mounts Alma and Aureus, near the Danube, in Illyricum and Mæsia.[3]

It would be interesting if Messrs. Price, in their future excavations to the foundations of this villa and its outworks, were to come upon any sockets for upright stones or posts to support the trellis-work for vines, as used in the south of Europe, or other arrangements for their culture in the form of vineyards. The aspect and locality is favourable to the growth of the vine, which was encouraged in

---

[1] *History of the Romans under the Empire*, by Charles Merivale, B.D., vol. vii, p. 139.

[2] Vopiscus, in *Probo.*, 18. "Gallis omnibus et Hispanis et Britannis hic permisit ut vites haberent, vinumque conficerent."

[3] *Ibid.* "Ipse Almam montem in Illyrico circa Sirmium militari manu fossum, lecta vite conservit, *ubi passim.*"

later ages in the monasteries often built on the sites of Roman villas.

HANTS AND THE ISLE OF WIGHT.

MORTON, between Sandown and Brading.[1]

The walls of a villa here were first discovered in 1880. One portion of the building has been since excavated and twelve rooms laid open, some of which display a beautiful series of mosaics, that is, the rooms numbered 3, 6, 9, and 12 in Messrs. Price's plan.

No. 3 was first uncovered, which lies on the south side of the building; adjoining this, and running up towards the north, is a long gallery, numbered 6 in the plan, in the centre of which is Orpheus, and on each side of the square containing this figure the pavement is filled up with chequers of large red and white *tesseræ*.

Further north, at the end of this gallery, is a long chamber running east and west, or nearly so, for the walls do not run at the exact points of the compass, but these points are named to facilitate the description.

9.—Chamber No. 3 measures 15½ ft. by 17½ ft.; the space containing the mosaic measures 9½ ft. by 10½ ft., and in the centre is a female head, a staff or *stemma* leaning upon her left shoulder. The angles of the outer square are cut off by quarter-circles, on one of which, that on the north-western side, is a head, perhaps one of the seasons. The subjects of the other three angles cannot be distinguished, by reason of decay, and between these are panels, on which three subjects are depicted, that to the east being totally destroyed.

---

[1] *Brit. Arch. Assoc. Journal*, xxxvi, p. 363. *Guide to Villa*, by Jno. E. Price, F.S.A., and F. G. Hilton Price, F.S.A., F.G.S., 1881. *Antiquary*, Jan. 1881, — Nicholson, F.S.A. C. R. Smith, *Collectanea Antiqua*, vii.

BRADING (Room No. 3, on Mr. Price's Plan).

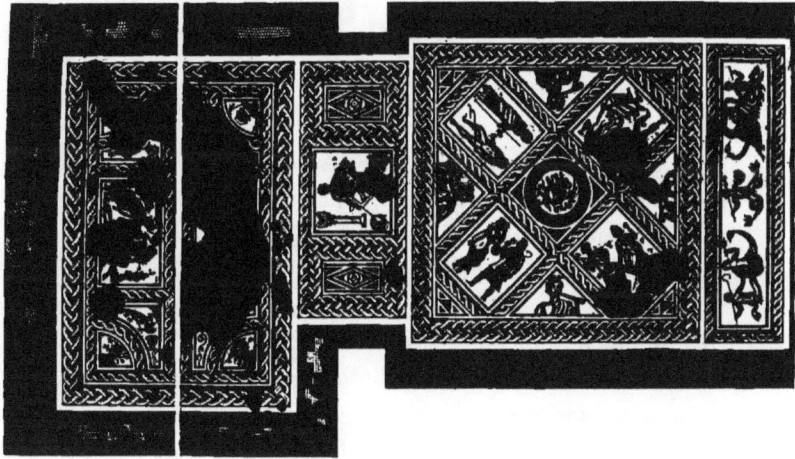

On the western side are two gladiators. One has a trident and net; the other is engaged in combat with him; but the figure is in great part destroyed. On the south side the panel is very perfect, and represents a man with the head and wattles of a cock, and with the legs of the same animal armed with long spurs. He is dressed in a tunic, with a wand in hand, and stands in front of a house with ladder of four steps leading up to it.

On the right hand of the building are two animals like panthers, moving in opposite directions, and they are each furnished with a pair of wings. On the north side is a fox under a tree, probably a grape vine. In the centre of the picture is a house with a cupola, perhaps a wine-press; the rest is destroyed.

10.—The colonnade or corridor, No. 6, extends from the margin of No. 3 to the step leading into the Medusa room, No. 12; the whole length is fifty feet. It is probable this corridor included the room No. 3, just described, as no wall had been discovered between them. In this case the whole length would be 65½ feet.

From the margin of the ornamental pavement of No. 3 to the commencement of the guilloche border is twenty-one feet; then occurs the figure of Orpheus, seated, wearing a red Phrygian cap and playing a lyre, by which he is attracting several animals, that is, a monkey, a coote or other bird, a fox, and a peacock.

Coins have been found here of Gallienus and Salonina, A.D. 253 to 268; Victorinus, 265 to 267; and Tetricus, 267 to 272. The paintings on the broken pieces of stucco, which once adorned the walls, lie about in great profusion; and on one of the pieces is a bird of the parrot species, well drawn, and the colours perfectly preserved.

11.—The large room, No. 12, measures 39 ft. 6 in. from east to west, by 19 ft. in the western portion; 15½ ft. in the eastern portion, and 11 ft. between the piers in the centre. The pavements in this room are of great beauty; that at the west end is almost square, its dimensions being 13 ft. 6 in. by 13 ft. 10 in., divided into compartments edged with guilloches in half-inch *tesseræ* of white, black, and red. The design may be described as consisting of a central circle within a square. The corners are marked off by a quarter-circle within a square, and between these figures are four oblong panels, on one only of which can the subject of the mosaic be deciphered; the others are destroyed. This subject consists of two figures, seated; the one holding up in right hand a human head, and in the left the weapon with which the head was severed; the other figure is nude, and seated; the mosaic is in dark brown and other *tesseræ*. At the feet of the figures is an indication of some object associated with the myth. In the corners are the seasons; that at the north-west corner alone being missing. Spring appears at the south-west corner, a female head decked with poppies, typical, perhaps, of Juno, as in the spandril of the circle is a peacock with flowing tail, the plumage beautifully worked in many colours, and pecking at a vase. In another corner is a female head, decorated with ears of corn, in illustration of Ceres and summer; she wears a torque round her neck. The last is winter, the most perfect of all; a female head, closely wrapped; her garment fastened across the left shoulder by a fibula; and attached to the dress is a *cucullus*, or hood, giving to the figure somewhat the appearance of a nun. In the left hand she carries a leafless bough, from which is suspended a dead bird.

Between the stone piers in the centre of the room, and dividing the two pavements, is a square panel in the centre, containing a male figure wearing a black beard, seated in what appears to be a chair; he is semi-nude, there being little drapery except at the lower part of the figure. At the left side stands a pillar, surmounted by an armillary sphere, the degrees corresponding with the number of the signs of the zodiac. Beneath this pillar is a globe, supported on three legs. The *tesserœ* are so arranged as to define four quarters of the earth. At his right hand is a bowl, in which is a point or pen, not yet identified with certainty ; this may be the gnomon of a horologium or sundial.

This illustration of an astronomer in the exercise of his profession is one of the most interesting yet revealed. The figure may perhaps be intended for Hipparchus, whose observations, made between 160 and 125 B.C., resulted in a catalogue of the fixed stars, which has been preserved by Ptolemy.

On each side of this panel is a geometrical pattern, composed of a centre with a circle, from which radiate four divisions, enclosed within a large circle ; this is again placed within a diamond or lozenge-shaped figure, the whole being contained in a parallelogram, in the angles of which are figures of triangles. The border, as in other cases, consists of the guilloche pattern.

The eastern division of this chamber contains the largest and most important of the mosaics yet discovered. In the centre is a large medallion, containing a Gorgon's head with head-dress of snakes. Springing from the centre are four compartments, arranged cross-wise, each bordered by the guilloche pattern. At the angles north, south, east, and west are triangular compartments, illustrating female heads wearing the petasus of Mercury. Over their left shoulders is a *pallium*, or other form of cloak, and each blows a horn.

The four oblong panels contain in each a male and female figure, but Messrs. Price have reserved the explanation of the figures for the present.

On the south-west panel, the female figure, dressed

after the manner of dancing girls of Greece or Italy, is
playing the *tympanum*, or tambourine, with right hand, and
the feet are crossed as in the act of dancing. The male
figure holds an object resembling the Pandean pipe in right
hand, and a crook in his left. Messrs. Price point out the
peculiarity of his costume. He wears a Phrygian cap, a
skirted tunic, with small cloak fastened on right shoulder,
and wearing *braccæ* or trousers, and *calceus*, or boot or
shoe, beneath.

On the north-west, the female figure is tall and closely
draped, bearing in one hand a staff, and in the other ears
of corn, which she is presenting to a man who, though perfectly nude, holds by the left hand the *bura* or *buris*, the
hinder part of the ancient plough.

On the north-east, a male figure, upper part destroyed,
pursues a nymph who is flying, and appears to have had
the upper part of her drapery torn from her back.

On the south-east, a nude male figure carries on right
shoulder a double-headed axe ; the female figure is draped,
and the attitude easy and elegant. The eastern end of
this beautiful mosaic is finished by an oblong panel containing two large marine deities, on each of whose scaly
backs sits a woman.

Outside the pictured pavement, extending to the wall,
is a paving of one-inch red *tesseræ*, adorned with a fret
pattern in white ; and at the west end, in the same colour,
is a semicircle enclosing a labyrinth fret.

The chamber No. 9 contains a geometrical pattern,
being a diamond within a square.

Examples of the following coins were found :—Alexander Severus, A.D. 222-235 ; Decius, 249-251 ; Gallienus,
253-268 ; Salonina, wife of Gallienus. Victorinus, 265-267 ;
Tetricus, 267-272 ; Claudius Gothicus, 268-270 ; Allectus,
293-297 ; Constans, 333-350 ; Magnentius, 350-353.

The interpretation of these mosaics at Morton by the author of the present work has been given at length in chapter iii, which he will supplement by drawing attention to the monkey in the Orpheus group, occupying the centre of the long corridor.

Ennius, in a line quoted by Cicero, says, " Simia quam similis turpissima bestia nobis." The poet, in acknowledging the monkey's resemblance to man, might have spared the epithet, which the poor beast hardly deserves.

Before taking leave of the Orphic and Bacchic myths, it will not be out of place to mention a discovery lately made in Rome of a *hypogeum*, forming the family vault of the Licinian family, a short distance outside the old Porta Collina, on the Appian way. One of the *sarcophagi*, out of seven discovered therein, had the emblems of Bacchus sculptured upon its marble front. The ashes of the young Piso Licinianus were placed in this vault after his murder, by order of the Emperor Otho, in the forum ; hurried out of this life in the midst of the *serta*, *unguenta*, *puellas*, and all the joys of a luxurious capital. " Per il corpo di Bacco", is still the familiar oath of the modern Italian ; eighteen hundred years have not sufficed to extinguish an expression on the lips long after the idea has died out in the mind.

CARISBROOK, *Isle of Wight.*

A pavement was discovered a few years before 1868, at Carisbrook, by Mr. William Spickernell.[1]

12.—On right or north of hall is room with chess-board pavement, in red and white *tessellæ*, 22 ft. square.

13.—In another room was a mosaic of half-inch cubes, in red, white, black, yellow, and blue; the rest is of coarse red and white *tesseræ*, formed of tile and calcareous stone.

[1] C. Roach Smith, *Collectanea Antiqua*, vol. v, plates xviii and xix.

There is a square in centre, enclosing cantharus and lilies, not unlike those found under the Excise office in London.[1]

GURNARD BAY, *Isle of Wight.*

14.—In a villa discovered by Mr. E. J. Smith, in 1864, tesselated pavements were found in two rooms, 15 ft. long by 9 ft. 9 in. broad; no pattern, but composed apparently of small square pieces of broken tile. Coins found: Vespasian, Faustina Major, Valens, Gratian or Valentinian, Maximus, with the *rev.* PAX AVG. Also some Greek coins.[2]

[1] See *Illustrations of Roman London*, pl. VI.
[2] *Brit. Arch. Assoc. Journal*, xxii, p. 351.

CHAPTER XVI.

IN the *Roman Gallery* of the British Museum, on the ground-floor, placed against the wall, are the following specimens of pavements found in Britain, which have been described in the previous pages. On the south wall, in compartments I, II, and III, are five pieces from Withington, Gloucestershire, and one fragment from the Woodchester pavement. On the north wall, in compartments VII and VIII, are mosaics found in Threadneedle Street, and in compartment IX that found at the Bank of England. In compartments X, XI, and XII are mosaics from Abbot's Ann, in Hampshire ; and in the *Roman Gallery*, on the *first-floor*, is a square piece discovered on the site of the old India House in Leadenhall Street, in 1803, on which is represented Dionysus or Bacchus on his tiger or panther, the figure nude, except where concealed by the folds of a *chlamys*, loosely thrown over the animal and thigh of the god, who wears *cothurni* on feet, and holds a *narthex* in left hand. The head is adorned with vine-leaves. This picture occupies a circle in the centre. The squares afford good typical examples of borders, the plain guilloche knot, the double-braided guilloche, the spiral, and the axe-head ; the spandrils between the circle and the square are filled by two *canthari* and a foliated axe-head ornament. This has been more particularly described in chap. xii, p. 179.

I I

Having now concluded my review of Romano-British mosaics, it will assist the study of their designs, their chronology, and their origin, if we penetrate into the lower recesses of the British Museum, where, in the *Græco-Roman Basement* with *Annex*, are brought together some of the finest specimens from Asia Minor and from North Africa which have ever been removed from the floors where they were first laid down. It is proposed in this chapter to offer some general remarks upon these pavements, and to illustrate them from the works of authors who have described them as they were found *in situ;* and in the next chapter to give a more particular account of them in their present position in the Museum.

The first object which strikes the sight, on descending the staircase, is the gigantic head of a marine deity, generally supposed to be Glaucus, which is placed against the eastern wall, at the end of a long gallery. This mosaic was brought from Carthage, and presented to the British Museum by Mr. Hudson-Gurney in 1844.[1] It will be seen, by the admirable skill of the artist, in reproducing a copy of the mosaic in its original colours, by way of frontispiece to this chapter, how appropriate to Roman Carthage ruling the seas was this emblematic head, and so may it be taken to symbolise Britannia's rule of the waves in our day, and to harmonise with our Romano-British mosaics. Glaucus is addressed by Bacchus, in the *Dionysiaca*,[2] as the broad-chinned descendant of Neptune, and a neighbour of his own in Bœotia : the birthplace of Glaucus being Anthedon, on the Aonian coast, not far from the Cadmean city of Thebes. The flowery plain of Anthedon was on the coast of the channel of Eubœa, on which Aulis was situated, from whence, in the dawn of Grecian history, the ship *Argo*

---

[1] It has been figured and described in the *Monuments of the Roman Institute*, vol. v, p. 38.   [2] xxxix, 99.

sailed for the Black Sea and to Colchis, at its far eastern
extremity. Here, too, the more important fleet of ships
assembled when—

"—— erst the princes twain went forth the war to wage,
And marching on with glitt'ring spear, and with avenging brand,
They led the flower of Grecia's youth against the Trojan land."[1]

How well the epithet εὐρυγένειον, broad-chinned, suits the
head on the mosaic ! how well the lower part of the face is
expanded to suit the description ; the flowing seaweed
taking the place of a beard when its human wearer was
transformed into an immortal. The pleasing smile is put
on as when he paid his addresses to the nymph Scylla, who
viewed him in astonishment after his metamorphose, though
with the same stone-like coolness she had shown towards
him before. His story, as related by Ovid,[2] is amusing.

A fisherman and a mortal, he was sitting on a bank
overlooking the Eubœic Sea, mending his rods and lines and
nets. A basket of fish lately caught was placed on the
sward by his side, when he was suddenly surprised by the
vivification of the fish, which he thought dead. They first
jumped about and then made a dart for their native element,
into which they plunged. Glaucus attributed something
magical to the sedgy grass, and began tasting some to try,
when lo ! he suddenly plunged into the water like the
fishes, and his whole nature was changed ; he cared no
more for the flowery meads, or the other delights of the
land, but his tastes became all aquatic. The sea-gods
poured a hundred streams upon his head, which quite
altered his nature. The flowing locks and beard assumed a
sea-green colour, intermixed with rusty-brown seaweed ;
and the marine deities, after this shower-bath, were glad to
welcome him among their crew.

[1] *Agamemnon* of Æschylus, translated by the Earl of Carnarvon.
Murray, 1879.   [2] *Metamorph.*, xiii, 900, *et seqq.*

The mountains at the back of Anthedon, and the country of Bœotia in general, smiled in the purple hues of ancient legends and stories. Mount Cithæron was famous for beasts of the chase, and as the spot where Actæon was changed into a stag, and where Œdipus in his cradle was exposed, that great architype of Greek tragic catastrophes. Here, also, the mystic orgies of Bacchus were held.

> " Thyias, ubi audito stimulant trieterica Baccho
> Orgia, nocturnusque vocat clamore Cithæron."[1]

Orchomenus was the city of the Graces, and where the river Cephisus runs into the lake of Copais. It was famous also as having been ruled over by the unfortunate sons of Œdipus. Mount Helicon is not far off, rendered classical as the abode of the Muses, and the wooded country around it where Itys, changed into a swallow, listened to Philomela, her sister, who, under the form of a nightingale, poured forth in plaintive melodies the sad tale of their mutual wrongs.[2]

> "Sola virum non ulta piè mœstissima mater
> Concinit Ismarium Daulias ales Itym."[3]

Claudian compliments Mallius Theodorus on the delight the Aonian woods would derive on hearing of his consul-ship, and how—

> "Concinuit felix Helicon, fluxitque Aganippe
> Largior, et docti riserunt floribus amnes."[4]

Sailors are proverbially superstitious, and Glaucus came to be looked upon by them as a prodigy and a prophet. His oracles were esteemed as infallible as are, in more scientific days, the forecasts of the weather in our daily journals. Once a year he was supposed to visit, with his marine

---

[1] Virgil, *Æn.*, iv.
[2] The swallow, often seen on the mosaics in connection with spring, has probably reference to this fable. [3] Ovid, *Epist.*, xv.
[4] Claudian, *De F. M. Theodor. Cons.*, 271-3.

assemblage, every part of the sea-coast, where his oracles were delivered, and it is difficult to say when they finally ceased.[1] A sailor saved from drowning would offer to Glaucus a lock of his hair.[2]

A strange affection for the human race is assigned to dolphins by the ancients, and they were said to save men from drowning by conveying them ashore on their backs, as was done in the case of Arion, the musician, when shipwrecked in company of Bacchus. The sailors on board mutinied to rob the singer of his gold and silver; Bacchus changed them all into dolphins, and one saved Arion, the musician and dithyrambic poet, by swimming with him ashore and landing him at Tænarus.

A mosaic, pictured with a triton and dolphin carrying a trident, was brought over by Mr. Wood from the temple of Ephesus in 1872, and another, representing fishermen in a boat, are two examples from Utica.

With the exception of the foregoing, all the mosaics placed here were brought either from Carthage or Halicarnassus. The former have been described by the Rev. Nathan Davis, in his work on the excavations made there by him in 1856-58; and the latter from *Halicarnassus in Caria*, by C. T. Newton, M.A. (assisted by R. P. Pullan, F.R.I.B.A.), from whose work on the discoveries there in 1856, as well as at Cnidus and Branchidæ (2 vols., 8vo.,

---

[1] Pausanias, ix, 22.

[2] As Lucillius, in the *Anthologia*, who had nothing else left to offer.

"Γλαύκῳ, καὶ Νηρῆϊ, καὶ Ἰνοῖ καὶ Μελικέρτῃ,
καὶ βυθίῳ Κρονίῃ, καὶ Σαμόθρᾳξι Θεοῖς,
σωθεὶς ἐκ πελάγους Λουκίλλιος ὧδε κέκαρμαι,
τὰς τρίχας ἐκ κεφαλήν· ἄλλο γὰρ οὐδὲν ἔχω."

Ino is the heroine, mentioned in the early part of this work, who nursed the infant Bacchus. Melicerte was her son.

plates, fol., 1862), I will extract some of the descriptions.[1]

The whole history of the mosaics from Carthage, as well as that of the country whence they came, has been summarised and explained by Augustus Wollaston Franks, M.A., late Director of the Society of Antiquaries, in *Archæologia*, xxxviii, in which the descriptions are very complete, and with numerous references to ancient authorities in support of the text. Mr. Franks, in calling to mind that the province of North Africa became the "celebrated centre of Christianity, illustrious by her bishops and consecrated by her martyrs", brings down its history to the times of St. Louis, King of France, when the unfortunate result of a crusade caused him to seek an asylum, and his death, at Carthage, six centuries after the Arabs, under Hassan, had destroyed the Roman city of Carthage, in A.D. 647. Near to the hill where the chapel of St. Louis now stands were found buried some of these precious mosaics, the works of the successors of the Roman conquerors of Carthage, and " near the village of Malkah, built on the ruins of the great cistern which supplied Carthage with water".

On comparing these mosaics with those found in England, though the workmanship shows various degrees of merit, both in the English as well as in the foreign examples, we find the realms of the sea to be a favourite subject in all, this being a theme no less congenial to the seafaring nation of the Carthaginians and the piratical merchants of the Ægean seaboard than it was to the islanders of Britain.

---

[1] In a very large, thick volume, in the MS. department of the British Museum, No. 31,980, are preserved the original photographs, among which may be seen, not only some of the mosaics and antiquities in detail which have not been brought over, but also views of the towns, sea-coast, and scenery of this most interesting locality.

HUNTING SCENE, FROM A DISH.

Gardens, flowers, and fountains were the natural result of wealth and the pleasures of ease and retirement, after the struggles and bitter distresses of the sea.

"*μετ' ἄεθλα, μετ' ἄλγεα πικρὰ θαλάσσης.*"

The scene on one of the pavements is a garden, wherein are three large flower-pots, and the words "FONTES, No. 49."

The chase of wild beasts has always been an engrossing amusement in all ages, as shown not only on mosaics, but on the Samian ware and sculpture of the Romans, whether in Asia, Africa, or elsewhere. On one of these mosaics, among other animals, is seen the ostrich, essentially the bird of Africa; and in another is a stag held by a thong fastened round his neck, of which a horseman holds the other end in his right hand. The antlers of this animal would cause a difficulty in catching him in this manner by a lasso: might not this represent a tame animal driven as a decoy, or kept for the purpose of being hunted?

A scene, No. 65 of the Museum Catalogue, is figured to illustrate this chapter, and shows the mode of catching wild animals in nets. Two boats with figures in each hold the ends of a net, placed around on the shore in a circle for the purpose of catching a number of wild animals, when the ends of the net are drawn together. The animals are frightened by means of brushes of many-coloured feathers, and thus become entangled in the meshes of the net. Ovid describes this kind of sport—

> " Retia cum pedicis, laqueosque, artesque dolosas
> Tollite; nec volucrem viscatâ fallite virgâ;
> Nec formidatis cervos eludite pinnis,
> Nec celate cibis uncos fallacibus hamos.'[1]

The *viscata virga* is seen catching a bird. The last line may be applied to the fishermen, as seen on another picture

---

[1] Ovid, *Metamorph.*, xv, 473, *et seqq.*

from Utica, No. 66, Mus. Cat. The basket of fish upset,
No. 52, is perhaps intended to represent the fishes in the
episode of Glaucus—

> " —— quos aut in retia casus
> Aut sua credulitas in aduncos egerat hamos"[1]—

and the flowers or fruit in the basket, the delights of the
land he had left.

There are two personal scenes, connected with hunting,
described on these mosaics, which are of especial interest
because the names are written over each figure, that is—

1st, *Meleager* and *Atalanta*. They are hunting, as
was their wont; though this does not seem to be the episode
of the Calydonian boar, for which they are famous, sent
against Meleager by Diana, in punishment for his neglect-
ing to offer to the goddess first-fruits, which were her due.
He was assisted by Atalanta, the virgin daughter of Iasius,
King of Arcadia, who gave the savage animal the first
wound, and Meleager, then despatching the beast, presented the fair huntress with the skin which she so well
deserved.

2nd, *Dido* and *Æneas*. How they came to hunt
together requires explanation, especially as Homer says
that Æneas never left Troy; however, let us not deny the
Romans their pedigree and pleasing vision of being descended from Æneas and Venus. The divine Julius, if he
did not in his heart believe a direct descent from Iulus,
was at least desirous that the illusion should be kept up;
and the artist on these mosaics acts up to the popular
belief that Æneas and Dido were contemporaneous, and,
therefore, would naturally engage in the favourite pastime
of hunting together when they met in the newly founded
Tyrian colony of Carthage.

---

[1] Ovid, *Metamorph.*, xiii, 933-4.

FISH FALLING FROM A BASKET, AND BASKET OF FRUIT

See Clup. xviii. and Brit. Mus Cut. No 3

AMPHITRITE AND TRITONS. FROM *HALICARNASSUS*.

"Venatum Æneas unaque miserrima Dido
In nemus ire parant."[1]

And again—

"Virginibus Tyriis mos est gestare pharetram,
Purpureoque alte suras vincire cothurno."[2]

We give an illustration of the myth of *Dionysus*, with his name over, and *panther*, No. 20; and another, coarsely executed, of *Europa* and the *Bull*, No. 19.

The subject of the seasons is well represented in that beautiful specimen from Carthage described by Mr. Franks, of which, however, we have only fragments, but he has furnished a plan of the whole design, once twenty-eight feet square.

The three months of March, April, July, and a portion of November, represented by figures and adjuncts, are all that remain out of twelve, and two only of the busts of the seasons, that is, Spring and Summer. The geometrical designs and borders are of great beauty and variety.

As a specimen of geometrical work, and at the same time of a clear and elegant design, that very large piece of mosaic brought from Halicarnassus holds a prominent place. It is no less than 40 ft. long by 12 ft. wide, and is an extraordinary example of chaste design, as well as of skill in Mr. Newton for bringing over from Halicarnassus so large a piece of ancient workmanship, which looks as fresh and perfect as when it left the Roman artist's hands.

Amphitrite and her attendants, on the upper part of this large pavement, are very well shown in our artist's coloured representation, but a portion only of the lower part is

---

[1] Vir., *Æn.*, iv, 117-8.
[2] *Ibid.*, lib. i, 336-7.

K K

reproduced, the borders being continuous. The break is shown on the Plate.

The lettered inscriptions on some of the foreign mosaics are interesting, because such are rare, and describe the figures represented, which thus admit of no misinterpretation, and five are especially remarkable, to which I will direct attention.

Three female heads, described in letters over each as *Alexandria, Halicarnassus,* and *Berytus,* the juxtaposition of these three great cities indicating some league or treaty between them.

The fourth of these lettered mosaics, to which I shall refer, has six words in Greek, equivalent in English to *Health, Life, Grace, Peace, Cheerfulness, Hope,* which seem to be coupled together as indicative of healthy life, graceful peace, and cheerful hope. This is from Halicarnassus, and it appears the building, of which it was the floor, was constructed out of the materials of an earlier building on the same site, and underneath the pavement of one of the rooms was found the statue of a winged female figure, in two pieces. After these preliminary observations upon the foreign mosaics, I will proceed to give more in detail the descriptions of those from Carthage and Halicarnassus, as furnished by the authors before referred to.

CARTHAGE.[1]—Hunting scene, No. 47, as well as another of a boar and dog, should be noted; and two dolphins with trident between them, No. 53; Victory, holding up a votive tablet, a fragment 7 ft. by 4 ft. Inscription in white letters on red ground; below the inscription are two youths, holding in right hand wreaths, and in left fans with long handles. This was found close to the seaside, at the foot of the slopes under Sidi Bou-Said, at

---

[1] See *Archæologia,* xxxviii, pp. 202-30.

the depth of four feet from the surface. The right-hand portion only remained of the following inscription :

```
............................NC FVNDAMENTA
.........................TEM DEDICAVIMVS
..............TIBIDETE—AMICI FLOREN
............DEVM INVOCANTEM—QVI
........................VIT GAVDENTES—
...................DOMINVS TE EXALTA
.................—FASTILANEM IN MIN
...............CONSVMMAVIT GAVDENS
...................E  M  T  E  M
```

"*Fastilanem* may be connected", says Mr. Franks, "with *fastella*, which Ducange explains as *ligamen* ;" No. 44.

The meaning of the inscription, being fragmentary, is "far from clear", says Mr. Franks; and he adds, "The style of art shown in this mosaic and the character of the inscription seem to belong to the fourth century after Christ."

Mosaic No. 52, found in a bean-field to the east of the hill of St. Louis, representing a basket of fish and panier filled with fruit; these designs are executed in very vivid colours ; some of the *tesseræ* are of glass ; round it is a wave pattern. Ornamental fountains (FONTES), No. 49.

Among the finest found by Mr. Davis at Carthage was a sea-piece with dolphins, tritons, and sea nymphs, No. 45 ; the remainder is ornamented with square panels containing female busts, and separated from each other by a delicate framework of leaves. The general effect is very pleasing. It has many *tesseræ* of coloured glass; it does not seem of early date; No. 45. Two deer drinking at a fountain; No. 50.

The pavements from Carthage were found at seven different spots; one of the most interesting is a square, originally of 28 feet, illustrative of the seasons and months, of which only two portions are preserved, described by Mr. Franks as now a square of 23 feet, having on each of its sides an oblong compartment, representing twining plants growing out of golden vases. In the middle of each there has been a circle containing a cruciform pattern. To one of the other sides of the square are attached small compartments, separated from each other by spaces, where the mosaic has either been destroyed or has never existed. The spaces were probably for columns and pilasters. The edge of square is ornamented with riband pattern, and at each corner is a circular medallion, 2 ft. 9 in. diameter, enclosing a head.

There are twelve panels or compartments with figures; three are nearly perfect, 4 ft. wide at base and 4 ft. 4 in. high. A fragment of a fourth has also been preserved.

Mr. Franks has interpreted these panels of the months by comparing them with a description of each month, attributed to the poet Ausonius, found attached to an ancient calendar, engraved in Kollarius, *Analecta Vind.*, tom. i, p. 946, and elsewhere.

First, No. 41, draped female leaning back on a square *cippus*, on which she rests her right hand. On another *cippus*, in front, are two cups, and at the foot of it a brazen bucket, on which lies a green branch. From behind the *cippus* rises a tree, and in it is a swallow.

> " Cinctum pelle lupæ promptum est cognoscere mensem ;
> Mars illi nomen, Mars dedit exuvias.
> Tempus ver hædus petulans, et garrula hirundo
> Indicat, et sinus lactis, et herba virens."[1]

The panel agrees with the description,—the swallow, the two little cups, and the pail, probably intended to hold milk, and a fresh bough for the *herba virens*.

[1] Or, rendered into free English verse—

> " In wolf-skin girt the month at once is known,
> March is its name, and Mars the spoils will own.
> Blythe kid and warbling swallow tell the time,
> And breasts of milk, green grass, and sweet woodbine."

On the next panel is a female dancing before a circular *cippus*, on which is placed a little statue, with a leafy bower behind it. The figure is strangely dressed; the robe ornamented with dark bands, terminating in barbed tongues, apparently snake-like ornaments. She holds in her hands long castanets; No. 42.

"Contectam myrto Venerem veneratur Aprilis;
Lumen thuris habet, quo nitet alma Ceres.
Cereus a dextra flammas diffundit odoras,
Balsama nec desunt, queis redolet Paphio."[1]

In the mosaic for April is the dancing figure, with metal plates on the dress, and holding castanets, and the statuette of Venus, under a bower of myrtle; the other adjuncts are wanting. The feast of Venus took place on the Calends of that month, and the Cerealia on the VII Ides.

On the third panel is a female resting with left elbow on a square *cippus*, and taking with a stylus some red fruit out of a glass bowl standing on another *cippus*, above which appears a fruit tree; No. 43.

"Ecce coloratos ostentat Julius artus
Crines cui rutilos spicea serta ligant
Morus sanguineos præbet gravidata racemos
Quæ medio Cancri sidere læta viret."[2]

The mosaic for July has only a portion of these emblems, —the shallow vessel with mulberries, and the tree from which they have been picked; but in its simplicity it agrees with the other panels.

[1] "In myrtle hid Venus, April adores,
Lit up with incense such as Ceres pours
In sav'ry flames, which Cereus spreads around,
And balsams near the Paphian goddess found."

[2] "Julius unfolds his red limbs to the wind,
And garlands sweet his auburn temples bind;
Weigh'd down by blood-red fruit the mulb'ry bends
When Cancer's star its season fit commends."

The fragment, No. 43*, is supposed to have been one of the inner panels, and represents the upper part of a female figure resting her left arm on a square *cippus* and holding in her right a *sistrum*.

> " Carbasco surgens post hunc indutus amictu
> Mensis, ab antiquis sacra Deamque colit :
> A quo vixavidus sistro compescitur anser,
> Devotusque satis ubera fert humeris."[1]

The lines describe a priest of Isis, whose feast took place on the Calends of November.

The five outer panels, for the months of January, June, September, October, and December, with the three described for March, April, and July, leave four months for the inner panels, February, May, August, and November, to which latter month the fragment is ascribed.

Of the seasons represented in the medallions two only remain ; that in the lower corner of mosaic No. 42 is a female head of forbidding aspect, without symbols of any kind. She wears ear-rings, and has a purple stripe to her dress.

The second, in the lower corner of mosaic No. 43, is a female head of great beauty, crowned with ears of corn and wearing a *torques* of gold round her neck,—this probably representing summer and the other spring.[2]

HALICARNASSUS. See the work on *Halicarnassus*,[3] beforementioned, to which I am indebted for the following descriptions of mosaics taken from one villa, which Mr. Newton believes to be "of the Roman period, built on the

---

[1] " Next, clothed in linen garb, the month appears,
True to great Isis' rites through these long years ;
The greedy goose no *sistrum* drives away,
But its fat carcase glorifies the day."

[2] The above are figured in *Archæologia*, xxxviii, with the descriptions by Mr. Franks.

[3] *History of Discoveries at Halicarnassus*, etc., by C. T. Newton, M.A., C.B.

ground occupied by an earlier Hellenic edifice on the same site. Its own plan was altered in several places after erection. Thus, under the pavement of Room C were four pieces of painted stucco and of an earlier tesselated pavement . . . . It is not probable that any of the pavements are earlier than the time of the Antonines ; the latest may be subsequent to the reign of Caracalla. These tesselated pavements are remarkable for the extent of the whole design, the variety of scenes and ornaments which they contain, the richness of the colouring in places, and the number of inscribed subjects."

Mr. Newton was engaged in disinterring the remains of the famous mausoleum erected to Mausolus by his widow, Artemisia, at the ancient capital city of Caria (now *Budrum*), but as we have only to do with the Roman period for the mosaics, it is not necessary to refer to his description of this marvellous monument.

The villa was a short distance to the west of the site of the Mausoleum, and the pavements were at a depth of 2 ft. to 4 ft. below the level of the ground. A ground plan of the villa is given on Mr. Newton's Plate XXXIX. The following is his description of the rooms and their mosaic floors.

"Room A, 26 ft. by 27½ ft. In the centre is sunk a rectangular area, 7 ft. 6 in. by 7 ft. 4 in. Round the square were four oblong pictures, each occupying the centre of one of the sides of the room. The subjects of these pictures were animals. The compartment on the west represented a group of three animals ; on the right a greyhound gallops towards a goat, which advances towards him from the opposite direction ; pursuing the goat on the left is another smaller hound. The opposite compartment, on the eastern side of the room, represented a lion and a bull rushing at each other ; between them was a tree. The subject of the north side was a lion pursuing a goat from left to right ; and on the south was a panther chasing a hind. The four angles of this room were severally filled up with a meander of the guilloche plait, the colours employed in which were blue, orange, red, and black, on a white ground. Each of the four pictures was set in a frame of indented pattern, black and white ; outside of this ran a border of guilloche plait. Outside this again a broad white margin, studded with stars, marked the boundary of the pavement on the west, north, and south sides. On the east side of the room was a border of six dolphins, arranged in pairs. These dolphins are blue, the fins red, the outlines black, on a white ground ; between each pair is a flower. The sunk square in the centre of this room was surrounded by a broad plait of red, orange, black, white, blue, on a blue ground. In the centre of each of the spirals formed by the plait was a lozenge, composed of orange, red, white, and black *tessellæ*. This border was very coarse, and appears to have been inserted in the general design at a later period. The animals in this room were designed with great spirit ; their movements were full of life. The colouring, though only partially true to nature, was very rich and harmonious."

The bad condition of the pavement in this room made it impossible to take up more than four of the animals. These were the dog, the goat, and two lions.

Room B, a rectangle, 62 ft. by 25½ ft. ; central part nearly all destroyed.[1] At the west end of the room was an oblong mosaic, representing Meleager and Atalanta hunting. Both are riding at full speed, from opposite directions, towards the centre of the picture, to attack a lion and a leopard. On the left is Atalanta, who wears a tight-fitting Amazonian jerkin and buskins ; at her back hangs a quiver ;

[1] Mr. Newton's Plate xl.

ΜΕΛΕΑΓΡΟΣ

a red chlamys flies from her shoulder; she is drawing a bow
to shoot a lion, who is galloping towards her. Over her
horse's head is inscribed ΑΤΑΛΑΝΤΗ. Her jerkin is coloured
yellow, her horse dark blue. On the right is Meleager,
thrusting his spear at a leopard, who is attacking him. He
wears a dark blue chlamys, buskins, and a white tunic
reaching to the knees, ornamented with vertical green
stripes. Behind this figure was inscribed his name,
ΜΕΛΕΑΓΡΟΣ. The colouring of the picture was rich and
harmonious, but the drawing was very bad, and the figures
out of proportion. The details of costume are curious.

In the corresponding oblong compartment at the eastern
extremity of the room was another hunting scene, in which
the personages represented Dido and Æneas. They are
both mounted, and galloping towards each other from opposite directions. On the left is Dido, aiming her spear at a
wild beast in the centre of the picture; but this part of the
design has perished. Dido is sitting sideways on her horse;
she wears a singular dress, apparently of leather, fitting
tight round the body and reaching to the knees; her right
shoulder and breast are bare; behind her head is inscribed
her name, ΔΕΙΔΩ. Her dress is coloured yellow; from her
shoulders flies a red scarf; her hair is yellow; her horse of
a dark blue colour.

Opposite to her, on the right, is Æneas, the greater part
of whose figure is destroyed; he is urging his horse at
speed; his spear is couched. Behind his head is inscribed
his name, ΑΙΝΕΑ(Σ). At his side is a dog galloping. In
front of Æneas, and nearly in the centre of the picture, is a
panther, rising to spring at him. A tree appears beyond
this animal. The horse of Æneas is coloured yellow. The
colouring and drawing of this picture are in the same style
as the opposite hunting scene. All the figures in this compartment were much injured, and no portion of it could be

taken up. Between the two oblong compartments were
two circular patterns, each inscribed in a square. The
circle on the west was formed of a guilloche plait, within
which were eight squares, so arranged round the inner edge
of the circle as to contain a star of eight points. These
squares had all been destroyed but two, one of which contained a flower, the other a guilloche knot. The portions
of the circle enclosed between the circumference and the
sides of two adjacent squares were filled up by a vase,
from which issued, on either side, a branch of ivy with
tendrils. The angles of the square within which the circle
was inscribed contained severally one of the Seasons,
represented by a female head, over which the name of the
season is inscribed.

At the north-west angle was the *Spring*, ΛIAP, personified by a youthful female bust, with long hair flowing down
her neck ; her garment was a white tunic, ornamented with
black and red vertical stripes, and fastened on either
shoulder by a circular fibula. Opposite to her, at the north-
east angle, was *Summer*, ΘE(P)OΣ. She was also represented
with long flowing hair, bound with ears of corn.

The south-east angle has disappeared.

At the south-west angle was *Winter*, inscribed (X)EIMΩN.
Her garment was a green tunic, fastened on the shoulder
with a circular brooch; her hair, flowing down her neck, was
covered behind with a veil ; on each side of her head was a
reed.

All these figures were represented with long wings ;
their bodies were cut off at the waist. The relative positions of Spring and Autumn seem to correspond with the
direction from which the wind, characteristic of either
season, blows. A small portion only of the great circle
was preserved, and only one angle of the square in which it
was inscribed. This angle was filled up by a vase, in form

like the *amphoræ* of Southern Italy of the latest period.
Out of this vase issued, on either side, an ivy branch.   In
consequence of the decayed state of the mosaic in this room,
only small portions of the figures could be taken up.

Room C is a gallery 40 ft. by 12 ft., running east and
west, and terminating at the west end in an apse.   The
pavement in this room was in very good condition, and the
excavators succeeded in taking up nearly the whole of it in
squares.   The design consisted of three compartments.   At
the west end was a group, representing a naked female
figure floating amid waves and dolphins ; on either side of
her was a youthful Triton, holding up the edge of her veil,
which floated behind her.   The heads of the two Tritons
were surmounted by horns, or perhaps the claws of shell-
fish placed upright.   The female figure, probably Amphitrite, was represented spreading out her long hair over her
shoulders.   The centre part of the design was formed of
squares, intersecting so as to form crosses and smaller
squares.   The colours used are red, crimson, blue, and
yellow.

At the east end of this room, two steps, 8 in. deep, led
down to the lower level of Room D and passages A and B.
On one of these steps was a mosaic of fish, remarkable for
the excellence of the drawing and colouring.

Room E.   This is a narrow strip lying north of Room
C, in length 14 ft., by 6 ft. 3 in. in width.   The design
was contained in an oblong compartment, bounded by a
frame formed by the interlacing of a guilloche plait, a band
striped in several colours, and a zig-zag band.   These inter-
lacings were continued from the frame over the inner area
of the compartment, so as to form three loops, within each
of which was a circular medallion.   The medallion on the
west represented a female bust ; round the head was
inscribed " Halicarnassus"—

A   N
ΛI   A
ΚΛ   CO
P   C

of which city this bust is a figurative representative. The
head was surrounded by a mitre, coloured crimson. The
tunic was light blue, bordered with black, having two
parallel vertical stripes in orange down the breast. These
were united by a zig-zag of black, red, and orange.

In the central medallion was a female bust, representing the city of Alexandria. The head was turreted; on
the shoulders was a tunic, ornamented with two parallel
vertical stripes, black and orange, between which were zig-
zags, red, orange, and pink. On either side of the stripes
was a zig-zag, black and orange, on a blue ground. Round
the head was inscribed the name

A
ΛE   ΔPI
XA   A
N

Medallion the third represents, in like manner, the city
of Berytus (*Beyrout*). This female head was surmounted
by a crimson mitre ; the hair was long. The tunic was in
like manner ornamented with vertical and zig-zag stripes ;
the colours employed were orange and black for the vertical stripes, and black, orange, and white for the zig-zags.
The ground of the tunic appeared to be pink. Round the
head was the name

BH
PY   TOC

The colours used in the three interlacing borders were blue,
red, crimson, orange, and black, on a white ground. The
triangular spaces were mostly ornamented by a bird. The
three heads were in a late, coarse style. The costume was
also of a very late period. The personification of cities as

female figures, with various attributes, was very common in the art of the Roman period, especially on the coins of Asia Minor struck in the reigns of the late emperors. It is not improbable that the combination of Halicarnassus, Alexandria, and Berytus on this mosaic may indicate an alliance (ὁμόνοια) between these three cities. The pavement in this room was too much decayed to be taken up.

Mr. Newton then proceeds to describe the pavements on a lower level. To these there is a descent of two steps, 8 in. deep each, to—

Room D, 51 ft. by 15 ft., the design consisting of two distinct parts. On the north an oblong strip, bounded on every side by a border of interlaced diagonals, black on a white ground ; within this outer border was an inner one of small medallions. At either end was a square compart-ment, in which was inscribed a circular pattern consisting of concentric rings. In the centre was a bearded and shaggy head with a wild expression, surrounded by a circle of leaves radiating outwards.

The principal outer circle was composed of the bead and reel ornament. The whole of this design much resembled that of an ægis or buckler, of which it was probably an imi-tation. The head of the centre was probably that of Phobos or Terror, often placed, like the head of Medusa, in the centre of bucklers.

Between these two circular patterns were three oblong compartments, each containing a picture ; the subjects were the following. The furthest to the east represented a male figure, probably a satyr, pursuing a nymph or mænad ; the head and shoulders of the male figure were destroyed. In his right hand he held a *pedum*, or shepherd's crook, from which hung a singular object, shaped like a bell and coloured yellow ; a panther's skin hung from his shoulder. The female figure was looking back to him in her flight. The

middle of the body was destroyed. Her tunic was blue,
edged with black.

The centre compartment of the whole was a very elegant
group of a Nereid seated on a hippocamp. The western
represented Dionysos with a panther ; above was inscribed
his name, ΔΙΟΝΥΣΟΣ. Dionysos is represented as a youthful, naked figure, moving to the right at the side of his
panther. In his hands, which were extended on either side,
he held up a red scarf bordered with black. The medallions
which formed a border round these inner designs were each
set in an octagonal frame. They are numbered consecu-
tively 1 to 41, and consisted in six or more cases of
the head of the youthful Dionysos, with long hair bound
with diadem and ivy leaves, and in the others of birds,
flowers, and fish.

These medallions were all on a white ground. Their
colouring was very harmonious, and the whole design of
Room D was very elegant. To the south was a rectangular
space, 31 ft. by 25 ft., containing the following designs.

On the extreme east was an oblong picture representing
a scene in a vineyard. Nearly in the centre, a bearded,
goat-legged figure of Pan was gathering grapes from a vine.
Before him stood a winged boy, probably Erôs, extending
his arms towards the same bunch. On the extreme right,
behind the goat-legged figure, were a panther and three
birds, one of which has a string fastened round its neck.
On the left, behind Erôs, was a lion galloping towards him,
and a greyhound running in an opposite direction towards
a hare on the extreme left, represented feeding on a bunch
of grapes. The colours of the animals in this scene were
arbitrary. The panther was dark blue with yellow spots ;
the greyhound also blue. The leaves of the vine were composed of *tessellæ* in cubes of green glass. This mosaic was
too much damaged to be taken up.

DIONYCOC

DIONYSUS OR BACCHUS, FROM *HALICARNASSUS*.

At the south end of this picture were two dolphins, their heads confronted with a trident between them, and on the west side was a white border studded with lozenges, twenty-nine in number. The colours used in these lozenges were red, orange, white, and black.

Next to this border were two pictures ; the one on the north represented Europa, standing by the side of the bull, whose head is turned back towards her. Europa wears a wreath ; her body is naked from the neck to half-way down the thigh ; a blue *peplos* passes across her lower limbs. The bull is of a tawny colour, with stripes of crimson and white. This group was in a better condition than any of the other mosaics in this field, and was interesting as a specimen of drawing.

To the south of this picture were two smaller ones, of which the upper had perished. That below it represented a water-nymph reclining; her right arm rests on an urn ; in her left hand she holds a flower. The upper part of her body is naked; over her lower limbs is thrown a blue *peplos;* at her feet is a tree. The head of this figure was destroyed. At the north-east angle of this picture was a bird pecking at a flower, and below it a dog pursuing a hare very coarsely executed in arbitrary colours. Round three sides of this picture was a border of birds.

The whole of the pictures were surrounded by a border of circular medallions, the subjects of nearly all which were a bird perched on a branch. Some of these are long-legged aquatic birds, like the ibis.

The circular frames of these medallions were formed by an interlaced guilloche plait, of which the colours were red, orange, blue, black, and white. This border terminated at its north-west angle with two ivy leaves set in an oblong frame. Outside the border of medallions was one of dolphins. All these dolphins were arranged in pairs, their

heads confronted. They were coloured in two shades of
blue, with red fins.

Passages A and B. A was 51½ ft. by 10 ft. The principal design of the pavement runs down the centre, occupying
rather more than half its width. It is divided into nine
rectangular compartments. Nos. 4 and 5 form one rectangle, the centre division of which (No. 5) is a square containing a laurel wreath. Within this wreath is the following
inscription :

YΓIA
ZOH
XAPA
EIPHNH
EYΘYMIA
EAΠIC.

The letters are in black on a white ground. The colours
used in the wreath are red, crimson, blue, black, and orange.
These colours are very harmoniously combined, and the
effect of this pattern is very pleasing.

Passage B. Length, 64 ft., by 14½ ft. in width. Mr.
Newton gives a description of the geometrical designs, and
of thirty-six medallions containing similar subjects to those
already described ; but several represent palm-trees, and
one a *pelta*, or Amazonian shield. The medallions in Room
E, and the pictures of Meleager and Dido in Room B, appear
to be of a later period than Rooms A and D.

The mosaic of Dido and Æneas, though referred to in
the foregoing description, was not brought over, in consequence of its imperfect condition.

The pavements in this basement consist of no less than
seventy specimens, which are noted and numbered in the
Museum Catalogue, Part II, "Græco-Roman Sculpture".
They are mostly referred to in this chapter, but those
omitted will be particularised in the next.

CHAPTER XVII.

SUCH of the various pavements referred to in the previous chapter as are now placed in the British Museum shall be summed up in the words and under the classification adopted in an article from the *Builder*, vol. xlii, p. 757 (1882), together with the excellent descriptions there given.

" They seem to fall easily into a few groups or classes, such as — 1. Mythological and legendary; 2. Hunting scenes and animal representations; 3. Birds; 4. Water scenes and fish ; 5. Ornamental and geometrical devices.

" In the *First Class* we will consider the picture derived from the mythology of Greece and Rome. The Halicarnassus pavement (No. 5 of the Museum numeration) terminates in a semicircular apse. The subject is a group representing the water goddess Amphitrite among dolphins and fish. On either side of her is a Triton, holding up drapery stretched behind her, their heads being surmounted by the claws of shell-fish. The goddess is clad with a mantle cast over the right thigh, but is otherwise undraped. In the right hand is a mirror which reflects her face ; with the left she smooths her tresses. This is an attitude not far removed from the conventional pose of the mediæval mermaid, of whom, perhaps, Amphitrite is the prototype. On the head is a golden-coloured fillet ; the mantle is of an olive-grey, and the drapery held by the attendant

M M

Tritons olive-grey, with yellow and red stripes. The bluish
grey background is evidently intended to represent the
watery element over which the goddess shed her lustre.
The border is intricate and harmonious. The mythic being,
the Triton, is a favourite subject. He appears in another
pavement (No. 69), wreathed about the head, and holding
a dish of pomegranates and a shepherd's crook. Here,
again, dolphins and fish are introduced as accessories. The
colouring is rich and harmonised, and the whole enclosed
in a guilloche border of red *tesserœ*, shaded delicately
through orange into white. This fine pavement, 5 ft.
by 8 ft., was discovered by Mr. Wood at the Temple of
Diana of Ephesus.

"Another (No. 63) represents a swimming Triton,
wreathed and mantled, and with a dish of fruit and crook
as before, looking back at a companion Nereid, who is seated
upon a fold of his fishy tail, on which also she rests her
left hand. In the right hand she holds a drinking-horn.
She wears a red *peplos*, armlets, and bracelets. Blue dolphins
with red fins disport around this animated group, which,
now measuring about 4 ft. by 7 ft., has originally formed
part of a larger mosaic, of which the border is composed of
flowers and knots.

"Carthage contributes another Tritonic pavement (No.
46), nearly 4 ft. by 12 ft., where two groups are represented.
In the first, a wreathed Triton extends his hand towards a
facile Nereid seated on his tail, and drawing forward a sea-
green veil, which swells out with the breeze behind her
head. Round her body is a yellow mantle, ornamented
with blue and red stripes. The second group is imperfect,
but not very dissimilar to that already mentioned. Here,
again, we meet the accessory dolphins, which, according to
the Greek canon of art, are introduced to represent the
surroundings of the scene. The water is artistically indi-

HEAD OF GLAUCUS, FROM POMPEII

cated by broken black lines on a white ground. The
border or frame, also on a white ground, shows the
guilloche plait and the embattled ornament, the colours
being red, pink, yellow, black, blue, and green.

"Another Nereid is seen on No. 64, on white ground,
with border of foliage, in company with a hippocamp
who bears the watery beauty on his tail, and holds out a
patera, or bowl, to his fair rider. In his hand is a red
crooked stick, and on his shoulders a *chlamys*, or mantle.
She wears a mantle, too, and her head is bound with a
diadem. The ancient reparation of this mosaic with a
fragment of another pavement representing fish and waves,
is of interest.

"Of marine deities, No. 68, nearly 6 ft. by 7 ft., presented
by Mr. Hudson Gurney in 1844, shows a head conjectured
to be that of Glaucus. The seaweed green of the hair,
the curling, plant-like beard, and the dark green lines on a
white ground below the chin of the figure, representing
waves, are worthy of notice.

"The head of a marine god appears also between
dolphins on a fragment from Withington in Gloucestershire, presented by Mr. H. C. Brooke in 1812, in the
gallery of Roman busts.

"A mask of the youthful Dionysus, with long hair bound
with a diadem, from a mosaic medallion (No. 30) found in
1856 in a large Roman villa at Halicarnassus, and a fine
pavement (No. 20), about 4 ft. 6 in. square, from the same
site, on which is the youthful god, wreathed with ivy, and
wearing a red scarf bordered black, accompanied with the
usual emblem, a panther, illustrate the Bacchus myth,
and perhaps come from rooms destined to convivial meetings.

"The same villa contained No. 19, a spirited picture in
tesseræ, of Europa, wreathed and girt about the lower limbs

with a 'mantle blue', standing to the right, beside the tawny
bull of Jove, whose body is marked with crimson and
white.

"Another room of this richly decorated villa supplies
three fragments (Nos. 6, 7, and 8), representing Meleager
and Atalanta engaged in hunting. They are riding at full
speed from opposite directions to attack a lion and leopard.
On the left hand, Atalanta, clad in the tightly fitting
yellow Amazonian jerkin and buskins, a red *chlamys* flying
from the shoulder, and armed with quiver and bow, aims
at an advancing lion. She is mounted on a dark blue
horse. Meleager, on the right hand, in blue cloak and
tunic of green and white stripes, thrusts his spear into a
panther which is attacking him. A border of black, wavy
pattern on white enclosed this subject, the original dimensions of which were 15 ft. 6 in. by 7 ft.

"A mask of Medusa's head, a not uncommon subject of
classical ornamentation, is seen on No. 22; the mask is
full-faced, dark red; the eyes, nose, and mouth heightened
with white; two concentric rings encircle it, from the outer-
most of which black, pointed leaves radiate on a white field.
This measures 3 ft., and comes from the same site.

"On the seashore of Carthage part of a large mosaic
pavement was found (No. 44), measuring about 4 ft. by
7 ft., the subject of which probably relates to some public
games. A figure of Victory is seen flying through the air,
holding a large rectangular label, on which are eight lines
of an inscription in Roman capital letters, white on red
ground. The goddess wears bracelets, a red and white
robe, and an over-garment, black bordered, reaching to the
hips.

"Terror personified is shown on No. 21, as a wild,
shaggy head, encircled by leaves radiating from it on a
white ground; the hair yellow; shades of red for the face;

and red, blue, green, white, and black for other parts. This is over five feet square, and comes from the Halicarnassus villa. Another similar subject (No. 39) gives yellow hair with black shading to the dread visage, the eyes being picked with white. Both of them are probably from the centre of an *ægis* or buckler, on which the heads of Terror or of Medusa were frequently portrayed, in order to cause dismay to the opponent—a custom, no doubt, surviving from the barbaric ages of Greece.

" The Temple collection gives another pavement to the Museum series. This is a mosaic now made into a table-top (No. 70), supported by a pillar, on which are sculptured in relief two Mænades and as many Satyrs, moving wildly under the influence of orgiastic frenzy. The subject is spirited and full of life, though treated in the conventional way, and replenished with the accessories of such scenes, with which most of us are familiar.

" At Halicarnassus Mr. Newton found in the villa a medallion mosaic, 1 ft. 9 in. diameter, with a female bust in tesselation, representing a personification of the city of Halicarnassus (No. 18), and inscribed with that name. The head is encircled with a crimson-coloured *stephane* or diadem. On the breast, light blue drapery bordered with black cubes is shown, having two parallel vertical stripes of orange-coloured *tesseræ* down the breast.

" Representations of the seasons may aptly terminate this first sub-division of pavimental subjects. They are favourite designs with the artist. Many such subjects have been discovered and recorded, not only in England—as at Cirencester, for example—but all over the ancient Roman empire. From the prolific site of Halicarnassus comes a fragment, 2 ft. 8 in. square, representing Spring, personified as a youthful girlish bust (No. 9), whose long hair flows down the neck, the drapery being a dark red tunic, fastened

on each shoulder by a circular brooch. From the ears
depend a pair of ear-rings. The name of Spring, in Greek
capitals, was inscribed in small cubes above her head.
Another female bust of Spring, from Carthage, is at the
corner of No. 42, her hair gathered over the forehead in a
top-knot; ear-rings in her ears ; and her dress a white
chiton or smock, with purple stripe on the right shoulder,
and a red mantle thrown over the left shoulder.

"Summer season is also represented on the Museum
pavements in two examples. The first (No. 10), from Halicarnassus, is a female bust with long flowing tresses,
crowned with ears of corn ; the other, from Carthage
(No. 43), a female bust, wreathed about the head with ears
of wheat, and wearing hooped ear-rings, a golden-coloured
torque, a white *chiton* with yellow stripes on the right, and
a red mantle over the left shoulder.

"The month of March is depicted in a Carthaginian
tesselation of more than ordinary interest, for it illustrates
a well-known pavement at Cirencester, which is adorned
with a corresponding subject. This fine pavement in the
British Museum (No. 41) exceeds in measurement 6 ft. by
7 ft. Here March is personified as a female figure, leaning
against a square *cippus* or altar, on which she rests her
right hand. She turns towards another *cippus* on the right,
on which are two cups ; and beyond it, at the extreme right
of the subject, there is a tree, in the foliage of which there
is a swallow, towards which she is pointing with the fore-
finger of the left hand, thus indicating the approach of
spring.

"In like manner the pavement found in Dyer Street,
Cirencester, in 1849, has a figure of Flora, on whose shoulder
the swallow, 'harbinger of spring', is vividly and faithfully
displayed. In this Corinian Flora nothing could better
symbolise spring than the ruby-gemmed flowers with which

the head of the figure is adorned. They heighten the
effect. They are composed of *tessellæ* of a bright ruby-
coloured glass, the only instance of the use of this material
in the Cirencester pavements,—but, as we shall show by-
and-bye, a not uncommon material for the richer sort of
tesselations found in Continental examples. In this Museum
pavement there are shown a bronze-coloured bucket with a
green branch across it, and containing a white liquid, either
water or milk; the personage wears an under-tunic, green-
bordered at the wrists, a saffron-coloured garment with
hanging sleeves, and a green mantle with a purple lining.
At her side is a plant growing in a two-handled vase,
yellow, shaded into red, and on each side of the vase foliage
of an arabesque kind.

"April's changeable month is given on No. 42, a female,
with a voluptuous expression, playing the castanets. She
may, perchance, represent one of the Gaditanian damsels,
famed of old, as now also, for their skill in dancing. On
the right is a circular *cippus*, on which is a little statue,
perhaps of Venus (for does not love hallow the April of
life?), with a leafy bower behind it. This is a charming
piece of tesseral art, full of poetry and feeling. It measures
6 ft. 9 in. by 10 ft. 6 in.

"Then comes ripe, matronly July (No. 43), another
female, picking a mulberry with a stylus, daintily, from a
dish of that fruit (which ripens in July) placed on a *cippus*
under a mulberry tree. Over her green *chiton*, reaching to
the heels, is a salmon-coloured garment with hanging
sleeves, green striped, with black and red.

"Last of the series comes November, a female, too,
holding a *sistrum* or musical rattle in the right, a *situla* or
bucket of libations in the left hand. Her sleeved under-
garment is green; over it a yellow and white dress; the
hair ruddy, with a flaxen yellow top-knot. We may place

at the end of this class (No. 29) a youthful male mask,
with long hair, wreathed, in a medallion.

"The *Second Class*, that of hunting-scenes and animal
representations, is not quite so numerously represented in
the British Museum collections. In Nos. 11 and 12 two
fragments of the same illustrative design, an ibex, of
bluish grey, speeding to the right, is pursued by a hound of
similar colour with a red collar; another dark red hound,
flecked with black, rushing forward, heads the quarry.

"No. 47, a rudely-made mosaic from Carthage, of the
size of nearly 4 ft. by 9 ft., has for its design a mounted
huntsman at full speed to the right, cheering on his dark
blue dog towards a lost game; at the right an orange-tree
laden with fruit; behind are tall plants, and the broken
lines of the rugged country-side. The dress of the hunter
is a red jerkin, with a black and white side stripe, and
black boots. The horse is of a drab colour.

"From Utica another hunting-scene is derived (No. 65),
measuring 5 ft. by 11 ft. Within a fence of network are
gathered a wild boar, a stag, a roe, fox, and panther, an
ostrich and two birds, all in their proper colours; at each
end of the net is a boat manned by two hunters, naked,
except that one has a cloth around his loins. The scene is
evidently laid near the shore of a lake or river; the ground
is white, besprinkled with a few green sprigs. In the
foreground are two lizards and a tree. Near the boat, on
the left, which, like the other one, has a sharp prow and
stern, blue-black and red, with a yellow streak from end
to end, are two fish. These water-hunters are hauling in
the end of the net, so as to narrow the space in which the
quarry is enclosed. It is an animated and interesting
glimpse into the sports of the past.

"On another pavement, not yet numbered, in this room,
is represented a hare coursed by a greyhound; and one of the

Withington pavements in the gallery of Roman portraits shows part of a boar-hunt, arranged in a circle, with an outer border of birds. The animal forms, which naturally fall into this second group, consist (some in addition to those already described) of the lion, leopard, panther, horse, stag, bull, goat, and deer. On four the lion occurs. In two of them the monarch of the beasts is rushing to his prey— a bull and goat—at full speed to the right (Nos. 13 and 14); in front of him, in each case, is a tree. The colours of these lions are yellow, red, blue, white, and black. Their form and design may be contrasted by the artistic student with those of the lion of the Orphic pavement at Ciren-cester,—the one spellbound under the musical numbers of the master's lyre, the other masterful, rampant, and full of life, in quest of his prey. Almost the same colours are employed in each case, but differently arranged. The leopard and lion in the scene of Meleager and Atalanta have been already pointed out ; so, too, the panther of Dionysus. The horse is seen in No. 1, where a wounded horseman is lying on a truck by the side of his charger, perhaps a part of a pavement representing the games of the Circus. This came from the Pourtales collection.

"Another fine Carthaginian pavement, not yet numbered, in the inner room, shows a horseman successfully lassoing a stag at full speed, to the right. The stag is seen not only on this pavement, but on one of the tesselated pavements found at Withington, and now on the wall of the gallery. A stag and deer drinking by a fountain may be seen on No. 47, from Carthage. The Jovian bull of Europa we have already noticed. Dogs are not uncommon, in many attitudes, and of various hues. The goat occurs in No. 48, where two are springing forward to the right ; one is pierced in the side, the blood falling to the ground. They are fawn-coloured, shading into grey, with black outlines. It is a late and coarsely-made pavement from Carthage.

N N

" Bird pictures form the *Third Class* of our division.
On nearly twenty of the British Museum pavements they
occur as subordinate accessories. They are mostly of the
domesticated kind, if we except the ostrich, which is found
in the draw-net scene. The eagle, a favourite military
symbol, strange to say, does not appear to occur. The
medallions of the Halicarnassian villa comprise a duck,
cocks, and other birds on branches (Nos. 23, 26, 28). A
bluish-grey bird, with wings, crest, and legs red, is shown
holding a twig in the beak in No. 31. A francolin is given
in No. 48, the scene of the wounded goat, speckled blue,
yellow, and red. A peacock, guinea-fowl, and other birds
occur in No. 67. The brightly coloured *tesseræ*, probably
glass, of many of these birds seem to have been in ancient
times wantonly picked out of the pavement. It is from
Utica, and some part of its design may be compared with the
gorgeous peacocks of the Cirencester pavement. There is
a drinking peacock in a fountain-scene (No. 49). Ducks
and pigeons occur on some pavements, not yet numbered, in
the lower room, and some birds are found on two British
pavements in the Bust gallery.

" Our next *Class* comprises fish and fishing-scenes.
Perhaps these subjects adorned baths and bathing-rooms.
The fish are not only subordinate to more pretentious
scenes where they are used to indicate locality, but frequently occur alone as the principal element of the composition. Just as we have already pointed out, in our recent
notice of the archaic Greek vases in the Museum,[1] objects
of marine origin entered largely into the ornamentation of
the early pottery of a people so pre-eminently maritime in
their proclivities as the Greeks, so here also in pavements
which, as a rule, must be attributed to a late period of
classical art. The dolphin in Nos. 5, 15, 16, 46, 53, and

[1] See *Builder*, vol. xlii, No 2049, 13 May 1881.

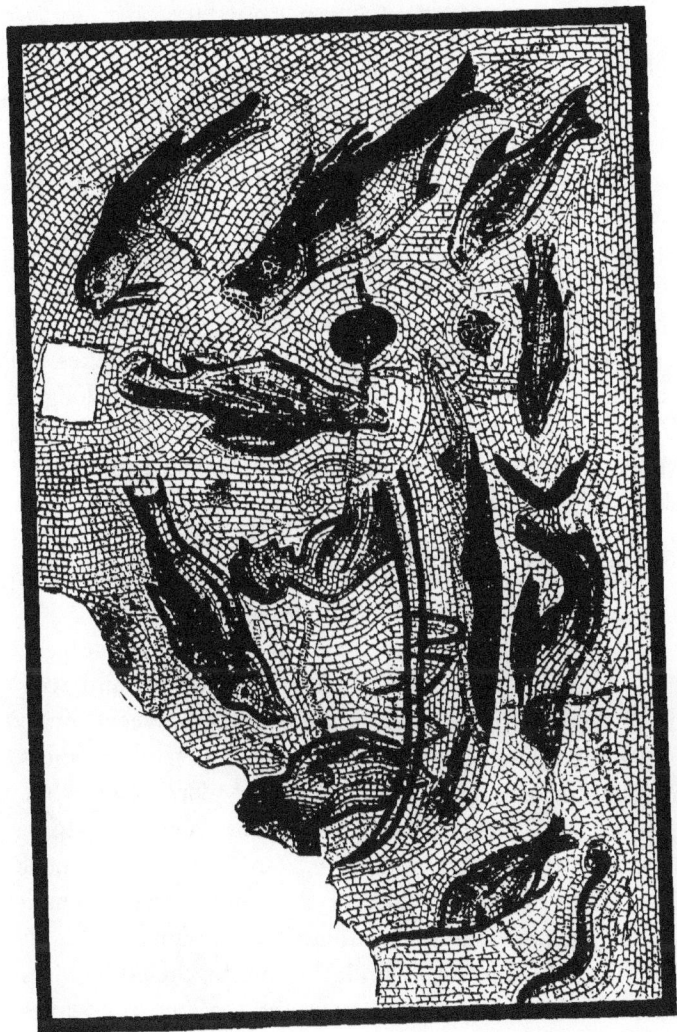

others, as well as in one of the Withington pavements; the long-snouted wrass and the sword-fish (No. 4); the dentex and the sparus (No. 27); a deep-bodied, thick fish (No. 33); a red and yellow perch, and black and purple lobsters (No. 51); the muræna, prawns, tunny, wrass, eel, sea-perch, and lobster, fallen from a fish-basket, all in natural colours, finely shaded (No. 52); the red and the grey mullet, dolphin, dentex, and wrass (No. 66), and several others, present themselves to the visitor as he makes the circuit of the room. Water-scenes and fishermen belong to this class. Boats occur in two pavements from Utica. Both examples are of pointed beaks; one has the curving neck and head of a swan for a figure-head (No. 66); over the gunwale hangs a line, or the edge of a net; one of the fishermen is raising out of the water a fish which he has hooked.

"The last *Class* into which we have divided the subjects of the tesselated pavements, that of geometrical and ornamental devices, may be illustrated from almost every existing specimen. These patterns are, in several instances, not subordinated as borders, but they form the whole ground of the design. Many of them, from the strong contrasts of their colour, and others for their subtly blended shades, stand out as marvels of the application of simple rules of geometry and of rudimentary designs to highly artistic ends. Hence the guilloche twists, cabled borders, threefold and fourfold plaits, mæanders, rosettes, ivy-leaves, quatrefoils, crosslets, and other simple devices, cunningly retained by the true feeling of the artist from the oldest periods, please and gratify the eye, that has already feasted upon far more complicated patterns, beyond expression, from their pure simplicity and chasteness; and we must go back 2,000 years to find the origin of patterns which, even to-day, form the stock-in-trade of the designer and colourist.

"The guilloche pattern is seen to good effect in three pieces of pavement from Abbot's Ann, Hampshire, presented to the Trustees of the British Museum by the Hon. and Rev. S. Best in 1854; the spiral, with radiating leaves, in the little bit of the Woodchester pavement, in the same gallery; the plaited border, enclosing a circle in which is a floriated cross, on the right hand of the gallery, in a pavement found on the site of the Bank of England, and presented by the governor and directors of that institution; and an elegant picture of alternate squares and lozenges, enclosing fourfold knots, rosettes, mæanders, and quatrefoils, is preserved on a pavement found in. Threadneedle Street, in the City of London, and presented by Mr. E. Moxhay to the authorities of the Museum in 1841.

"The chequer pattern, representing rows of parallelopipeds seen in perspective, coloured white, black, yellow, red, and green, is shown in two pavements bequeathed by Sir William Temple (Nos. 2 and 3); squares and lozenges, enclosing a quatrefoil, in No. 37; cubes in diagonal rows, with an embattled border, in No. 59; the lozenge, guilloche, and *pelta*, or Amazonian shield, a very archaic ornament, in No. 5; the guilloche and black-and-white wave pattern in No. 8; guilloche and checky border in No. 45; intersecting circles, green and red, embracing crosses and quatrefoils, in No. 54; ivy-leaves in No. 57; and star and flower patterns in No. 60. Of this class a fine pavement at Leicester has nine octagonal compartments, enclosing quadrilateral and triangular figures, interlaced by a rich guilloche of various colours. It was discovered in 1830, and originally about 24 ft. square.

"Inscriptions and explanatory words or names occur on several pavements in the Museum collection.

*　　*　　*　　*　　*　　*

"Interesting as these pavements are as monuments of the

past, they have, says Mr. Westmacott, a further claim on our attention for the qualities of art which they exhibit, and in this respect they claim a superior place among antiquities. The execution is somewhat coarse sometimes, but this is owing to the nature of the materials and the mode of workmanship. The details and drawing may be rude, but, apart from these mechanical and technical defects, there is a style in them which elevates them to the best period of art. Another point of comparative excellence is the quality, breadth, and distribution of their colour ; there is a picturesque grandeur about them, a strong love of nature, and a thorough acquaintance on the part of the designer with the full extent of their applicability. Hence their success and esteem in old times ; their appreciation and importance as teachers of true art in our modern collections."

CHAPTER XVIII.

Comparison of the subjects of Romano-British and foreign Roman mosaics generally, with extracts from the Orphic Hymns and the Golden Poems of Pythagoras, together with some opinions of eminent modern archæologists on the subjects treated of.—On the materials employed by the Romans in tesselated work.

IT will be seen that in the foreign examples in the British Museum, which have been so well summed up and described by the writer of the article from *The Builder* in the foregoing chapter, hunting scenes, garden scenes, and the realms of the sea and the air, as they relate to the pleasures and occupations of life, form the stock ideas of the artists who designed the mosaics. They were more conversant with the gardens of Epicurus than with the porticos of Zeno or the baptisteries of Eusebius. In our British examples, astronomy in connection with mythology, and the succession of the seasons, preponderate as subjects. This fact appears to yield another link in the continuous chain of British history, by pointing to the progressive advance in the human mind which prepared it for the reception of Christianity. Erôs, the supreme god in mundane affairs among the ancients, became spiritualised into a love divine and a spirit of goodwill among men. The refined idea of the ancient Orpheus was accommodated to the feelings of advancing civilisation. A quotation from the Orphic hymns may suffice to show this :

" Φρικτὸς, ἀήττητος, μέγας, ἄφθιτος, ὃν στέφει αἰθὴρ,
Δεῦρο νεῇ, οὐατά μοι καθαρὰς ἀκοάς τε πετάσσοις,

Κέκλυθι τάξιν ἅπασαν ὅσην τεκμήρατο δαίμων
Ἐκ τε μιῆς νυκτὸς ἠδ' ἐξ ἑνὸς ἤματος αὔτως."[1]

> " Fearful, invisible, eternal, great,
> Whom the blue firmament surrounds,
> Come hither and arouse my ears
> To feel these everlasting sounds.
> This harmony to hear I pray,
> Ordained of God, through one long night and day."

The following lines from the "Golden Poems" of Pythagoras, the philosopher of Southern Italy, may be quoted as an early instance of aspirations after a future existence among the Greeks of the Italian peninsula—

> " Ἔν τε λύσει ψυχῆς κρίνων, καὶ φράζευ ἕκαστα,
> Ἡνίοχον γνώμην στήσας καθύπερθεν ἀρίστην.
> Ἢν δ' ἀπολείψας σῶμα ἐς αἰθέρ' ἐλεύθερον ἔλθῃς,
> Ἔσσεαι ἀθάνατος θεὸς ἄμβροτος, οὐκ ἔτι θνητός."[2]

> " Think of the soul's release, and weigh well all ;
> Deeming the charioteer above, the wisest mind.
> The body left, you'll reach the boundless sky,
> And reign a god, never again to die."

—though, at the same time it must be admitted that neither the date nor the authorship of the above poems has been satisfactorily settled. Could we credit half the fine things which have been attributed to Pythagoras, he would be not the lover only, but the very impersonation of wisdom itself. Both the proportionate movements of the heavenly bodies and the numeration of the intervals of musical notes have been equally ascribed to his philosophy and invention. The high opinion entertained of him at Rome in the days of the Republic, is shown by the following history of two

[1] *De Deo*, iii, 3-6.
[2] Πυθαγόρου, Χρυσᾶ ἔπη, 68-71.

statues, related by F. M. Nichols, M.A., in his account of the Roman Forum.[1]

"On occasion of the reverses which befell the Roman arms in the second Samnite war, about three centuries before the Christian era, the Senate applied to Delphi for advice, and were commanded by the oracle to dedicate, in some frequented site, a statue to the wisest, and another to the bravest, of the Greek race. The philosopher and warrior chosen were Pythagoras and Alcibiades; and the statues were placed, to use Pliny's expression,[2] on the horns of the *comitium*,—that is, apparently at its two corners or extremities. These statues retained their position until the rebuilding of the Curia by Sulla."

I will now quote the opinions of some of our first archæologists in support of various statements set forth in this work. Mr. C. Roach Smith, F.S.A., says: "While mythology supplied by far the greater portion of subjects in tesselated work, pastoral and hunting scenes are comparatively rare. .... The extent and splendour of tesselated pavements often afford the strongest evidence of the importance of the buildings they decorated, although scarcely any traces of those buildings remain, the very foundations having not unfrequently been removed for building materials. .... Symbolically, the myth of Orpheus was adopted by the early Christians in the pictorial embellishments of the catacombs and churches, and in the latter it continued to retain a place for centuries. The tolerant Emperor Alexander Severus, Lampridius states, associated in his *lararium* the figure of Orpheus with those of Christ and Abraham."[3]

The Rev. Dr. Collingwood Bruce, the historian of the Roman Wall, among other remarks made at the Congress of the Royal Archæological Institute at Gloucester in 1860,

---

[1] Longmans, 1877, p. 173.　　　　[2] *N. H.*, xxxiv, 12.
[3] C. Roach Smith, in *Arch. Cant.*, xv, p. 136.

compared the remains of Roman occupation in the north of England with those found in the south, and said : " The tesselated pavement which forms so beautiful a feature in the Roman villa of the south, is unknown in the three northern counties of England and Scotland. There is no tesselated pavement north of Aldborough in Yorkshire. The floors of houses in stations on the Watling Street and on the Wall are usually paved with rough flags, occasionally with tiles. The comparative, nay, the almost entire absence of any Christian monument is a perplexing circumstance. We have altars to old gods and to new ; to the gods of Rome and the gods of the country ; to gods and goddesses without name, but we have no dedication to the only living and true God. We have occasionally the simple inscription ' Deo'; but there is reason to suppose that this was a dedication to Mithras, whom we may regard as a sort of Antichrist—a deity whose worship was introduced into Europe when polytheism began to fall before the advance of Christianity. Nearly all the monumental inscriptions in which we might hope to find some trace of Christian sentiment are dedicated to the divine manes of the departed. We find no dedication of any Christian temple. We must not, however, thence conclude that Christianity had not made progress even in the north of Britain. To the very close of the Roman period heathenism displayed itself, and so might Christianity. The one showed itself in stone altars, the other in holy living."[1]

Mr. C. Drury Fortnum, F.S.A., announced the discovery at Rome, in 1871, at S. Clemente, "at the side of the Basilica of Constantine, of a Mithræum intact : the mosaic roof in imitation of a cavern. The *altare* was there, the sacred stone, an ara with the usual mystic bas-relief, a statue of Mithras, the niches for the

[1] Proceedings at Gloucester, *Archæological Journal*, vol. xvii.

genii; also the division set apart for the initiated." This
author, in one of his papers on finger-rings of the early
Christian period, quotes Clement of Alexandria for the
emblematic representations recommended by him to members of the Christian Church, for use as signets engraven
upon their rings—the dove, the fish, the ship running
before the wind, the lyre, the ship's anchor, a man fish-
ing, by which the wearer will be reminded of the apostle
and of the children drawn out of the water.[1]

Mr. S. W. Kershaw, M.A., Librarian of Lambeth
Palace Library, upon Symbolism, after passing from the
illuminations in MSS., remarks that "Christians at first
restricted their visible representations of sacred personages
and actions to mystic emblems. Thus the cross expressed
redemption; the fish, baptism; a sheep, the Church; a
serpent, sin, or the spirit of evil. The relation between
pagan and Christian art holds a strong place in the history
of symbolism, and shows that pagan forms adapted to
Christian meanings have been the great key to classic
Christian art." Of this connection he observes, "The walls
and ceilings of the Catacombs in Rome offer many illustrations, in which almost the first outlines of sacred art appear
clothed in the classic garb which continued to exist till
the twelfth century." The phases of symbolism are too
numerous to allow Mr. Kershaw more than the mention of
a few leading examples, e.g., "the palm-branch, assigned to
martyrs; the crown of the royal saints; the roll to pro-
phets; the book to apostles and evangelists; the nimbus,
aureole, triangle, circle, and square either accompanying or
typifying events and persons."[2]

Mr. J. W. Grover, F.S.A., has summed up what sym-

---

[1] *Archæological Journal*, vol. xxviii, p. 266.
[2] *Art Treasures of Lambeth Library.* By S. W. Kershaw, M.A.
London, 1873.

bols are to be found in Britain of pre-Augustine Christianity, and supposes the owner of the beautiful Frampton villa to have been "one of the semi-Christians who composed the bulk of the population of the empire after the age of Constantine. Like that great man, he loved to mingle the old wine with the new; for Constantine, long after he had adopted the Christian *labarum* as his standard, retained his favourite Apollo, the *Sol invictus*, upon his coins. In the very catacombs of Rome, some of the Christian inscriptions commence with pagan addresses to the gods and shades. In the baptistery at Ravenna the Jordan is represented by a river-god. These facts point evidently to the conclusion that the imperfect state of the faith, when it became universal, was such as to permit the combination of Christian and pagan symbols in the manner shown at Frampton."[1]

The Rev. John McCaul, LL.D., President of University College, Toronto, refers to the mystic rites of the Taurobolium and Criobolium in connection with the Magna Mater and Mithras, and shows the mixture of these cults with some Christian principles and terms. He quotes the following remarks from Mr. King's *Gnostics*, p. 48 : "There is very good reason to believe that, as in the East, the worship of Serapis was combined at first with Christianity, and gradually merged into it with an entire change of name, not substance, carrying with it many of its ancient notions and rites ; so in the West a similar influence was exerted by the Mithraic religion. Seel (*Mith.*, p. 287) is of opinion that ' as long as the Roman dominion lasted in Germany we find also traces of the Mosaic law : as there were single Jewish, so there were also single Christian, families existing amongst the Gentiles. The latter, however, for the most part, ostensibly paid worship to the

[1] *Journal of the Brit. Arch. Assoc.*, vol. xxiii, p. 221.

Roman gods, in order to escape persecution, holding secretly in their hearts the religion of Christ. It is by no means improbable that, under the permitted symbols of Mithras, they worshipped the Son of God and the mysteries of Christianity. In this point of view the Mithraic monuments, so frequent in Germany, are evidences of the secret faith of the early Christian Romans.'"[1]

Mr. E. P. Loftus-Brock, F.S.A.,[2] in writing upon Christianity in Britain in Roman times, produces evidences of Roman architecture in Christian churches, particularly instancing the discoveries lately made in the churches of St. Pancras and St. Martin at Dover. He also refers to a "hexagonal bath of remarkable construction, believed", as he says, "and with very weighty reasons, to have been a baptistery,"[3] in the villa at Chedworth, described by Mr. J. W. Grover.

These extracts and observations are rather beyond the scope of our mosaics, but it seemed necessary in some way to account for the absence in them of Christian symbols, of which there appears to be only one instance on the mosaics, even if that is to be depended on; for a star of six points, a common emblem in Roman as well as in Mithraic monuments, would only require a loop to change it into the ☧. After all, it is not in the dining-hall where we should expect to find emblems of a new faith in times of great political and religious change.

In conclusion, something must be said of the great skill of the Romans in selecting those materials best suited for these and other works of art. A volume might be written upon the various marbles and hard stones found

[1] *Journal of the Brit. Arch. Assoc.*, vol. xxix, p. 377.

[2] *Archæologia Cantiana*, vol. xv, pp. 38-55.

[3] *Journal of the Brit. Arch. Assoc.*, vol. xxiv, p. 129, where it is figured.

both in England and elsewhere, which were freely made
use of by the Romans for the composition of mosaic-
work. Those ready to hand would naturally be the
most generally used, on the score of expense ; but it will
be seen that economy was not always an object, as in the
fine specimens found in Gloucestershire. Those from North
Africa, in the British Museum, have the advantage in the
variety of material employed, and the wide choice of
marbles and hard stones within reach. This will be seen
by the following extracts from two lectures delivered by
Mr. G. Aitchison, A.R.A., at the Royal Academy, on the
18th and 25th February 1884, upon the subject of marble
and glass employed by the ancients, and brought down to
later times. He informs us that "there are forty dif-
ferent-coloured marbles in the quarries at Sienna, ranging
from white to black ; that there are marbles in every
division of the world's surface ; and that in France alone
about 600 have been already catalogued. First may be
mentioned the imperial purples ; the amethystine ; the
Tyrian, of the colour of clotted blood ; the Hysginian or
puce ; and the crimson. The first marbles in rank are the
purple Egyptian porphyries, which are truly imperial from
their fine colour, excessive hardness, and great durability ;
they will, moreover, take a polish like glass. Both purple
and green Egyptian porphyry may be seen on Henry III's
tomb in Westminster Abbey. Still more splendid in colour
is red serpentine, mottled with dark green and black, and
flecked with gold ; the dappled blood-red antique breccia of
Numidia, and the Griotte d'Italie, with its white veins and
partridge eyes. The Rosso Antico is no longer antique,
since the quarries have been found in Greece. The Langue-
doc is of a still more vivid red, powdered with flames of
white ; the Greek red, with fragments of pink and yellow
imbedded in it ; the Cork red, speckled with white ; the

dusky red and grey of rouge royal ; and red Devonshire.
After these come the soft-coloured mottled yellowish-pink
of emperor's red and Verona ; the deeper pink of St. Juan,
fretted with pinkish white; the brilliant Devonshire spar,
mottled with violet-pink or brownish red; and the red-
veined alabasters. Splendid alabaster is found in the
English quarries, tinted with purple, not to speak of the
pink granites and porphyries. For yellows there is the
lordly sienna, with its deep orange ground streaked with
purple, veined with black, and here and there spotted with
white; the pure yellow of Giallo Antico ; the pale yellow
of the Ivorio Antico of Numidia ; the yellow Egyptian
alabaster, with its eddying veins of white; brocatello, which
may be classed with yellow or red, as in its fine brocade one
or the other colour predominates ; and the Rose du Var,
light tawny yellow with red marks. Nearly approaching
the yellows are some of the tawny marbles of Numidia. Of
all the greens, some of the five Verdi Antichi are the most
splendid and the noblest. Next to these come the Genoa
green, Greek green from Laconia, and the dark green Vert
de Corse ; the Vert Maurin, intersected in every direction
with light green veins ; the Campan Vert ; the Campan
mélange, of a full green, streaked with red and flowered with
white ; the Cipollino; the Irish green, that varies from bold,
eddying streaks of dark grey to a pale yellow, here and
there interspersed with translucent spots of dark green ;
the cool green marble of Anglesea, spotted with black and
brindled with white ; the green Egyptian and Irish porphyries; green serpentines, of which the dark bands on
Italian buildings are made ; the grey, green, and purple
Purbeck and Petworth marbles, of which so many of the
shafts in our Gothic cathedrals are made. For white, are
the Carrara, Parian, and Pentelic, and the blue-white from
Carrara, besides others. For black, Nero Antico, Irish

black, Belgian black, English black, black basalt, and black granite, though this latter is grey. For greys, the grey granites, dove, Belgian grey; the pale grey Bardilla, with its net-work of darker veins and black rivulets; and blue imperial. For black and white is Hachette and Grand Antique. But perhaps the most splendid marbles are those which can be put into no category of colour, the different sorts of variegated breccias; the pale, fawn-coloured Caserta, diapered with crimson patches; the violet breccias from Rondona, with large round patches of purple, red, grey, and yellowish white, bound with dark grey and black veins; the breccia of Palermo; the gorgeous antique breccias of Africa; the grey Sarrancolin veined with red; the dark brown breccia of Belgium, with black patches and red spots; the breccias of Septimus Bassus, and all the antique breccias of Numidia. The Egyptian, in which green and purple pebbles of porphyry start out from a golden ground, are to be seen at St. Vitale, Ravenna, and at the Campo Santo, Pisa.

"From these are omitted the gems and precious stones, lapis lazuli and malachite, coral, onyx, agate, real jasper, chalcedony and blood-stone, rock crystal, and cornelian, all which may be found used in the altar-pieces abroad. Thanks to Il Cavaliere Giovanni Battista, we can see at the Natural History Museum many of the famed marbles of Numidia, and at the Geological Museum Corsi's slab, containing 1,012 specimens of antique marbles."[1]

The same author, in speaking of ancient glass, its manufacture and adaptation to the purposes of mosaics, as described very fully by Pliny, remarks that this Roman writer "uses a strong argument to prove that glass mosaic was not known in B.C. 27, when Agrippa built the Pantheon, and either glass must have taken a rapid stride between

[1] See *Builder*, vol. xlvi, p. 281.

that time and Pliny's death in A.D. 79, or else glass mosaic must have been introduced from some country where this mode of decoration was practised, for we find glass mosaic used in fountains at Pompeii."

It will be seen by the separate descriptions of the mosaics in England that glass, though judiciously introduced at times, yet was but sparingly used, but in the African and Asiatic specimens it is more frequently employed. If the plan of this work were to follow up the history of mosaic-work in after ages, it would be seen how the material of glass came to be more and more employed in the decorations, but the scope of it must be limited to Romano-British examples; nor can the subject of Continental mosaics be entered upon, which would carry us beyond our limits, otherwise it would have been useful to record such magnificent specimens as the Battle of Arbela, found in the House of the Faun at Pompeii, and now in the Museum of Naples; the Doves of Pliny, now in the Capitoline Museum, Rome; and the Combat of Animals, brought from Hadrian's villa.[1] There are several small pieces of foreign mosaics of minute design placed against the wall in the vase-room, on the first floor of the British Museum, which are worthy of careful examination.

It must strike the observer, on inspecting the large pavements in the British Museum, how skilfully they must have been handled, before removal as well as after, when the difficulties had to be overcome of transporting to a great distance such friable materials. It were to be wished that those mosaics still *in situ* in our own country could be preserved for posterity, and measures taken without loss of time to prevent decay, which is already destroying many,

---

[1] Many of them are figured in a comprehensive manual, *La Mosaïque*, par Gerspach (Bibliothèque de l'Enseignement des Beaux-Arts). Paris: A. Quantin, 1881.

from the effects of damp, frost, and the hands of curious visitors. This can be accomplished in other ways besides the not very satisfactory one of covering them up again with earth. The mode of fixing and levelling the *tessellæ* is now pretty well understood—as witness the very large pavement brought from Halicarnassus, in the British Museum—that is, by gluing the surface upon canvas stretched on a flat slab; then, reversing the whole, the concrete at the back, in which the *tessellæ* are imbedded, may be adjusted or renewed. This process has been successfully accomplished in the case of the large pavement from Bucklersbury, London, now in the Guildhall Museum, and many other examples of pavements removed, referred to in the preceding pages. Once levelled and secured, three modes could be adopted of taking care of the pavements, if private proprietors were content to waive their rights for the public good. First, by retaining the pavement *in situ*, and building a cover over it to keep out wintry frosts and damp; or, secondly, by sending it to the nearest local museum, where it would be taken care of, and a special interest given to it from vicinity to the place of its origin ; or, lastly, failing a good local museum, to send it to the British Museum in London.

CHAPTER XIX.

Descriptions of Thirty Coins, selected from the British Museum Collection.
—Amplification of the descriptions to illustrate the period travelled
over in this work with reference to the Mosaics.—Remarks upon
the value of certain Coins, and on the importance of Numismatic
Science.

DESCRIPTION OF THIRTY COINS IN THE
BRITISH MUSEUM.

PLATE I.

Claudius (A.D. 41-54).

1.—TI . CLAVDIVS CAESAR AVG . P . M . TR . P . IMP . His head to right,
laureate.

Rev. DE BRITANNI., inscribed on an arch surmounted by an equestrian
figure between two trophies. (*Aureus.*)

Claudius, desirous of military fame, crossed over into Britain in A.D. 43
and completely defeated the British chief, Caractacus, whom he took
prisoner, but immediately liberated. For this success he was, on his
return to Rome, rewarded with a military triumph, and the surname of
Britannicus was decreed both to himself and his son, who was originally
named Claudius Tiberius Germanicus.

Trajan (A.D. 98-117).

2.—IMP . CAES . NERVAE TRAIANO AVG . GER . DAC . P . M . TR . P . COS .
V . P . P . His head to right, laureate.

Rev. S . P . Q . R . OPTIMO PRINCIPI . S . C . View of the Circus Maximus. (*Sestertius, or large brass.*)

This piece was struck to commemorate the enlargement of the Circus
Maximus, which is here represented with the Egyptian obelisk of Augustus
in the centre of the spina. This structure was capable of holding upwards
of 20,000 spectators.

Hadrian (A.D. 117-138).

3.—HADRIANVS AVGVSTVS . His bust to right, laureate, and wearing the
paludamentum.

Rev. FELICITATI AVG . S . C . A prætorian galley, with the gubernator
and rowers. (*Sestertius, or large brass.*)

ROMAN IMPERIAL COINS AND MEDALS

In A.D. 119 Hadrian quitted Rome on a personal visit to all the provinces of the State. His journeys extended from Britain to the far East. This piece was struck, upon his departure, by the Senate, so that he might carry with him their wishes for a successful voyage.

Antoninus Pius (A.D. 138-161).

4.—ANTONINVS AVG . PIVS P . P . TR . P . COS . III . His head to right, laureate.

Rev. IMPERATOR II . S . C . Victory walking to left, bearing palm-branch and shield, inscribed BRITAN. (*Dupondius.*)

In A.D. 139 Lollius Urbicus, who commanded in Britain, chastised a revolt of the Brigantes, and having carried his arms beyond the frontier, completed the defences of Agricola with a continuous rampart of earth from the Clyde to the Forth.

Faustina Junr. (Wife of Marcus Aurelius).

5.—FAVSTINA AVG . PII AVG . FIL . Her bust to right, draped.

Rev. IVNO. Juno seated to left, having one child on her knee; before her is another, with hands outstretched. (*Aureus.*)

On this coin Faustina is personified by Juno.

Commodus (A.D. 180-192).

6.—M . COMMODVS ANTONINVS AVG . PIVS BRIT . His bust to right, laureate, and wearing the paludamentum.

Rev. BRITANNIA P . M . TR . P . X . IMP . VII . COS . IIII . P . P . Britannia seated to left on a rock, wearing close-fitting dress and mantle over her shoulders; she holds in her right hand a standard, and in her left a spear; her left arm resting on her shield. (*Medallion in bronze.*)

This well-known medallion commemorates the victories gained by Ulpius Marcellus in Britain, for which Commodus was saluted Emperor the seventh time, in A.D. 184. It is said that this piece suggested the type of the Britannia on English copper coins in the reign of Charles II, which, with but slight alterations, remains to the present time.

7.—IMP . COMMODVS AVG . PIVS FELIX . His bust to right, laureate, wearing the paludamentum.

Rev. VOTIS FELICIBVS . Commodus standing near a "pharos", on a rock near the sea, sacrificing at an altar; at his feet lies a slain ox; in the distance is a fleet and several small boats; at the stern of the central large ship is seated Jupiter Serapis. (*Medallion in bronze.*)

In the year A.D. 186, after a long dearth, Commodus sent a fleet to collect grain in Africa. This fleet is here represented, and the moment chosen is its return to the port of Ostia; the Emperor received the fleet on its arrival and offered up sacrifices for the bounteous provision which it brought.

PLATE II.

Septimius Severus (A.D. 193-211).

1.—SEPT . SEVERVS PIVS AVG.   His bust to right, laureate.
Rev. VICTORIAE BRITTANNICAE . S . C .   Two winged Victories, holding a shield against a palm-tree, at the base of which are seated two bound captives. (*Sestertius.*)

This coin was struck in A.D. 210, to commemorate Severus's defeat of the Picts, who offered so strong a resistance that it is said the expedition cost the Emperor upwards of 50,000 men.

Caracalla (A.D. 211-217).

2.—ANTONINVS PIVS AVG .   His bust to right, radiate.
Rev. VICTORIAE BRITTANNICAE . S . C .   Victory, with her left foot on a helmet, stands to right, and is writing on a shield placed on a palm-tree. (*Dupondius.*)

Caracalla accompanied his father Severus in the expedition to Britain, and after his death continued the war against the Picts, with whom he soon concluded a peace, and returned with his brother Geta to Italy.

Geta (A.D. 211-212).

3.—P . SEPTIMIVS GETA CAESAR .   His bust to left, wearing the paludamentum and cuirass, and holding a staff (?) over his right shoulder.
Rev. CONCORDIA MILITVM .   Geta standing between five signa, three on *his* right, and two on *his* left, and holding a staff in his left hand; he is clad in the paludamentum and cuirass. (*Medallion in bronze.*)

Geta did not receive the title of Augustus till A.D. 209, so that this piece was probably struck between A.D. 205-207, at which time he was in Britain with his father Severus.   He was much beloved by the troops, and this medallion testifies to his valour and activity as a general.

Elagabalus (A.D. 218-222).

4.—IMP . CAES . M . AVR . ANTONINVS PIVS AVG .   Bust of the Emperor to right, laureate, wearing the paludamentum and cuirass.
Rev. SACERDOS DEI SOLIS ELAGAB . S . C .   The Emperor, in a long Oriental dress, stands nearly facing, near a garlanded and lighted altar. He holds a patera and a palm-branch.   On his right is a star.   (*Sestertius.*)

The Emperor, whose early name was Bassianus, is here represented in his character of high-priest of the sun, to which post he was appointed during his residence at Emesa in Syria, before his assumption of the title

of Emperor and the name of Antoninus. The sun was worshipped at Emesa under the name of Elagabalus (Ela-Gabal), and in the form of a black conical stone, which was said to have fallen from heaven. To this protecting deity Antoninus ascribed his elevation to the throne, and therefore sought to raise the god of Emesa over all the religions of the earth. In a solemn procession through Rome, this conical stone was decked with precious stones, and placed in a chariot drawn by six white horses, which the Emperor himself drove, decked in his sacerdotal robes of silk and gold.

Severus Alexander (A.D. 222-235).

5.—IMP . CAES . M . AVR . SEV . ALEXANDER AVG. His bust to right, laureate, and wearing the paludamentum and cuirass.

Rev. P . M . TR . P . V . COS . II . P . P . S . C. An elegant and highly ornamented structure, decorated with statues and surrounded by a portico. (*Dupondius.*)

The reverse of the piece, struck about A.D. 226, represents the celebrated *thermæ*, or baths which bore the Emperor's name, and which were frequently illuminated at night. "*Addidit et oleum luminibus thermarum, quum ante non antea auroram paterent, et ante solis occasum clauderentur.*"

Maximinus (A.D. 235-238).

6.—IMP. MAXIMINVS PIVS AVG. His bust to right, laureate, wearing the paludamentum.

Rev. LIBERALITAS AVGVSTI . S . C. The Emperor seated on a curule chair, placed upon a suggestum, which is decorated with a frieze; behind him are two warriors, and before him Liberalitas holding a *tessara* and a cornucopiæ. (*Sestertius.*)

This coin refers to some act of *largesse* on the part of the Emperor Maximinus. It may be the distribution of money amongst his troops, which was chiefly made out of the gold and silver offerings taken by him from the temples.

Gordian II (A.D. 238).

7.—IMP . CAES . M . ANT . GORDIANVS AFR . AVG. His bust to right, laureate, wearing the paludamentum and cuirass.

Rev. ROMAE AETERNAE . S . C. Roma seated to left, holding a Victory and a spear; at her side her shield. (*Sestertius.*)

"This device alludes to the eternity promised to the city of Rome by all the oracles of antiquity, and echoed by the Latin poets"—

"His ego nec metas, rerum nec tempora pono ;
Imperium sine fine dedi."

PLATE III.

Gordian III (A.D. 238-244).

1.—IMP . GORDIANVS PIVS FELIX AVG . His bust to left, wearing the
paludamentum, and armed with spear and shield ; the latter decorated with
a relief representing the Emperor on horseback, preceded by Victory and
followed by a soldier.

Rev. MVNIFICENTIA GORDIANI AVG . View of the Flavian amphitheatre
or Coliseum from above ; within are seen the spectators, who are witness-
ing a contest between a bull and a hippopotamus with rider ; outside, on the
left, is the Meta Sudans, and a figure holding a rudder ; and on the right a
porch, within which is a figure. (*Medallion in bronze.*)

This famous amphitheatre was begun by Vespasian and completed by
his son Titus. In the reign of Macrinus it was struck by lightning, and so
much damage done to the interior that for several years no games were
celebrated in it. Its restoration was commenced by Elagabalus and completed by Severus Alexander. There appears no special record of the
games held in that theatre which are commemorated by this medallion.

Philip I, Otacilia, and Philip II (A.D. 244-249).

2.—CONCORDIA AVGVSTORVM . Busts jugate to right of Philip I and
Otacilia ; he wears the paludamentum and cuirass ; and she is draped
and wears stephane ; facing them is Philip II, laureate, and wearing the
paludamentum and cuirass.

Rev. SAECVLVM NOVVM . The two Emperors, Philip I and II, each
accompanied by two attendants, sacrificing at an altar placed in front of an
octostyle temple. (*Medallion in bronze.*)

This piece was struck in A.D. 248, and commemorates the New Era.
The legend *Saeculum Novum* intimates that the thousandth year from the
building of Rome having expired, another age has commenced. The temple
may be that of Jupiter Capitolinus.

Otacilia Severa (A.D. 244-249`.

3.—MARCIA OTACIL . SEVERA AVG . Her bust to right, draped ; her hair
is draped, and plaited behind.

Rev. SAECVLARES AVG . S . C . A hippopotamus walking to right.
(*Sestertius.*)

This coin commemorates the celebration of the secular games in

1.

2.

3
5
4

6
7

A.D. 248 ; in which no doubt were introduced combats with hippopotami, as shown in the medallion of Gordian III, above described.

Trajan Decus (A.D. 249-251).

4.—IMP . C . M . Q . TRAIANVS DECIVS AVG . His bust to right, laureate.
Rev. DACIA . S . C . A draped female figure, standing facing, and holding staff surmounted by an animal's head. (*Sestertius.*)

In A.D. 250 Dacia was liberated from the incursions of the Barbarians, an event commemorated by this coin. The origin of the staff with the animal's head is unknown ; it may, however, represent some Dacian instrument, such as the trumpet.

Postumus (A.D. 258-267).

5.—POSTVMVS AVG . His bust three-quarters to right, head facing, wearing the cuirass.
Rev. INDVLGENTIA POSTVMI AVG . Postumus seated to left on a curule chair ; before him a suppliant with uplifted hands. (*Aureus.*)

Postumus stands second on the list of the thirty tyrants enumerated by Trebellius Pollio. He ruled in Gaul, and his government was a contrast to that of Gallienus, being marked by moderation and justice. This coin, no doubt, refers to some unrecorded act of indulgence on the part of the Emperor.

Victorinus (A.D. 265-267).

6.—IMP . VICTORINVS P . F . AVG . His bust to right, laureate.
Rev. LEG . XXX . VLP . VICT . P . F . Jupiter, naked, leaning on his spear and holding thunderbolt, standing facing ; on his left a capricorn. (*Aureus.*)

The "legio Ulpia", or the 30th, was originally raised by Trajan, and was stationed in the north, probably during the reign of Victorinus, in Gaul, and of which he had the command. Victorinus was also one of the thirty tyrants, but his character appears to have been the opposite of that of Postumus.

Marius (A.D. 267).

7.—IMP . C . M . AVR . MARIVS P . F . AVG . His bust to right, laureate, wearing the cuirass.
Rev. CONCORDIA MILITVM. Two right hands united. (*Aureus.*)

This coin marks the ephemeral reign in Gaul of Marius, who was raised to the purple by the voice of his army, and two days afterwards killed by a soldier who had worked with the Emperor when he served as a blacksmith.

PLATE IV

Diocletian (A.D. 284-305).

1.—IMP . C . C . VAL . DIOCLETIANVS P . F . AVG . His head to right, bare. (*Medallion in gold.*)

The reverse of this medallion has a figure of Jupiter, leaning on his sceptre, and holding a globe surmounted by a Victory, and the inscription IOVI CONSERVATORI. The letters S . M . N . (Signata Moneta Nicomediae) also on the reverse, show that it was issued at Nicomedia. This piece was struck about the year A.D. 296, and the reverse type is probably an allusion to the assumption by Diocletian of the name of *Jovius*, as his colleague Maximian took that of *Herculius* (see the next piece).

Maximian I, Hercules (A.D. 286-305).

2.—IMP . C . M . AVR . VAL . MAXIMIANVS P . F . AVG . His head to left, wearing the lion's skin. (*Medallion in bronze.*)

On the reverse are the figures of the three Monetæ, each holding a pair of scales and a cornucopia, and the inscription MONETA AVGG. These figures are symbolical of the three metals used for the coinage, viz., gold, silver, and copper. Maximian is here represented in the character of Hercules (see the preceding).

Carausius (A.D. 287-293).

3.—CARAVSIVS P . F . AVG . Bust of Carausius to right, laureate, wearing the cuirass.

Rev. CONSERVAT . AVG . M . L . (Moneta Londinii). Jupiter, standing, leaning on his sceptre, and holding a thunderbolt; at his feet an eagle. (*Aureus.*)

This is one of the earliest coins of the London Mint.

Allectus (A.D. 293-296).

4.—IMP . C . ALLECTVS P . F . AVG . His bust to right, laureate, wearing the cuirass.

Rev. ORIENS AVG . M . L . (Moneta Londinii). Male figure (the Sun), radiate, standing to left, raising his right hand and holding a globe; at his feet two captives, seated. (*Aureus.*)

Constantius I, Chlorus (A.D. 305-306).

5.—CONSTANTIVS NOB . CAES . His head to right, laureate.

1.

3.

2.

4

6.

5.

7.

9.

8.

8.

Rev. HERCVLI VICTORI S . M . N . (Signata Moneta Nicomediae.) Hercules, standing, holding club and lion's skin. (*Aureus.*)

This coin was struck before Constantius was raised to the purple, but after A.D. 296, when the coinage was reformed by Diocletian.

Constantine I, the Great (A.D. 306-337).

6.—Head of Constantine to right, with diadem.

Rev. GLORIA CONSTANTINI AVG . SIS (Siscia). A Roman soldier, carrying a trophy and dragging a captive after him by the hair ; his foot is placed on another captive, whose hands are tied behind him. (*Aureus.*)

This coin was struck by Constantine when he had become sole master of the Empire.

Constans (A.D. 337-350).

7.—FL . IVL . CONSTANS PIVS FELIX AVG . His bust to right, diademed, and wearing the paludamentum and cuirass.

Rev. TRIVMFATOR GENTIVM BARBARARVM . TES (Thessalonica). The Emperor, standing facing, holding a vexillum, his left hand on his shield. (*Medallion in silver.*)

The barbarians referred to are no doubt the Gauls, Britons, and Celts, who were subdued by Constans in A.D. 342-3.

Constantius II (A.D. 337-361).

8.—CONSTANTIVS AVGVSTVS . His bust to right, diademed, wearing the paludamentum and cuirass.

Rev. VICTORIAE DDNN . AVGG . TR (Treves). Two Victories, holding between them a shield, inscribed VOT . XX . MVLT . XXX . (*Solidus.*)

This coin records the vicennalian vows of the Emperor, with the expression of the hope that he might live to the tricennalian.

Magnus Maximus (A.D. 383-388).

9.—DN . MAG . MAXIMVS P . F . AVG . His bust to right, diademed, wearing the paludamentum and cuirass.

Rev. VICTORIA AVGG . AVG . OB . (Augusta, 72). Magnus Maximus and Flavius Victor, seated facing, and holding between them a globe ; behind the chairs is seen a Victory. (*Solidus.*)

This coin was struck at London, the name of which place had been changed to Augusta. The numerals O B = 72 record the fact that that number of *solidi* went to the Roman pound. This was one of the last coins struck in Britain. The sovereignty of Gaul, Spain, and Britain was confirmed to Magnus Maximus by Theodosius I, who also recognised Flavius Victor, the son of Maximus, as his associate in the Empire.

A history of the Roman Empire might almost be compiled from the figures and inscriptions stamped upon the
coins and medals of the Emperors. Britain comes in for its
share of mention on some of them, and many of these coins
have been engraved in plain outline by Camden, Horsley,
and others ; but the new process by which they can be
reproduced on paper in exact *facsimile* has induced me
to present to the reader, in four plates, some of the coins
which bear upon the subject-matter of these pages. The
identical coins found upon or near the pavements have not
been attainable, but the types herewith are from coins of
the Emperors, in the British Museum, and of the greatest
rarity. I am enabled to reproduce them by the privilege
and through the kind assistance of Mr. Herbert Appold
Grueber, who, besides co-operating with Mr. Prætorius in
the photographic process, has furnished me with descriptions of the coins, which are given above in his own words.
Their connection with events referred to in these pages
will be sufficiently apparent through Mr. Grueber's descriptions, but a few amplifications may not be without their
use.

The first of the series is the beautiful aureus of Claudius, recording, as it were, the annexation of Britain consequent on his triumphs over the Britons; though as to
mosaic pavements, the time for such elegancies had not
yet arrived. (See pp. 58-9.)

The next Emperor, Trajan, No. 2 in the series, well
deserved the epithet by which he was addressed as *Optimo
Principi*, and in the matter of coinage he had the sagacity
to recoin and reissue many of the old consular or family
coins of the republic. A writer in the first volume of the
Journal of the Numismatic Society (p. 247) has said, as
to this recoinage, that " it was a noble as well as refined
stroke of policy, to refresh and keep alive in the minds

of the people the pride of ancestry, the renown of brave
achievements, the memory of the origin and growth of
Roman power and independence, the associations produced
by revered traditions and distinguished names."

The value of the consular series of coins as records of
contemporary history has been well pointed out by Mr.
H. A. Grueber, in a letter to the author, published in the
Journal of the Brit. Arch. Assoc., vol. xxxiv, p. 226 ; but
these early coins are seldom found in this country.

The journey of Hadrian to Britain with his wife
Sabina in A.D. 119 is represented by the interesting coin
No. 3, which conveys the good wishes for their safety at
the time of departure from Rome. I have referred to the
water-supply of London, and the works connected there-
with, at pp. 164-5, and these works were probably completed in the reign of this Emperor or his predecessor.
(Coin at Woodchester, see pp. 6 and 78.)

The next coin, No. 4, of Antoninus Pius, records a name
especially connected with Britain, even if for nothing else
than the accurate " Itinerary of Roads" (the British portion
printed at length in the Appendix to this work, according to the most approved readings) ; and for his wall in
Scotland, between Edinburgh and Glasgow, and for the
exploits of Lollius Urbicus, his propraetor. (See p. 153 for
coin at Wingham.)

An aureus of the frail and beautiful Faustina, No. 5,
wife of Marcus Aurelius, represents her as the *mater-
familias*, and personified as the stately Juno. We can
hardly congratulate the lady upon having acted up to this
her part in history.

The medallion of Commodus, No. 6, will be remembered
for the figure of Britain on the reverse, seated on a rock,
and for the victories of his propraetor, Ulpius Marcellus, in
A.D. 184. May the rock long remain as stable as it has
been from that time to the present !

Another medallion, No. 7, commemorates the same
Emperor welcoming the corn-ships coming in from Africa,
after a long dearth, and sacrificing at an altar on the occasion. This may have stimulated his successor to make
ample provision against a famine, as he did by collecting
a very large public store of corn. (See p. 135.)

This successor was Septimius Severus, who heads
Plate II, No. 1, on a fine sestertius, struck the year before
his death at York. The two figures of winged Victories
holding up a shield are a counterpart of those sculptured
on his arch at Rome, and a similar design is on the pediment of the temple at Bath, as restored from the fragments found. (See p. 170, and p. 37.)

The next two Nos. 2 and 3, a dupondius and a medallion in bronze, are of his two sons, Caracalla and Geta, of
whom some account has been given in connection with Bath,
on p. 167.

The priest of the sun, Elagabalus, is represented on a
sestertius, No. 4. The next, No. 5, a dupondius of Severus
Alexander, is interesting as having on the reverse a view
of his Thermæ, which, as Mr. Grueber informs us, he lighted
up with oil lamps for the first time, as before then, baths
were closed at sunset and opened at early dawn.

On a sestertius, No. 6, is the likeness of the hardy
Thracian, Maximinus. The largess referred to on the coin,
if it kept up his popularity with the soldiers during three
years, did not prevent the massacre of himself and his son
at the end of that term. (See p. 7.)

No. 7 is a sestertius of Gordian II, who seems to
have believed in the eternity of the city of Rome, though
his own rule in it ended before the year of his election
was out.

Plate III.—No. 1 represents, on a medallion, Gordian III,
and records his munificence at the Coliseum at Rome. He

is referred to on page 7 ; and from and after this time the greater part of the mosaic pavements appear to date.

No. 2 gives, on a medallion, the likeness of Philip I, the Arab, and his wife Otacilia and son Philip II. The secular games to commemorate the thousandth year of the foundation of Rome were held in his reign, in A.D. 248 (see p. 8), and a new era was henceforth to commence, a *sæculum novum*.

No. 3 is a sestertius, and represents the Empress Otacilia, wife of Philip. A hippopotamus on the reverse records the secular games above referred to, the great event of the day.

No. 4. Trajan Decius probably had this coin, a sestertius, ready in anticipation of victories in Dacia, which, however, never came off. This successor of the two Philips, Cnæus Metius Quintus Trajanus Decius, aimed at and expected to reconquer Dacia, and thus emulate the fame of the great Trajan, from whom he claimed descent and whose name he bore; but on marching at the head of a large army against the Goths, he found them already south of the Danube, investing Nicopolis ; and though he raised the siege of that place, the barbarians marched further south to Philippopolis, a city of Thrace, at the Balkans, which they sacked, murdering the inhabitants. Decius in vain tried to infuse the ancient spirit into the Roman army, and he appears to have lost his life fighting in that desperate engagement at Forum Trerebonii in Mæsia, where a marshy swamp proved fatal to his army. The son, appointed to succeed his father, lost his popularity through buying off the Goths by payment of an ignominious tribute, an expedient which had been before resorted to by the Philips.

Nos. 5, 6, 7 are aurei of the tyrants or usurpers Postumus, Victorinus, and Marius. As the latter reigned less than a month, it is wonderful there are so many types of his coins; but they were doubtless struck in anticipation of his success, and for liberal donations to the troops. The full face of Victorinus is no less uncommon than it is beautifully designed.

I regret that room could not be found for some of the coins of Tetricus, to illustrate what has been said of him. (See p. 8.)

The last series of coins, on Plate IV, commences with No. 1, a fine medallion in gold of Diocletian, struck at his new capital of the East, where he personified Jupiter—to his own edification perhaps, if not to that of his subjects. His colleague in the West, Maximian, figures on coin No. 2 as Hercules, the lion-skin forming a head-dress. The personification of the three metals of the coinage on the reverse celebrates the rectification of its values at this period, and at the same time recalls the fact that the weights also, by which merchandise was bought and sold, were kept in temples dedicated to Hercules ; and in the matter of weights the Romans was scrupulously exact, as is seen by the distinction they made in comparing rain-water, spring-water, and boiled water as a standard of weight. (See p. 9.)

No. 3 is an aureus bearing the portrait of the bluff Carausius, styled the Preserver of the Empire (*Conservator*). Dr. Stukeley collected the many types of this bold usurper's coins to write the history of his reign in Britain. The coin here shown is of extreme interest, being " one of the earliest coins of the London Mint". (See p. 10.)

For the same reason that it was struck at London, No. 4, an aureus of Allectus, is interesting. His boastful figure on the reverse, as the sun in the East, soon set when his successor appeared on our shores, who is represented by the next coin, No. 5, of Constantius Chlorus, a beautiful aureus struck at Nicomedia. (See pp. 10 and 12.)

Constantine the Great appears on a fine aureus, No. 6, struck at Siscia, in Pannonia, and the way he triumphs over his competitors is seen on the reverse.

Constans, his successor, is shown on a beautiful medallion in silver, No. 7. He holds the labarum bearing the Christian monogram in right hand; and the letters in the exergue show that it was struck at Thessalonica.

The last two of the series are solidi counterparts to the aurei of the olden time.

No. 8, one of Constantius II, struck at Treves.

No. 9, another of Magnus Maximus; and this coin is doubly interesting as being struck at London, called at this time Augusta (Trinobantum), and also as having numerals to record the number of solidi (72) then coined out of the Roman pound of gold.

This small selection of coins serves as a numismatic sketch of the period travelled over, without perplexing the reader with too many specimens ; and what may be deduced from them will serve as an incentive to further medallic researches into the history of Britain. Many questions are to be solved by such a study ; as an instance of this, the value of the silver denarius, of which seven were coined to the ounce, bears upon the pay of the soldier, and this very often upon the election even of the emperors. In very ancient times, when payments were made by weight rather than by tale, the denarius was equivalent to ten *asses*, whence its name, and each *as* was said to have been originally a pound of copper ; but the silver denarius was not struck till B.C. 269, at which time the *as* weighed either four ounces (triental) according to Mommsen, or two ounces (sextantal) according to others. As silver became more abundant its relative value to copper or brass would adapt itself to the circumstances of the times, and payments by tale were found expedient, the *as* becoming

uncialis, or of the weight of an ounce instead of a pound,
and this was, by the Lex Papiria, in B.C. 89, made
semuncialis, or of half an ounce. Some little compensation
was afforded the soldier by paying him in silver, and reckon-
ing in military pay the old ten asses as equivalent to a
denarius, instead of sixteen, according to the current mintage; much in the same way as our soldiers in India have
their sterling money commuted into rupees at an old exchange of the rupee, whereas, if this were reconverted into
English money at the current exchange, there would be a
loss of over 20 per cent.; but with this difference, that in
the case of the Roman soldier he derived the benefit of the
difference in the increased rate of pay, whereas in the case
of the British soldier the difference is made a saving to the
State, by diminishing the pay to that extent.

When the relative value between silver and brass was
altered, whether it adapted itself to the natural law of
metals and other commodities, or was established arbitrarily
at particular dates, as recorded by Pliny (xxxiii, 3), must
be referred to the many learned authors who have written
on the subject. It is sufficient for my purpose here to take
the silver denarius as the fixed quantity in metal, seven
being coined out of the ounce of pure silver, and therefore
the full-weighted ones would be worth about eightpence,
valuing silver at 56*d.* the ounce. The sub-divisions of
value in brass by tale and not by weight would be as
follows:—The *sestertius,* being a fourth part, would be two-
pence ; the *as,* or sixteenth, one halfpenny ; the *dupondius,*
one penny, in this ratio, or when of two uncial *asses,* two-
pence.

The separation of the empire into East and West probably influenced in some degree the depreciation of the
aureus, by making gold scarce in the West. This gold
coin, up to the reign of Nero, was about equivalent in

weight to our sovereign, or more nearly to our guinea of twenty-one shillings. The depreciation is seen by the weight of the coins, of which forty-five in Nero's time were coined from a pound of pure gold, and seventy-two at the time of the last coin of our series, when the aureus would thus be worth 13*s*. 4*d*. instead of 21*s*., its original value as to weight.[1]

The historical, mythological, social, and artistic incidents displayed on the coins often afford a more accurate insight into the life of the Romans than history can teach, and many of its blank pages can only be filled up by numismatic science.

[1] A brief account of the Roman coinage will be found in *Coins and Medals, their Place in History and Art*, edited by Stanley Lane-Poole (chap. iii, by H. A. Grueber), London, Elliot Stock, 1885.

R R

APPENDIX.

Notes on the *Itinerary* of Antoninus and the Text of such portion thereof as concerns Roman Britain.—Table of the Mosaics referred to in this work, distinguishing the Plain and Geometrical from the Figured Designs.

THE text of the *Itinerary* of Antoninus, as far as concerns Britain, is given herewith, as a guide to the map on which the lines of this military roadster are laid down ; and it will show the direction given to colonisation at an early period of the Roman dominion, for this *Itinerary* seems probably to have been compiled in the time of the first of the Antonines, rather than in that of either of the other *imperatores* bearing this name, though some of the older antiquaries assign its composition to the time of Septimius Severus.

The text I have made use of is from the excellent edition of Messrs. G. Parthey and M. Pinder (Berlin, 1848). In a preface they have given their views as to the time of its compilation, which in the main dates, probably, from the first of the Antonines ; though Marcus Aurelius, who paid much attention to the roads of the Empire, may have had it corrected to date ; and the same may be said as to Severus and Caracalla, who adopted the name of Antoninus, and who ordered the milestones, ruined through age, to be restored, as is seen by an inscribed stone preserved at Vienna, and described by Scipio Maffei (in *Museo*

Veronensi, p. 241).[1] Some amended copies of the *Itinerary* are as late as Diocletian, to judge by the two names given to Legionary stations,—the one, I *Jovia*, and the second, II *Herculea*, indicating the time of Diocletian and Maximian. There is mention made in one of the latest copies of Constantinopolis, instead of Byzantium, its name before the reign of Constantine. Still, it is shown that the main work was not as late as this, by the fact that Constantinople is not made a centre to which roads converge, for between Sirmium and Nicomedia the road does not even stop at Byzantium. The editors have consulted about forty different MSS., but have made particular use of twenty for the composition

---

[1] The Rev. Prebendary H. M. Scarth (*Roman Britain*) records the fact that "about fifty-six milliaries or mile-stones have been found on the lines of Roman roads in Britain, and some have inscriptions which are legible (p. 119) ; one was discovered near Leicester (*Ratæ*) in 1771 (p. 68), with this inscription (p. 120) :

IMP . CAES .

DIV . TRAIANI . PARTII . F . NER . NEP .

TRAIAN . HADRIAN . AVG . P . P. TRIB .

POT . IV . COS . III

A.RATIS . II

None have as yet been found earlier than the reign of Hadrian, or later than that of Constantine the Younger, A.D. 336" (p. 120).

"A very perfect one was found in Wales, in the year 1883, at Gorddinog, near Llanfairfechan. It is a stone pillar 7 feet high and about 4½ feet in circumference, and bears the following inscription :—

IMP . CAES .

TRAIANVS . HADRIANVS

AVG . P . M . TR . P .

P . P . COS . III .

A . KANOVIO

M . P . VIII .

thus marking the distance of eight miles from Caer-Hun in Caernarvonshire (*Canovium*)" (p. 244).

For this last discovery Mr. Scarth refers to a letter by Mr. W. Thompson Watkin, in *The Academy*, March 1883, No. 565. This stone is now in the British Museum, in the room of Romano-British antiquities.

of their notes and various readings, and have given a *fac-simile* of one page of a MS. of the tenth century, in the Royal Library at Paris, 4806. They have affixed an index of modern names, answering to the ancient, according to various authors, such as Lapie, Mannert, Reynolds, Gale, Horsley, Just, and others. We have, besides these, had the benefit of the latest investigations of Thomas Wright, C. Roach Smith, the Rev. Prebendary Scarth, Gordon-Hills, W. T. Watkin, and others.

Commentators have paid too little regard to the general scheme of the *Itinerary*, laid out as it was in accordance with the configuration of the whole island, and of the localities in reference to their military concatenation. It is for this reason I have given a view of the *Itinerary* on a map, omitting all other roads made before or since, in order to show the scheme which influenced the direction of the roads on this valuable piece of contemporary evidence. The following observations, however, are necessary to justify some of the deviations from usually accepted schemes of identification.

In No. 1, the terminus *Prætorium* was fixed at Patrington by Camden, and later writers appear, without sufficient cause, to have removed it elsewhere.

No. 7.—The position of *Clausentum*, *Regnum*, *Venta Belgarum*, *Calleva Attrebatum*, and *Pontes* has been altered by Mr. Gordon-Hills, in his identification of these places. He says: "An inscribed stone was dug up in the North Street at Chichester in 1723, of the time of the Emperor Claudius; and from the occurrence on it of a part of a name, GIDVBNI (the first portion of the word being broken off), which has been suggested to be COGIDVBNI, it was concluded that we have here the name of the native prince, of whom Tacitus relates that certain states out of the conquests of Ostorius Scapula were given, 'Cogiduno regi.' This con-

clusion led to another assumption, viz., that the states
given to Cogidunus rex must have been those of the Regni;
and, lastly, to another, viz., that the capital town of the
Regni must be Regnum; and the discovery of the stone
here declared Regnum to be Chichester. Depending on
this chain of conjecture, the town Regnum has been invented
out of the name of a people or district, and has by antiquaries been ever since annexed to Chichester. We know
from Ptolemy that the Regni were a people; therefore, when
we read that this *iter* starts from Regnum, I conclude that
it started from some place not given by name, but in the
territory of the Regni, which territory stretched across
Sussex; the present rape of Bramber forming about the
centre of it." Mr. Hills removes the starting point to
Cissbury, near Worthing, for reasons which he gives.
Clausentum, conjectured to have been at Bittern, near
Southampton, Mr. Hills would place at Chichester; both were
important Roman stations, from the evidence of remains
found; but these will not specially identify them with particular stations on the *Itinerary*. It has been thought that
the word Clausentum indicates the shut-in or land-locked
situation of Bittern; but the same definition would also
apply to Chichester. Venta Belgarum has been attributed
to Winchester by most authors, because Henry of Hunting-
don, in the twelfth century, called it Caer Gwent; but he
merely says, in endeavouring to identify the chief cities
named by Nennius, " Kair Gwent, id est Winccastria";
but he does not say that Kair Gwent was Venta Belgarum.
The Belgian territory extended as far east as the seaport
of Havant; for this and other reasons given by Mr. Hills,
he would place here their chief town. Calleva Attrebatum
the same learned antiquary separates from Calleva Segontiacum, which is Silchester, near Reading, and he places
the former at Haslemere, in Surrey, and Pontes at a place
called Pointers, also in Surrey.

No. 10.—This *iter* has long puzzled antiquaries, from their not having settled where it begins, that is, where is Clanoventa, or Glanoventa ? It will be seen by the direction of the roads that this London road requires to be continued to the coast, thus running nearly parallel to the other further east, which went to Carlisle. Hence I would place the starting point, or Clanoventa, at Cockermouth, which was an important station to guard this coast, much exposed to attack ; and the next station, Galava, would be at Ambleside, at the head of Windermere lake. The distance of eighteen miles between these Roman stations has deterred many antiquaries from starting at Cockermouth, the real distance to Ambleside being so much greater ; but if we remember that the Romans were much in the habit of using water carriage by inland lakes and rivers—and we know from other cases that the distances given in the *Itinerary* were only land distances—we shall find that, by using the navigation of the Bassenthwaite and Thirlmere lakes, the eighteen miles will just be about the land distance to Ambleside.

The next station, Alone, I would place at Kendal, an important place since the time of the Romans, much inhabited by miners, and giving its name to the hundred and barony of Kendal. Calacum would be at Lancaster or Halton, or somewhere in the neighbourhood, and Bremetonacæ at Preston ; or if at Ribchester, then the road would have crossed the Ribble many miles from the station—probably at Walton, near Preston, which lies in the straight line of road, discovered by Mr. W. T. Watkin, leading to Wigan, which has been proved by that antiquary to be Coccium ; and this perfectly reconciles the distances as far as Manchester, thus far bringing down the road to London from Cockermouth. It is as dangerous to hazard an origin for the name of a place as of a people, but, subject to a better derivation, χλαινόεντα may mean the mart for woollen cloaks, called χλαῖναι, of the native manufacture, and perhaps of the texture still in use. Britton and Brayley describe the inhabitants as much occupied in woollen manufactures. " The clothing of the men was of the native fleece of the country, home-spun and woven by the village weaver; the wool of a black sheep, slightly mixed with blue and red, was the favourite colour of this cloth, which was very thick and heavy . . . . The women's apparel was of the finer sort of the native wool, woven into a kind of serge, dyed of a russet, blue, or other colour; and, like the men's, made up by the tailor at the weaver's own fireside." And as to woollen fabrics, Kendal was especially famous. Leland calls it "*emporium laneis pannis celeberrimum*"; and Camden describes it as "eminent for its woollen manufacture and the industry of its inhabitants, who carry on a great trade in woollen cloth all over England."[1]

" At Keswick, Roman coins of Antoninus Pius and Gordian, as well as a Roman eagle of brass, were found, and a paved road is in many places visible towards Ambleside."[2] This road being continued below Manchester, through Condate (Congleton) to Mediolanum, or Chesterton, near Newcastle-under-Lyne, a few miles of river navigation would unite it with the main London road at Venonæ, or High Cross, in Staffordshire.

As modern antiquaries did not see their way to commence this road to London from Cockermouth, by reason of the distance from thence to the neighbourhood of Kendal, which I have endeavoured to reconcile by the water-way through the lakes, they have thought fit to place Clanoventa at Penrith (Mr. Gordon-Hills) and Whitley Castle (Mr. W. T. Watkin), bringing the road down the valley of the Lune ;

[1] *Britton and Brayley*, vol. xv, p. 191.
[2] *Ibid.*, p. 219.

but we have a road direct from London to Penrith already, and Whitley Castle is equally out of the natural direction of this more westerly course.

Overborough, at the junction of the Burrow and Lune rivers, has been fixed upon for Galacum, because the distances agree, and a fine Roman camp has lately been explored there; but this is no reason for carrying the road out of its natural course, which should run parallel, or nearly so, with the Carlisle and London road, communicating with the coast, and where the remains of Roman occupation are almost more numerous than anywhere else in the county. Overborough would be a fine situation for a camp between the two roads, and to command the intermediate country and the valley of the Lune; and the fact of a Roman road having been found in the neighbourhood tending towards Penrith, does not detract from the probability that the road to Cockermouth is that intended by the author of the *Itinerary* of Antoninus as laid down on the tenth *iter*.

ITER BRITANNIARUM.

A GESSORIACO DE GALLIIS RITUPIS IN PORTU BRITANNIARUM.
STADIA NUMERO CCCCL.

No. 1.—*A limite, id est a vallo, Prætorio usque, m. p. m.* CLVI.

A Bremenio Corstopitum	.	m. p. m.	xx
Vindomora	.	„	viiii
Vinovia .	.	„	xviiii
Cataractoni	.	„	xxii
Isurium .	.	„	xxiiii
Eburacum leg. vi victrix		„	xvii
Derventione	.	„	vii
Delgovicia .		„	xiii
Prætorio		„	xxv

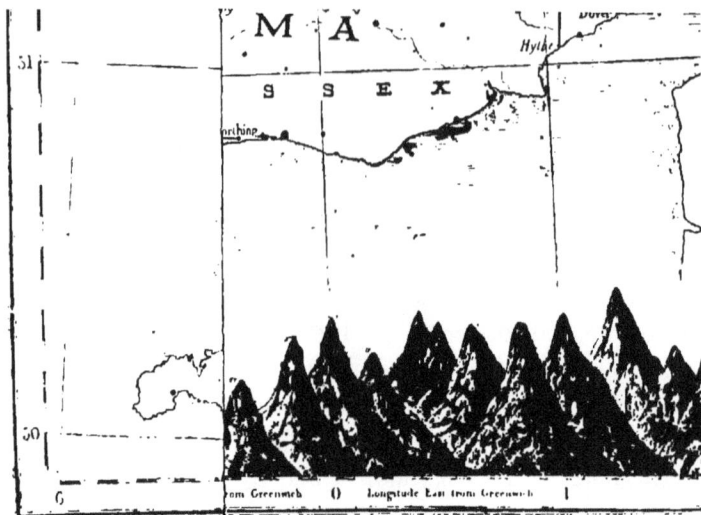

ITINERARY OF ANTONINVS THROUGH ENGLAND & WALES.

No. 2.—Item a vallo ad portum Ritupis, m. p. m. CCCCLXXXI (*sic*).

A Blato Bulgio Castra exploratorum	.	m. p. m.	xii
Luguvallo	.	.	.	„	xii
Voreda	.	.	.	„	xiiii
Brovonacis	.	.	.	„	xiii
Verteris	.	.	.	„	xiii
Lavatris	.	.	.	„	xiiii
Cataractone	.	.	.	„	xvi
Isurium	.	.	.	„	xxiiii
Eburacum	.	.	.	„	xvii
Calcaria	.	.	.	„	viiii
Camboduno	.	.	.	„	xx
Mamucio	.	.	.	„	xviii
Condate	.	.	.	„	xviii
Deva, leg. xx vict.	.	.	.	„	xx
Bovio	.	.	.	„	x
Mediolano	.	.	.	„	xx
Rutunio	.	.	.	„	xii
Urioconio	.	.	.	„	xi
Uxacona	.	.	.	„	xi
Pennocrucio	.	.	.	„	xii
Etoceto	.	.	.	„	xii
Manduesedo	.	.	.	„	xvi
Venonis	.	.	.	„	xii
Bannaventa	.	.	.	„	xvii
Lactodoro	.	.	.	„	xii
Magiovinto	.	.	.	„	xvii
Durocobrivis	.	.	.	„	xii
Verolamio	.	.	.	„	xii
Sulloniacis	.	.	.	„	viiii
Londinio	.	.	.	„	xii
Noviomago	.	.	.	„	x
Vagniacis	.	.	.	„	xviii
Durobrivis	.	.	.	„	viiii
Durolevo	.	.	.	„	xiii
Duroverno	.	.	.	„	xii
Ad portum Ritupis	.	.	.	„	xii

No. 3.—Item a Londinio ad portum Dubris, m. p. m. LXVI (*sic*).

Durobrivis	m. p. m.	xxvii
Duroverno	„	xxv
Ad portum Dubris	„	xiiii

S S

No. 4.—Item a Londinio ad portum Lemanis, m. p. m. LXVIII (*sic*).

Durobrivis .	.	.	m. p. m. xxvii
Duroverno .	.	.	„ xxv
Ad portum Lemanis .	.		„ xvi

No. 5.—Item a Londinio Luguvalio ad vallum, m. p. m. CCCCXLIII (*sic*).

Cæsaromago	.	.	m. p. m.	xxviii
Colonia	.	.	„	xxiiii
Villa Faustini	.	.	„	xxxv
Icinos	.	.	.	„ xviii
Camborico	.	.	.	„ xxxv
Duroliponte	.	.	.	„ xxv
Durobrivas	.	.	.	„ xxxv
Causennis .	.	.	.	„ xxx
Lindo	.	.	.	„ xxvi
Segeloci	.	.	.	„ xiiii
Dano	.	.	.	„ xxi
Legeolio	.	.	.	„ xvi
Eburaco	.	.	.	„ xxi
Isubrigantum	.		„	xvii
Cataractone	.		„	xxiiii
Levatris	.	.	„	xviii
Verteris	.	.	„	xiiii
Brocavo	.	.	„	xx
Luguvalio .	.		„	xxii

No. 6.—Item a Londinio Lindo, m. p. m. CLVI (*sic*).

Verolami .	.	.	.	m. p. m. xxi
Durocobrivis	.	.	.	„ xii
Magiovinio	.	.	.	„ xii
Lactodoro .	.	.	.	„ xvi
Isannavantia	.	.	.	„ xii
Tripontio .	.	.	.	„ xii
Venonis .	.	.	.	„ viii
Ratas	.	.	.	„ xii
Verometo .	.	.	.	„ xiii
Margiduno .	.	.	.	„ xii
Ad pontem	.	.	.	„ vii
Crococalana	.	.	.	„ vii
Lindo	.	.	.	„ xii

No. 7.—*Item a Regno Londinio, m. p. m.* XCVI (*sic*).

Clausentum	.	.	. m. p. m. xx
Venta Belgarum	.	.	„ x
Calleva Atrebatum	.	.	„ xxii
Pontibus	.	.	„ xxii
Londinio	.	.	„ xxii

No. 8.—*Item ab Eburaco Londinium, m. p. m.* CCXXVII (*sic*).

Lagecio	.	.	. m. p. m. xxi
Dano	.	.	„ xvi
Ageloco	.	.	„ xxi
Lindo	.	.	„ xiiii
Crococalana	.	.	„ xiiii
Margiduno	.	.	„ xiiii
Vernemeto	.	.	„ xii
Ratis	.	.	„ xii
Venonis	.	.	„ xii
Bannavento	.	.	„ xviii
Magiovinio	.	.	„ xxviii
Durocobrivis	.	.	„ xii
Verolamo	.	.	„ xii
Londinio	.	.	„ xxi

No. 9.—*Item a Venta Icinorum Londinio, m. p. m.* CXXVIII (*sic*).

Sitomago	.	.	. m. p. m. xxxii
Combretonio	.	.	„ xxii
Ad Ansam	.	.	„ xv
Camoloduno	.	.	„ vi
Canonio	.	.	„ viiii
Cæsaromago	.	.	„ xii
Durolito	.	.	„ xvi
Londinio	.	.	„ xv

No. 10.—*Item a Clanoventa Mediolano, m. p. m.* CL (*sic*).

Galava	.	.	. m. p. m. xviii
Alone	.	.	„ xii
Calacum	.	.	„ xviiii
Bremetonaci	.	.	„ xxvii
Coccio	.	.	„ xx
Mancunio	.	.	„ xvii
Condate	.	.	„ xviii
Mediolano	.	.	„ xviiii

No. 11.—*Item a Segontio Deram, m. p. m.* LXXIIII (*sic*).

Conovio	.		m. p. m.	xxiiii
Varis	.		„	xviii
Deva	.		„	xxxii

No. 12.—*Item a Muriduno¹ Viroconium, m. p. m.* CLXXXVI (*sic*).

Leucaro	.		m. p. m.	xv
Nido	.	.	„	xv
Bomio	.	.	„	xv
Iscæ leg. II Augusta			„	xxvii
Burrio	.	.	„	viiii
Gobannio	.	.	„	xii
Magnis	.	.	„	xxii
Bravonio	.	.	„	xxiiii
Viroconio		.	„	xxvii

No. 13.—*Item ab Isca Callera, m. p. m.* CVIIII (*sic*).

Burrio	.	.	.	m. p. m.	viiii
Blestio	.	.	.	„	xi
Ariconio	.	.	.	„	xi
Clevo	.	.	.	„	xv
Durocornovio		.	.	„	xiiii
Spinis	.	.	.	„	xv
Calleva	.		.	„	xv

No. 14.—*Item alio itinere ab Isca Callera, m. p. m.* CIII (*sic*).

Venta Silurum		m. p. m.	viiii
Abone	.	„	xiiii
Trajectus	.	„	viiii
Aquis Solis		„	vi

---

¹ We are indebted to Messrs. Parthey and Pinder for pointing out that by the error of a scribe, the places of *Iter* No. 15 have been generally placed at the head of, and added to, No. 12, as the said scribe had confused the Muridunum of No. 15 with the Muridunum (Carmarthen) of No. 12. This unnatural excrescence in No. 12 being now left out, the road is made perfectly intelligible.

The reader is reminded by Messrs. Parthey and Pinder that the three letters M. P. M. are intended to signify *Millia plus minus* (miles more or less), the fractional parts of miles being omitted.

Verlucione	m. p. m.	xv
Cunctione	„	xx
Spinis .	„	xv
Calleva .	„	xv

No. 15.—Item a Calleva Isca Dumnuniorum, m. p. m. cxxxvi *(sic).*

Vindomi .	m. p. m.	xv
Venta Belgarum	„	xxi
Brige .	„	xi
Sorbiodoni	„	viii
Vindogladia	„	xii
Durnonovaria .	„	viii
Muriduno .	„	xxxvi
Isca Dumnuniorum .	„	xv

TABLE OF ROMANO-BRITISH MOSAICS,

Distinguishing the Plain, or with Geometrical Designs only, from those which have Figured Delineations upon them.

Chapter.	Numbers.	County.	Plain and Geometrical.	Figured.	Total.
VI Introduction	1 to 19 ———	Gloucester . . } „ . . }	10	{ 9 } { 1 }	20
VII	1 to 13	Somerset . .	6	7	13
VII	{ 14 to 16 } { 18 to 20 }	Monmouth . .	1	5	6
VII	21 to 29	Wilts . . .	4	5	9
VII	30 to 32	Shropshire . .	2	1	3
VIII	1 to 21	Oxford . . .	17	4	21
VIII	22	Leicester . .	—	1	1
VIII	23	Nottingham .	1	—	1
VIII	24 to 41	Northampton .	15	3	18
IX	1 to 12	Lincoln . . .	9	3	12
X	1 to 5	Berks . . .	4	1	5
X	6 to 8	Essex . . .	3	—	3
X	9 to 19	Kent . . .	11	—	11
XII	1 to 29	Middlesex . .	21	8	29
XIII	1 to 7	Sussex . . .	2	5	7
XIII	8 to 9	Surrey . . .	1	1	2
XIII	10 to 17	Dorset . . .	4	4	8
XIV	1 to 8	Hants . . .	3	5	8
XV	———	Isle of Wight .	3	3	6
			117	66	183
XVI and XVII		Mosaics from Halicarnassus and Northern Africa preserved in British Museum (basement with annex)			70
					253

INDEX.

320 INDEX.

www.ingramcontent.com/pod-product-compliance
Lightning Source LLC
Chambersburg PA
CBHW032307280326
41932CB00009B/735